Creative Economies in Peripheral Regions

Patrick Collins • James A. Cunningham

Creative Economies in Peripheral Regions

palgrave
macmillan

Patrick Collins
National University of Ireland Galway
Galway, Ireland

James A. Cunningham
Northumbria University
Newcastle Upon Tyne
United Kingdom

ISBN 978-3-319-52164-0
ISBN 978-3-319-52165-7 (eBook)
DOI 10.1007/978-3-319-52165-7

Library of Congress Control Number: 2017940826

Printed on acid-free paper

This Palgrave Macmillan imprint is published by Springer Nature
The registered company is Springer International Publishing AG
The registered company address is: Gewerbestrasse 11, 6330 Cham, Switzerland

To Aideen, and our girls, Lua, Allie and Molly
To Sammi (JC)
In loving memory of Brendan J. Collins and Jean Ena Cooke

Foreword

The celebrated scholar Raymond Williams, in his classic monograph *The Country and the City*, explored some of the key ideas that had respectively been associated with rural and urban places in Anglophone culture. The country, he suggested, had long been described as backward, limited and ignorant, while the city was associated with learning, innovation and creativity. This deeply entrenched alignment of creativity with the city is not surprising – cities have been throughout history places where things were made, where artists practised and where intellectuals congregated. Yet, in recent years this notion has assumed greater potency as 'creativity' has been seized on by analysts and city planners as a key ingredient for economic growth. One of the main advocates of this approach, American geographer Richard Florida, has described cities as 'cauldrons of creativity', a metaphor that emphasises creativity as a product of the mixing of components. Cities foster creativity, Florida and others argue, because they are agglomerations of people, materials, languages, cultural influences and capital. In contrast, creativity in the countryside, it might be inferred, is frustrated by disaggregation and dispersal.

However, as Patrick Collins and James Cunningham persuasively demonstrate in this book, the alluring notion of the creative city is only part of the story. Rural and peripheral regions are not devoid of creativity, but also boast vibrant creative economies that have thrived despite being overshadowed and neglected in policy and analysis. As the case studies in this book show, creative industries in peripheral regions have confounded some of the assumptions of the creative city model, replicating the productive practices and business strategies of urban creatives in non-metropolitan settings through 'creative' adaptations to context. Moreover, in doing so, they have recovered older perhaps more 'rural' expressions of creativity that had been marginalised in the urban-centred discourse: individual artistry, self-reliance, adaptability and dexterity, working with nature and refashioning local resources. At the heart of this is the importance of place to creative economies in peripheral regions, not only as sites for exchange and cooperation, but also as inspiration for creativity.

By developing this argument in this volume, and by extensively documenting examples of good practice in non-metropolitan creativity from Ireland, Sweden and Finland, Collins and Cunningham have produced a valuable resource for researchers, policy makers, practitioners and entrepreneurs that deservedly refocuses attention on the creative energies of peripheral regions and supports the embedding of creative industries of all types in regional development.

Aberystwyth University Professor Michael Woods

Preface

Cultural and creative production has received increased attention from academics and policy makers in the recent past. The reason for this, we contend, is that the economy is becoming more creative. This work hopes to contribute to the growing literature that is pointing to this recent upsurge in creative activity not being bound to urban places. Here, we make the case for vibrant creative and cultural economies existing in peripheral areas.

More broadly speaking, this work takes place within the context of an evolving consumer society. There is increasing recognition of a change in consumer patterns as the modern consumption era matures. As more and more people buy goods that they feel reflect their own individual identity, more of us are expressing ourselves by how we dress, what we eat, what we listen to and where we go on holiday. In doing this we are turning our back on mass-produced goods and services. As the market for these kinds of goods, ones laden with expressive values, increases, the products of our peripheral regions become more desirable. We argue here that it is the connectedness to place; the use of more traditional production techniques; and the imbued sense of authenticity in the produce of the peripheral regions that makes them more and more marketable in a maturing consumer society.

By looking at the production of these products in more remote areas, we contend that the productive practices seen in our case-study regions are reflecting those of leading innovative industries. How creatives in remote regions collaborate, co-produce, switch codes (writers and visual artists become theatre makers and game designers) is demonstrative of an agility that is seen by many as key to productive success. By shining a light on the array business models adopted by these industries we see a sector that is more connected to its place and its society in a way that is unique in the modern context.

This book will be of value to those from a social science and business background. But it will also be of interest to those within this growing sector and those that support it. We make explicit our policy recommendations for supporting the growth of creative economies in peripheral areas. As a sustainable model for development, one that relies on the infinite resource of human creativity, it has the potential to act as a vital agent in the future growth of peripheral regions.

Acknowledgements

The writing of this book has been a culmination of many years work and this reflects numerous conversations and discussions we have had with colleagues, policy makers and creatives. The Creative Edge project funded by the Northern Peripheries Programme provided a catalyst for us to focus on peripheral creative industries and economies on a pan-European basis. In bringing this book to fruition we would like to thank Micheál Murphy for the research assistance support he provided at the early stages of this endeavour; Pauline White and Ian Brannigan of the Western Development Commission; and Paul Kavanagh and Niall Drew of the Armagh Banbridge, Craigavon Borough Council; and colleagues who collaborated with us on the Creative Edge project, with special mention for Dr. Aisling Murtagh and David Kelly (NUI Galway) for their help. We would also like to thank Rachel Sangster and Gemma Leigh of Palgrave for their support in developing and publishing this book and all the members of creative industries that offered their time to our work.

Finally, we would like to thank our families for their ongoing support and understanding that has allowed us the time and space to complete this book.

Contents

List of Abbreviations

BM	Business Models
CA	Creative Application
CE	Creative Expression
CT	Creative Technology
DCMS	Department of Culture, Media and Sport (United Kingdom)
EI	Enterprise Ireland
EU	European Union
IDA	Industrial Development Agency (Ireland)
NPA	Northern Periphery and Arctic Programme
NPP	Northern Periphery Programme
NUIG	National University of Ireland, Galway
SEED	South East Economic Development (Northern Ireland)
UNCTAD	United Nations Conference on Trade and Development
UNESCO	United Nations Educational, Scientific and Cultural Organisation
WDC	Western Development Commission (Ireland)

List of Figures

List of Tables

1

Creative Economies and Industries in Peripheral Regions

1.1 Introduction

The past 20 years have seen an increased awareness of the importance of creativity in economic development. Policy makers and politicians are now realising the contribution of creative economy and industries, both economically and socially. Those public-supporting institutions that are tasked with developing the economic potential of creative economy are utilising support interventions used successfully in other sectors to support the establishment of new businesses and the internationalisation of established firms. While cognisant of the growing interest and support for the creative economy, some creatives are also cautious about embracing the economic potential that may damage or constrain the creative spirit, genius and expression that is the fundamental core ingredient of their cultural work. Herein lies the conflict between the production of Art and commercial produce that we reflect on throughout this book as something that helps define the creative economy. Of importance here is the significant rise in academic research in the form of academic journal articles that are focussed on issues pertaining to the creative economy. Taking just one measure of this interest via Google Ngram viewer allows users to track the instances of phrases in books

P. Collins, J.A. Cunningham, *Creative Economies in Peripheral Regions*, DOI 10.1007/978-3-319-52165-7_1

published over the last 500 years. Applying this to the creative economy we can see an exponential increase from 2000 onwards.[1] This context gives rise to some interesting and challenging issues facing all stakeholders in creative economy. For example, how should the creative economy be supported by public policy? What are the appropriate public policy support tools that really make a difference in supporting creatives? Should the same interventions be used for all sub-sectors of the creative industry? How should peripheral creative economies be supported and should this be different from urban creative economies? For us, ensuring the flourishing and growth of creative economies is of strategic importance to national economies. Most crucially, for peripheral regions the creative economy provides real opportunities to sustain communities culturally, socially and economically.

Against this context we begin our chapter by exploring some of the definitions, approaches and models of the creative economy. We then outline our approach to categorising creative industries and turn our attention to outlining some of the key drivers of the creative economy. Our focus then shifts to discussing some of the critiques of the creative economy before concluding our chapter examining the importance of place and making the case for the peripheral creative economy.

1.1.1 Our Framework Approach

Much of the focus has been on creative economies and industries in urban areas with a less of a focus on peripheral or rural areas. Our intention is to explore further the different facets and dimensions of the creative industries and economies in peripheral regions. Figure 1.1 acts as a visual representation of the framework on which this book lies and our approach to understanding the creative economy and industry in peripheral regions. Our framework comprises of distinct layers that provide a conceptual structure and to better understand the combination of the broader creative industry and economy context and the distinctive dimensions of peripheral regions. First, we

[1] https://books.google.com/ngrams/graph?content=Creative+Economy&year_start=1950&year_end=2006&corpus=15&smoothing=1&share=&direct_url=t1%3B%2CCreative%20Economy%3B%2Cc0

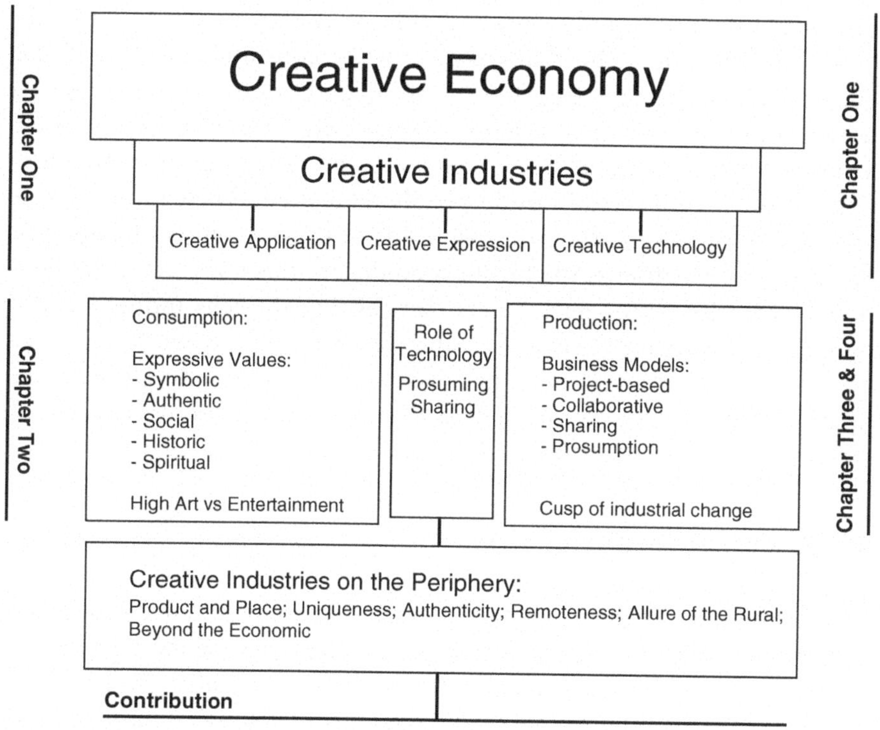

Fig. 1.1 Our framework

categorises the creative economy into three elements – creative application, creative expression and creative technologies. Emanating from this is the unique role of culture (values and expression) and how it is consumed. We consider the distinctive dimensions of the creative economy and industry in the peripheral regions namely, product and place, uniqueness and authenticity of rural, remoteness, non-economic motivations and the allure of the rural. This is set against the business models approaches of creative industries and the challenges faced by policy makers. Our framework provides a starting point and a basis to stimulate for future analysis and discussion.

In terms of monograph structure, Chapter 1 considers the creative economy and the industries that comprise it. This requires reflecting on previous approaches to defining the newly emerging entity and placing our interpretation alongside them. Chapter 2 adds to the small, but growing, literature on the demand side of the creative economy. By better understanding the changes in how we consume culture and the effects of technology on those consumption patterns we are better able to understand the productive side of the economy. We bring our level on analysis down to the case-study regions in an effort to explore how it is that culture is celebrated in those peripheral regions. These same regions are used to investigate the production side of the economy in Chapter 3. In Chapter 4 we discuss the business model approach and consider how it differs in the peripheral context. By shifting the lens inquiry to the periphery in gauging the extent of the creative economy we believe that we are making a unique contribution to better understanding the nature of creativity as a whole, as well as the new and emerging models of sustainable development for peripheral regions.

1.1.2 Our Approach

One of the most challenging aspects of understanding creative economies and creative industries in peripheral regions is access to data that captures the extent, scope and unique characteristics of this sector. Other challenges lie with respect to definitions and interpretations of creative economies and industries across different national contexts. To deal with these and other challenges and associated complexities we adopted mixed methodology approach for our data collection. Our methodological approach is varied owing to the fact that much of the data referred to here was gleaned from a 30-month project focussed on the creative economy of Europe's Northern Periphery. The Creative Edge project was funded by the Northern Periphery Programme and set out to promote the active participation of local creative organisations and businesses in global markets, while also aiding them in their ability to attract and utilise local emerging creative talent in these markets. The project involved four regions from Europe's northern periphery; these regions act as our case-study regions (see Fig. 1.2). A key element of this involved the collation of a large dataset to better understand the sector in peripheral regions. As one of the first attempts to uncover the extent of creative economy practices in peripheral regions, much of the data was gathered through secondary sources. A database of Creative Industries,

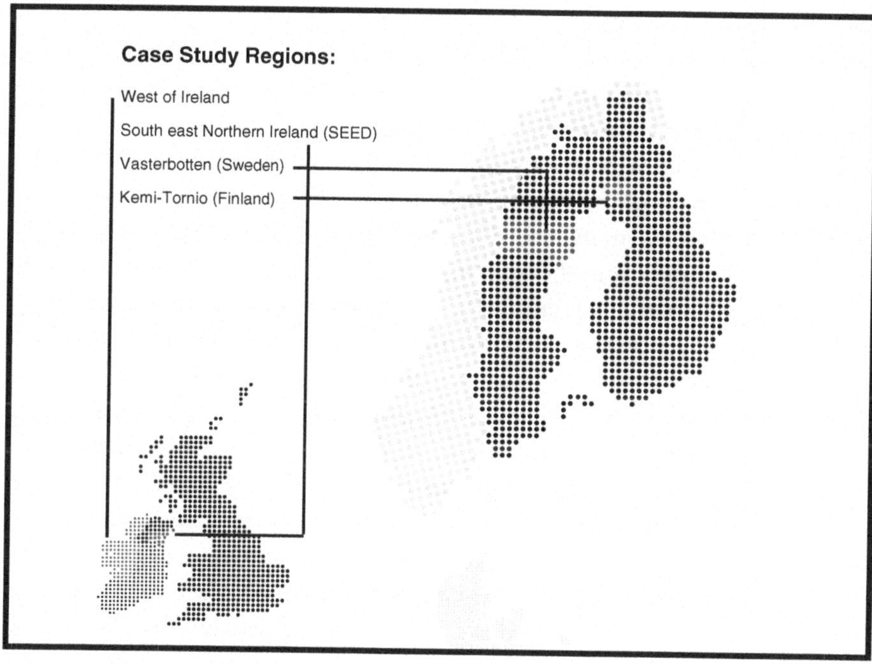

Fig. 1.2 Case-study regions
Source: Authors creation, via Noun project and Stock Image Folio

defined by type (see definition below), size and location, was drafted from the main statistical agencies of the four countries of the respective regions in focus. Different agencies make use of different methods in gathering this data, to ensure the greatest level of coherence across all the sectors, we make use of NACE codes to categorise the creative economy industries and their respective subsectors.

Viewing the creative economy as resting on three pillars, People, Production and Place, with a focus on the latter the data gathering element of the project set out to understand how creativity and culture was enacted, celebrated and sustained in places. Undertaking this involved an extensive trawl of literature and web resources. This was added to data sourced from artistic agencies and promoters to get an understanding of the cultural infrastructure of our case-study regions. The data here serves to help us better understand how the culture of the periphery is consumed, and it forms a key part of Chapter 2 in this book. More information on the Creative Edge project is available at www.creative-edge.eu.

In order to gain a better understanding of the production side of the creative economy and the work carried out by the creative industries of the case-study region, we made use of a survey, carried out in 2015. The survey set out to gain insight into the working practices of creatives in the case-study regions, with a particular emphasis on business approaches (networking and learning practices), as well as more general characteristics (numbers employed, market focus). Access was gained though the web portal mycreativeegde.eu a platform used by over 500 creative industries in our case-study regions (and supported by the Creative Edge and a creative momentum projects). More detail of the responses can be seen in Chapter 3, but the survey gained a representative response rate of 167 respondents. The survey is supplemented by a number of interviews carried out with creatives over the course of the project. Most face-to-face interviews took place in the west of Ireland (23), with other interviews (14) being carried out by the use of telephone and email. These interviews provide more context and in devising of our case-study industries (Chapter 3).

In an effort to explore the use of business models in the creative sector, we have made use of an extensive literature review. With an analysis of 62 empirical papers we provide a comprehensive overview of work carried out in relation to the varied approaches taken to business in the creative sector. Each chapter uses a solid backbone of theory to further develop our perspective. This involves a unique collection of reflections on producing and consuming culture as well as best practice in sustaining economic development in peripheral areas.

1.2 Creative Economy: Definitions, Approaches and Alternative Models

We live in a time of great change politically, economically and socially. In this monograph our intention is to focus on the creative economy as a bellweather of this change. In today's developed world, everywhere we look, we see the growth of the creative economy. Computer mediated technologies have aided the advance of the creative economy over the past 20 years, indeed the case can be made that cultural and creative content has driven the exponential growth of the digital economy. Consumer tastes have also evolved and we now spend more and more of our money on culturally imbued products and services. The maturation of the consumer society in the most developed parts of the globe has witnessed a discernible shift away from mass-produced goods towards produce that better reflect individual preferences. Adapting to the changes in consumer sentiment have inspired changes in the way we work. Creative economy firms (the Creative Industries), while diverse and multifaceted, share many unique traits in how they do business: they are young, they are small, they are agile, entrepreneurial and innovative. Their approach, in the form of the business models they adopt, mark them as a unique entity and place at the cusp of change in how business is being done. They are blurring the lines between the consumer and producers and the adoption of collaborative business models is particularly unique to the sector. In many ways these firms defy many traditional business conventions with their definition of success being more nuanced and their sense of purpose reaching beyond the commercial. To begin our exploration of creative economies and industries in peripheral regions we begin by considering the creative economy and the multitude of different approaches to defining it.

1.2.1 The Creative Economy: A Growing Economy

The creative economy is subject to many different definitions and as such this leads to challenges in measuring the economic contribution it makes to national economies. What sectors should be included or excluded when categorising a creative economy? For example, should the information economy or the information society be included? While the inclusion or exclusion of certain subsectors (be it tourism, heritage or electronic engineering) has been the subject of much debate there is a general consensus on the fact that the creative economy as a whole is a growing entity.

Recently published reports by UNESCO and Ernst and Young place the revenues of cultural and creative industries at $2,250 billion in 2013, a figure that would place it in the top ten of the world's richest countries in comparison to Gross Domestic Product (GDP) (Ernst and Young 2015). UNCTAD records statistics on the trade of creative goods and services; global trends for the period 2003–2012 show export growth rates of 8.6% for creative goods and 8.8% for creative services. In absolute terms this is an increase in the trade of creative products from $223,795 million in 2003 to $473,791 in 2012 (unctad.org).

In an analysis of employment in the Creative Economy Nathan et al. (2015) estimates 11.2 million workers in the Creative Economy across all 28 EU member states. This is equivalent to 5.21% of all employment across the Union, with degrees of variation between countries. This most recent figure, derived from more precise industry classifications, shows that previous efforts to gauge the importance of the Creative Economy under-reported its extent. Analysis over the three years from 2011 to 2013 shows continuous growth in the creative economy across the continent. More globally, the creative economy has been receiving a boost from the increase in South–South trade. The Global South's exports of creative goods to the world reached $176 billion in 2008, accounting for 43% of total creative industries trade with an annual growth rate of 13.5% during the 2002–2008 period (UNCTAD 2010).

The evolution of the creative economy is an interesting one. While conceived of as a recent phenomenon in the literature, the fact remains that since the clay pots of the Byzantine period, there has been an economy of cultural produce. Indeed it is the cultural produce of previous ages that we use to account for the rise and fall of civilisations. More recently, with the rise of industrial productive capacities, we have witnessed the increased commodification of culture. The advent of what Horkheimer and Adorno (2009) term 'the culture industry' is best recognised in the form of Hollywood studios or the prevalence of large record labels still holds huge sway today. These large multinational corporations were responsible for the most recent commercialisation of culture. In this monograph, it is our intention to move the focus beyond mass cultural producers to a different tier of creative producers, ones that are not household names, but combined are having a significant impact on what we consume and the way we work.

We know that increasing amounts of our disposable income are being spent on culturally imbued products and services (UNCTAD 2010). The maturation of the consumer society in the most developed parts of the world is marked by a movement away from mass-produced goods and services towards products that are narrative laden, products that better reflect our individual tastes, products that reflect the culture and creativity of their time and place. These trends are also reflected within the creative economy, where consumers are in search of culture in non-massified form. This is reflected in the growth of independent labels in music, art house cinema in film or indeed the growth of craft beers in the brewing industry.

The European Union Green Paper (European Commission 2010) *Unlocking the Potential of the Creative and Cultural Industries* contends that the immaterial value increasingly determines the material value as consumers search for a new and enriching experience. This echoes notions of taste, associated by Bourdieu (1984) with cultural capital and is considered a more important factor in relation to the demand for cultural goods. Moreover, Van der Ploeg (2002: 339) has classified culture as an acquired taste, 'an experience good in that the more one tries it, the more one gets out of it'. Furthermore, almost all cultural goods are investments in one's own cultural capital (Van der Ploeg 2006). The UNCTAD (2010) report notes that increasing income in industrialised countries has heightened demand for creative goods and services. In addition, it contends that the prices of the products and the means for their mediated consumption have declined as technology has advanced, ensuing an upward pressure on demand. Examples of products imbued with cultural content are increasingly pertinent in the literature. Such products are oft inculcated with notions of authenticity, similar to the immaterial value referenced above. An instance from the global periphery of this has been the rise in popularity of Aboriginal art (Belk and Groves 1999) as the authentic nature of this cultural product has played an integral role in this increase as well as in gaining access to successful markets (Myers 2002; Gibson and Connell 2004; Christen 2006).

1.3 Creative Economy Industry Classification and Our Classification

Such is the ambiguous nature of standard industrial classifications, precise quantitative assessments of the full extent of these industries and the cultural economy are almost impossible. The fact is that so much of this economy and the value accrued by it is based on ephemeral qualities that the traditional metrics of explaining the extent of the economy will likely undervalue it (Scott 2010).

As a starting point we consider the creative economy as comprising of those firms and individuals that make use of creative practices in the production of their culturally imbued output. Before we delve deeper into the definition that we use in this monograph, we must consider the current landscape and contemporary approaches to defining the economy and the industries upon which it depends (see Table 1.1). Despite a relatively recent proliferation in studies germane to the creative economy and the creative industries, there still remains a contentious debate surrounding its definition and what industries it incorporates. Nebulous definitions dominate (Santos Cruz and Teixeira 2015) and thus blur the subsequent assimilation of industries and wider sectors (McGranahan and Wojan 2007; Markusen et al. 2008; De Propris et al. 2009; Mangematin et al. 2014). This has obvious impacts on cross-analogies/comparisons of creative economy or creative industry studies as there is no set definition or methodological approach to their analysis. This lends to disparities in estimations of the impacts of the creative economy (see for example Clifton and Cooke (2009) in comparison to estimates by Clark (2009)). Set against this, Gibson and Kong (2005) provide a detailed account of the inadequacy of classification but argue that this 'polyvalency' retains its value provided that we deliberate on the multiple contradictions and interpretations. We need first to consider the most popular definitions before explaining how they have inspired our approach.

Table 1.1 Creative economy and industry definitions, advantages and disadvantages

Author/ Institution	Definition	Rationale/ Criteria	Sectors accounted for	Advantages	Disadvantages
(DCMS 1998, 2001, 2010) Sectoral model	Industries which have their origin in individual creativity, skill and talent and which have a potential for wealth and job creation through the generation and exploitation of intellectual property	Creativity as a central input to the production process, with intellectual property being the identifying characteristic of creative industries' output.	Advertising, Architecture, Arts and Antiques, Crafts, Design, Designer Fashion, Video, Film and Photography, Music and Visual & Performing Arts, Publishing, Software, Computer Games and Electronic Publishing, TV and Radio	Set a standard approach Easy to use Based on a supporting template for policymaking and governmental decision.	• Selection of a restrictive number of creative sectors. • Arbitrary exclusion of certain activities from the listing (e.g., heritage, museum, recreation). • Difficulty in separating the creative from non-creative component of industry codes related with activities that are not entirely 'creative'. • The Crafts sector cannot be captured by means of industry codes.

(continued)

Table 1.1 (continued)

Author/ Institution	Definition	Rationale/ Criteria	Sectors accounted for	Advantages	Disadvantages
Thorsby (2001) Concentric circle model	Creative ideas originate in the 'core creative arts' and then disseminate outwards to the 'borderline' and 'peripheral' cultural industries	Focus on Activities that produce culture/creative content vs. Activities using creativity as input to diffuse it through distribution networks	Core creative arts Literature, Music, Performing arts, Visual arts **Other core cultural industries** Film, museums and libraries Wider cultural industries Heritage services, Publishing, Sound recording, television and radio, video and computer games	Emphasis on fine arts and on cultural production. Importance of fine arts/culture as the epicentre of the creative economy. Representation with concentric layers, useful in policy analysis.	• Mapping the Core of Cultural and Arts activities is strongly limited to the industry classification system. • Some industry codes cannot be disaggregated into more detailed level implicates inability of separating production from distribution.
Hesmondhalgh (2002) Symbolic texts model	Cultural industries essentially concerned with the production of social meaning through production and circulation of texts.	Focus on processes which produce, disseminate and consume symbolic texts or messages.	**Core cultural industries** Advertising, Film and Video, Internet Music, Publishing, TV and radio, Video and Computer Games	More narrow and selective process of grouping the creative industries.	• Cultural content and creativity can be resources and the outcomes not only of cultural activities, but also of the entire creative economy

			Peripheral Cultural Industries Creative arts **Borderline cultural industries** Consumer Electronics, Fashion, Software, Sport		
WIPO copyright model Intellectual property and copyright model (2003)	Those industries whose primary purpose is to produce or distribute copyright materials. These industries include newspapers, book publishing, recording, music, and periodicals, motion pictures, radio and television broadcasting,	Copyright is a characteristic of the industry's output.	**Core copyright industries** Music, advertising, Collecting societies, Film and video, Performing arts, Publishing, Software, Television and Radio, Visual and Graphic art **Interdependent copyright industries** Blank recording material, Consumer	More objective methodology on the selection of copyright based activities, since criteria lie on copyright goods and intellectually protected contents.	• Set of broad and all-inclusive industry codes involving the wholesale, retail sale and rental activities. • Difficult to assess the creative or copyright-based part of each of the industry code considered. • Difficulties in obtaining an appropriate copyright factor for

(*continued*)

Table 1.1 (continued)

Author/ Institution	Definition	Rationale/ Criteria	Sectors accounted for	Advantages	Disadvantages
	and computer software		Electronics, Musical instruments, Paper, Photocopiers, Photographic equipment **Partial copyright industries** Architecture, Clothing, Footwear, Design, Fashion, Household goods,Toys		interdependent and partial copyright based industries.
Americans for the Arts (2004)	Creative industries are composed of arts-centric businesses that range from nonprofit museums, symphonies, and theaters to for-profit film, architecture,	Businesses involved in the production or distribution of the arts.	Museums & Collection Performing Arts Visual Arts & Photography (Crafts, Visual arts, Photography) Visual Arts & Photography (Supplies and services)		

	and advertising companies.		Film, Radio, & TV Design & Publishing Arts Schools & Services		
KEA (2006)	N/A	All the outputs can be protected by copyright	**<u>Core Arts Field:</u>** Visual arts, Performing arts, Heritage, **<u>Cultural industries:</u>** Film and Video, TV and radio, video games, books, music, press **<u>Creative industries:</u>** Design, architecture and advertising **<u>Related Industries:</u>** i.e. Mp3 and mobile manufacturing	Attempts to improve the original DCMS classification Representation with concentric layers, useful in policy analysis. Emphasis on fine arts and on cultural production.	• Industrial classification-based approaches cannot encapsulate the convergence of the information technology, communications, cultural and content industries. • Makes it difficult to accurately differentiate between different economic and industrial activities. • Standard industrial classifications do not always capture emerging industries, such as

(continued)

Table 1.1 (continued)

Author/ Institution	Definition	Rationale/ Criteria	Sectors accounted for	Advantages	Disadvantages
					digital content industries. • Many specialist creative activities may get lost among broad industry categories.
NESTA 2006	The creative industries as industrial sectors rather than as a set of creative activities based on individual talent	Focus on industries with capacity to create, own and exploit intellectual property through the ability to distribute and reproduce content on a large scale.	4 cross-cutting but distinct groups: **Creative service providers:** Those who dedicate time and Intellectual property to other businesses. Advertising, architecture, design consultancy and new media agencies **Creative content producers:**	Better reflects the perspective of private investors'	• Neglects economic significance of the creative sector

Those IP producing industries who distribute it to customers.
Film, TV, fashion designers, publishers.
Creative experience providers:
Those who sell the rights to experiences or live performances to consumers.
Theatre, opera, dance, live music organizers.
Creative original producers:
Those involved in the creation, manufacture or sale of one-off physical artefacts. Craft makers, design makers and visual artists (NESTA 2006, pp. 54–55)

(continued)

Table 1.1 (continued)

Author/ Institution	Definition	Rationale/ Criteria	Sectors accounted for	Advantages	Disadvantages
Higgs and Cunningham (2008) Creative trident	Collective term for those businesses in the economy which focus on creating and exploiting symbolic cultural products (such as the arts, films and interactive games), or on providing business-to-business symbolic or information services in areas such as architecture, advertising and marketing and design, as well as web, multimedia and software development.	**Specialist mode:** People in defined creative occupations within the defined creative industries. **Support mode:** People employed within the defined creative industries not working in defined creative occupations performing ex-creative functions (sales, secretary,) **Embedded mode:** Those people employed in defined creative occupations but who are working	Advertising and marketing, Architecture, visual arts and design; Film, TV, radio and photography; Music and performing arts; Publishing; Software, computer games and electronic publishing.		

		outside the defined creative industries.			
Work Foundation/ DCMS (2005 Concentric circle model		Focus on Activities that produce culture/creative content vs. Activities using creativity as input to diffuse it through distribution networks	**Creative Core** All acts of original creation of expressive values **Cultural Industries** Commercialisation of expressive product (TV, Radio, Film, Music etc.) **Creative Industries** combination of expressive and function values (architecture, advertising, fashion, design **Wider Economy** Expressive input into manufactured and service goods (Dyson, Virgin)	Representation with concentric layers, useful in policy analysis. Emphasis on fine arts and on cultural production. Importance of fine arts/culture as the epicentre of the creative economy. Representation with concentric layers, useful in policy analysis.	• Mapping the Core of Cultural and Arts activities is strongly limited to the industry classification system. • Some industry codes cannot be disaggregated into more detailed level implicates inability of separating production from distribution.
Potts *et al.* (2008) Social networks market model	The creative industries are the set of economic activities that involve the	The CIs are not about the allocation of resources: they are about the	**Systems that build and maintain social networks:**	Higher formalization in the modelling of agents linkages and interactions in	• Complexity. • Limitations of mathematical methods in modelling a high

(*continued*)

Table 1.1 (continued)

Author/ Institution	Definition	Rationale/ Criteria	Sectors accounted for	Advantages	Disadvantages
	creation and maintenance of social networks and the generation of value through production and consumption of network-valorized choices in these networks.	creation of new resources.	advertising, architecture, media, ICT software, etc. **Systems that create value on these social networks though content** film, TV, music, fashion, design, etc.	the network, and in the study of social interactive processes.	density of flows and linkages that characterize pure social processes.
UNESCO Framework for cultural statistics	The cultural domains include cultural activities, goods and services that are involved in all of the different phases of the culture cycle model. The related domains are linked to the		**Cultural domains:** Cultural and Natural heritage Performance and celebration Visual arts and crafts Books and Press Audiovisual and Interactive Media Design and Creative services **Transversal domains:**	Employs International Standard Industrial Classifications (ISICs) which allow for more cross-comparisons than simple SICs. Utilization of Central Products Classification (CPC) which	

	broader definition of culture, encompassing social and recreational activities.		Intangible Cultural Heritage Education and Training Archiving and Preservation Equipment and Supporting materials **Related Domains:** Tourism Sports and Recreation	reduces the effects of limitations in the ISIC approach.	
UNCTAD (2010)	The creative industries: are the cycles of creation, production and distribution of goods and services that use creativity and intellectual capital as primary inputs;	Creative activities are grouped as upstream or downstream creative activities. Upstream creative activities include cultural activities of a traditional nature. Downstream creative activities encompass	**Heritage** Traditional cultural expression – arts and crafts, festivals and celebrations Cultural sites-archaeological sites, museums, libraries **Arts** Visual arts, performing arts **Media** Publishing and printed media	Simple to use. Distinction between creation/production activities and distribution/broadcasting activities. It facilitates the analysis of the interdependencies between creation and distribution activities.	• Limitations of industry classification codes in mapping either creation or distribution industries. • Some industry codes, even at their maximum breakdown, include both creation and distribution activities, therefore no way of

(*continued*)

Table 1.1 (continued)

Author/ Institution	Definition	Rationale/ Criteria	Sectors accounted for	Advantages	Disadvantages
		activities that are closer to the market and generate commercial value from reduced production costs and linkages to other economic domains	Audiovisuals **Functional creations** Design New Media Creative services		separating production from distribution activities. • Difficulties in quantifying linkages and interdependencies(e.g. spillovers, externalities, flows that surpass national borders) throughout the value chain.
Collins etal., 2013	At its most basic, the creative sector is made up of those industries that rely on human creativity to generate wealth.	Creativity is the fundamental factor of production, without new, creative ideas, the industry could not exist.	**Creative Application** Covers industries that develop products or services primarily for the purpose of selling. Their existence is dependent upon market demand. Art/Antiques		

trade
Architecture
Fashion
Publishing
Advertising Crafts
Creative Expression –
Covers products that may not primarily be driven by commercial considerations. These products are typically defined as 'art for arts' sake' and are developed for audiences and consumers with an expressive story in mind.
Music, visual and performing arts
Video, film and imaging (photography)
Radio and TV broadcasting

(*continued*)

Table 1.1 (continued)

Author/ Institution	Definition	Rationale/ Criteria	Sectors accounted for	Advantages	Disadvantages
			Creative Technology – includes creative industries that rely most on technology and digital media. Internet and software Digital media Design		
OECD 2014	Knowledge-based creative activities that link producers, consumers and places by utilising technology, talent or skill to generate meaningful intangible cultural products, creative content and experiences.	Definition altered to incorporate focus on tourism.	Advertising, Animation, Architecture, design, Film, Gaming, Gastronomy, Music, Performing arts, Software and interactive games Television and radio.	More nuanced definition with relation to tourism.	

DCMS (2015) Industry and Occupation-based approach - Creative Intensity (Bakhshi et al. 2013)	A Creative Industry is defined as being one which employs a significant proportion of creative people, i.e. those employed in a creative occupation.	An industry passes a certain threshold in order to be classified as a creative industry.	Advertising and marketing Architecture Crafts Design: product, graphic and fashion design Film, TV, video, radio and photography IT, software and computer services Museums, galleries and libraries Music, performing and visual arts Publishing	Novel approach justifies the inclusion of IT, software sector. This approach draws on a key feature of the DCMS classification: it includes a definition of both industries and occupations. This distinguishes it from most other industrial classifications, including the SIC system itself, which define only industries.	
Santos Cruz and Teixeira (2015)	All the activities whose primary purpose is to produce creative goods. All those dedicated to the	Creativity in its broader sense, which involves not only artistic and cultural creativity, but also scientific/	Advertising and Marketing Architecture and Engineering Design and Fashion Design, Crafts,	A definition more suited to a Mediterranean context where creativity said to be more heritage-inclined	• industry classification systems' inherent limitations mean that these were also present here.

(*continued*)

Table 1.1 (continued)

Author/ Institution	Definition	Rationale/ Criteria	Sectors accounted for	Advantages	Disadvantages
	diffusion/ broadcasting/ reproduction services in straight correlation with production activities.	analytical creativity in the form of literary, academic, and scientific works.	Film, Video and Photography, TV and Radio, Music and the Performing Arts, Publishing, Software Publishing and Computer Consultancy, Research and Development	than its technologically oriented counterpart in Northern Europe.	

Source: DCMS, 1998, 2001, 2010, 2015; Throsby 2001; Hesmondhalgh 2002; WIPO, 2003, American for the Arts, 2004; KEA, 2006, pp. 56; NESTA 2006; Work Foundation/DCMS, 2005; Higgs and Cunningham 2008; Potts et al., 2008; UNCTAD, 2010; Flew 2012; Bakhshi et al. 2013; Collins et al., 2013; DCMS, 2015, Santos Cruz and Teixeira 2015, pp. 90–91

1.3.1 Department of Culture Media and Sport (DCMS) UK

In its most recent iteration, many writers see the modern reflections of the Creative Economy dating back to Horkheimer and Adorno essay on the Cultural Industry (2001: 2009) (O'Connor 2010; Steiner and Prettenthler 2015). The concept grew in popularity in the 1980s when it was used to denote the affiliation between the arts and economic activities. The UK is regarded as the key endorser of the discourse, a notion that is epitomised in the shift from 'cultural industries' to 'creative industries' introduced by the Blair-led Labour government, elected in 1997. O'Connor (2010) argued that with this slight shift in discourse, these industries transformed themselves from an undervalued, ignored arts-related sector into a frontrunner in the establishment of a novel contemporary image for Britain, thereby inserting themselves into the regular vernacular of government policy circles.

With the subsequent establishment of a creative industries taskforce, the Department of Culture, Media and Sport (DCMS) released the 1998 *Creative Industries Mapping Study*. The creative industries were defined to be those 'which have their origin in individual creativity, skill and talent and which have a potential for wealth and job creation through the generation and exploitation of intellectual property' (DCMS 1998: 3). Thirteen industry sectors comprised their classification, namely: Advertising, Antiques, Architecture, Crafts, Design, Fashion, Film, Leisure Software, Music, Performing Arts, Publishing, Software, TV and Radio. Curran and Van Egeraat (2010) contend that this definition ratified itself as an archetype for national, regional and city-level studies of the creative industries worldwide. A proliferation of studies followed in the subsequent decade reflecting on this classification (see Caves 2000; Scott 2001; Hesmondhalgh 2002; Power 2002).

Criticisms of the DCMS approach such as Garnham (2005) described the idea of the 'creative industries' as alien to artists' self perceptions. Cunningham (2002: 54) criticised the 'eclectic' listing of industries, while others such as Pratt (2005), Scott (2004) and Bakhshi et al. (2013) cited the arbitrary nature of some industries' inclusion as one of the main limitations of the approach. Similarly, O'Connor (2010: 49) characterising the approach as 'backed by some rather optimistic statistics (. . .) a handy definition and a list of 13 subs-sectors with clear links to statistical sources' and contended that the definition did not contribute towards a description of the complex structure of the sector. Furthermore, Higgs and Cunningham (2008) criticised a lack of comparability with available classification systems. In essence, the definition sparked an intense debate as noted by Flew (2012: 19) 'as to whether it was primarily an economic policy associated with promoting generating successful industries and new forms of IP (Intellectual Property), or primarily a policy to support the arts and cultural sectors, particularly those reliant upon public sector funding'. Mangematin et al. (2014) argued that the inclusion of the software factor was questionable given that it had little relation to the original cultural industries concept. Moreover, considering the view that the incorporation of this sector was essential in raising its economic value, it has been compared to a Trojan horse-like political agenda vehicle (Garnham 2005).

1.3.2 Alternative Classification Models

While we outlined some of the limitations of the DCMS approach, it must also be acknowledged that it established a platform and a basis for the creative industry discourse to have a voice at government and policy levels. Nevertheless, given the extant drawbacks of the approach, others researchers and organisations have put forward alternative models that have attempted to address some pitfalls in the DCMS approach (see Table 1.1; Throsby 2008; Hesmondhalgh 2002; WIPO 2003; KEA 2006).

The concentric circles model developed by David Throsby and later elaborated upon by the Work Foundation-DCMS (2005), contend that creativity is in most pristine form in the core creative arts (literature, music, etc.). However, there is amplified divergence from the centre towards 'peripheral' and borderline cultural industries, diminishing in creative and cultural value while increasing is the monetary value. Throsby's concentric circles model (2001) attempted to differentiate between the core creative arts (literature, music, etc.), other core cultural industries (films, museums etc.), wider cultural industries (publishing, TV) and related industries (advertising, design). The Work Foundation, in conjunction with the DCMS (2005) proposed a model that also draws on Throsby with the creative core incorporating forms of 'original product'. O'Connor (2010) argues that its value resides in the reinsertion of the specificity of culture into creativity which results in a more coherent model than previous DCMS approaches. These approaches along with others and their advantages and disadvantages are summarised in Table 1.1.

1.3.3 Creative Intensity: Towards a Benchmark?

The most current approach was produced by Bakhshi et al. (2013) who adopted Freeman's (2004) 'creative intensity', that is: the proportion of workers in any given creative industry that are engaged in a creative occupation. Following a public consultation exercise in January 2014, the DCMS adopted this methodology. Authors and institutions have such as CCI (2013) and Novak-Leonard (2014) argued that this approach has helped reduce the challenge posed in previous approaches as it helps determine which industries should be included in the analysis. Thus, this can assist in overcoming the arbitrary and 'eclectic' nature of industry listing previously cited as problematic in the DCMS approach. Moreover, it has the added benefit of permitting the IT sectors to be reinstalled (Bakhshi et al. 2013) as they normally surpass the threshold required for inclusion.

The creative intensity methodology has had a profound effect in the reworking of the DCMS classifications, which as of the 13th January 2015 features 9 subsets in contrast with the original 13 in the previous mapping studies (DCMS 2015). These are Advertising and Marketing, Architecture, Crafts, Design: product, graphic and fashion design, Film, TV, Video, Radio and Photography, IT, Software and Computer services, Publishing, Museums, Galleries and Libraries, Music, Performing and Visual Arts. Given its relative novelty, the classification has not been implemented in many studies of note. However, the creative intensity approach has gained certain currency, as it is extant in some academic and policy publications. Lazzaretti and Capone (2015) employed it as a narrow analysis alongside the broader Green Paper definition (European Commission 2010) in an analysis of the creative industries in Tuscany. Indeed, they argue that the approach appears to be a better standard that provides more representative results of the reality. Similarly, DCMS (2015) utilised it in an examination of employment in creative industries in the UK. Other studies in which it is apparent include Lazzaretti et al. (2015), Nathan et al. (2015), Bakhshi and Windsor (2015).

Some authors have argued that the creativity present in Northern Europe is dissimilar to that of the Southern region such as the Mediterranean. They contend that the former's is more related to technology rather than the more cultural heritage-inclined creativity of Southern Europe. For example, Santos Cruz and Teixeira (2015) in the Portuguese context argue in all previous classification systems that there was an intrinsic inability to capture the majority of activities involved in culture and fine arts. Thus, they employ a distinct industry-based approach focussing on core creative industries that departs from the WIPO copyright model as they view it as the most objective. The primary rationale behind their approach is to include all the activities whose principal objective is to produce creative goods, creativity here being considered it its broader sense (artistic, cultural, scientific, analytical forms of creativity). In contrast, Steiner and Prettenthler (2015) envision creativity as a continuum and emphasise the trans-sectoral character of creativity. Thus, instead of repeating a traditional focus on distinguishing between creative and non-creative activities, they focus on the question of how the service is provided, which allows for a better capture of the creativity external to the traditionally considered creative industries.

1.3.4 Our Classification Approach

Against the ongoing debate with respect to creative industry classification and recognising the dissimilar definitions extant in the creative economy, the challenge for us is: what is the most appropriate approach to take to define and classify creative industries that is relevant to peripheral regions? Solace can be taken from Thorsby (2008: 156), who noted 'There is no "right" or "wrong" model to analyse creative and cultural industries, but simply a range of alternate constructions based on different sets of assumptions and employing different mechanisms for putting the parts together'. The study by Santos Cruz and Teixeira (2015) provides a good example of this, employing all the models that we have discussed. Moreover, the employment portion of the creative industries varies ranging from 2.5% (DCMS 1998, 2001) to 4.6% (WIPO) according to the approach utilised. However, we argue that a distinct benchmark would be hugely beneficial allowing cross-national comparisons as well as providing an adaptable and workable framework for countries such as Ireland who have no set policy for creative industries.

While academic debate on the definition of the creative economy is a necessary part of the introduction of a new form of analysis, the reality made clear by Allen Scott (2010) on the ambiguities of standard industrial classifications holds sway. In our approach to defining the creative industries as evidence of the extent of the creative economy in peripheral area we are cognisant of the constraints of carrying out research in a heretofore under researched area. Within the literature there is an acknowledgement of some differences between urban and rural/peripheral creative industries and economies (Bell and Jayne 2006; Scott 2010).

Our definition and classification is informed and speaks to previous work carried out under a number of projects undertaken with colleagues in NUI Galway and in collaboration with other organisations in Ireland such as the Western Development Commission Ireland (WDC). As will become clear, the availability of statistical data, for our own region in the West of Ireland and that of the peripheral contexts we are concerned with, is far below that of average cases. This reality confines our definition and forces us to make use of standard industrial classification as employment data at the level that we are concerned with is not available. For these reasons our definition most closely aligns to that of the DCMS. For the purposes of our research on the creative economy in peripheral regions we (taking the lead from work done by Oxford Economics and the WDC (2009)) have chosen a classification that splits individual creative industries into three distinct categories: *Creative Application; Creative Expression;* and *Creative Technology*. In taking this approach we are attempting to balance the acknowledged under representation of the industry, the classification challenges against drawing on a broad enough classification that has the flexibility and robustness to be applied in peripheral regions for the purposes of cross country analysis. Moreover, the utilisation of our classification approach was informed by the academic and policy debates and also was shaped and influenced by our partners on the Creative Edge project funded by the Northern Peripheries Programme and by our interactions and engagement with creatives, policy makers and supporting agencies. Our definition draws on and adopts our work on the Creative Edge project (see Collins et al. 2013; Oxford Economics, 2008; WDC, 2009) outlined our definitions and classifications as applied to peripheral creative industries (see Fig. 1.3). Although there is some overlap between each of the categories and blurred edges, this classification represents a majority rules approach. Each industry has been classified according to its core activity i.e. the primary reason for its establishment.

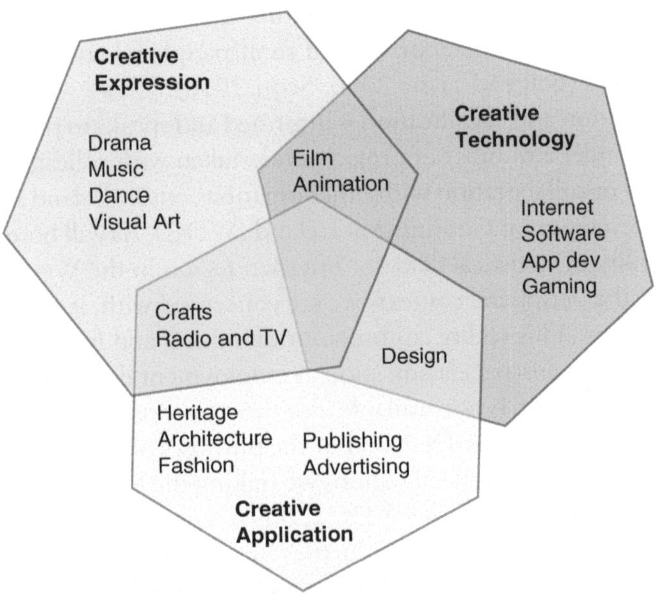

Fig. 1.3 Creative industries by subsector
Source: Adopted from WDC (2009)

The overlap can be seen as a reflection of the interaction that is indicative of creative industries as we explore further in Chapter 3.

1.4 Key Drivers of the Creative Economy

So what are the key drivers of the creative economy? We suggest that there are two main drivers. First, there is an increased *demand for creative product* and, second, *changing the ways we produce and consume creative produce*. Taken together these are significant drivers within the creative context irrespective of urban or peripheral locations. These drivers provide us with an initial point of reference, one to which we will return to many times throughout the book.

1.4.1 Increased Demand for Creative Produce: Global, Societal and Technological

The rate of that change makes our lived world experience today a vague reflection of that 30 years ago. We contend that the coalescence of culture, society and technology have been instrumental in this change and all three have direct and obvious consequences on the growth of the creative economy across the globe.

One most obvious driver of the creative economy is that we simply spend more of our money on 'Culture' than we have ever done. There is more demand for creative produce, which can be defined in many different ways as we have discussed earlier. The simple facts such as global spending on entertainment and media (E&M) rising at 4.9% in 2011 (PWC 2015) or that spending on cultural services and cultural admittance in Ireland and the UK has risen 15% in the last four years (Visa Europe 2015) proves the above observation. This further highlights that the demand for culture produce is on the increase. Many see this as evidence of the maturation of the consumer society that grew out of the post-war boom (circa 1950). Others describe it as evidence of the movement away from massification towards goods and services that better reflect individual tastes and identity (see Caves (2000) and Townley and Beech (2010)). Within this main driver are the *experience economy, slow fashion* and *technology* that are driving the demand for creative produce.

The Experience Economy: The concept of the experience economy originated in the early 1980s with Hirschman and Holbrook (1982: 99) who refer to hedonic consumption as 'those facets of consumer behaviour that relate to the multi-sensory, fantasy and emotive aspects of product usage'. Pine and Gilmore (1999) were the first to build on this to construct the notion of the experience economy. In essence, the act of consumption becomes a holistic experience that involves a person as opposed to a customer (LaSalle and Britton 2003). It is this experience and use value that determines the quality and memorable nature of the product or service. As Pizam (2010: 343) suggests, the quality of the experience is the intervening variable between 'the independent variables of quantity and quality of tangible and intangible products and services and the dependent variables of consumer satisfaction and willingness to pay high prices'.

In the experience economy, rather than compete on price, firms add value to products and services by enhancing their aesthetic and experiential dimensions (see Leslie et al. 2015). Consumers no longer desire mass-produced goods, preferring to purchase products by small industries that are instilled with local narrative, products whose small production environment harks back to pre-industrial methods of production (McRobbie, 2003). This driver presents a real opportunity for peripheral areas where there is also an increasing demand for local intangible-imbued produce.

Slow Fashion: Related to the experience economy and the focus on the customer experience we are seeing the emergence of Slow Fashion. This parallels with the shift away from consumption of mass produce towards the experience economy. This movement is characterised by the growth of small independent producers, who differentiate themselves from mass-production models by offering customers an alternative retail experience (Leslie et al. 2015). Clark (2009) identifies three components of slow fashion: placing value on local resources and economies, transparency in the production system and creating products with a longer usable life. Similarly, this relates to the slow food movement that strived to support local farmers and their produce. Indeed, both are constituents of the wider

'Slow Living' concept which as Leslie et al. (2015: 92) describes 'as premised upon an ethic of care – a concern for the materials that go into the foods we consume, the longevity of products and the lives of those involved in their production'. Part of the concerns includes issues related to environmental sustainability and social impact (Siegel et al. 2012; in Pookulangara and Shephard 2013) which are disregarded as the polar-opposite 'Fast' equivalent of these productions. In relation to slow food, people are motivated by a desire to gradually move away from the institutionalised, mass-produced business model hitherto dominant (Fletcher 2010; for more on this, see Pookulangara and Shephard 2013). The emergence of slow fashion exhibits a paralleled path.

Technological Change: While the rate of technological advance over the past 40 years has impacted on virtually every part of the economy, we contend that the creative economy as we know it would simply not exist were it not for the recent rate technological innovation and its socialisation. Digital technologies such as Information and Communication Technologies (ICTs), the evolution of Web 2.0 and its consequential upsurge in the abundance of user-generated content are highly conducive towards growth in creative industries. They represent a vital component in abating traditional barriers and in democratising creative and cultural production (Power 2002). Moreover, an equally pivotal component in this progress has been the emergence of improved mobile infrastructure, including smartphones, tablets and e-readers, devices which demand quasi-ubiquitous quality internet provision. The establishment of 3G and 4G networks has enhanced the bandwidth afforded to consumers, thus improving the experience and quality of service provided.

Data from Eurostat, OECD and other agencies show the rate of penetration of new technologies into homes across the world. A watershed was reached in 2007, when a majority (55%) of households in the EU–28 had internet access. This proportion continued to increase and in 2014 reached 81%, a 2% rise from the year previous (Eurostat 2015). We are cognisant of the fact that the roll out of these technologies has been far from and that in some cases these notionally aspatial technologies have had very real impacts on geography (see Malecki 2003; Collins 2007). That said, the more recent advances in mobile communications have shown a higher rate of equalisation of access, monetarily and geographically.

Documenting the addition of 122 million new mobile broadband subscriptions in its 34-country area, the OECD notes a year-on-year rise of 13.5%, driven by growth in smartphone and tablets, culminating in a total of 1.03 billion subscriptions for the area as a whole (OECD 2015). In excess of 50 million Europeans now go online on tablets and 68% own an internet-enabled mobile phone, an increase of 46% since 2010 (Ernst and Young 2014). Indeed, by 2025, it is estimated that 13.7 billion internet-enabled devices will be shipped worldwide (IHS Technology 2015). This proliferation is represented by the fact that in 2012, 36% of individuals aged 16 to 74 in the EU–28 used a mobile device to connect to the internet, with this figure rising by a further 15% in 2014 (Eurostat 2015).

Beyond access, the rise of mobile internet has had a real impact on the way we consume, 42% of UK online sales were via mobile and tablet devices in the second quarter of 2015 (IMRG 2015). Moreover, mobile e-commerce represents 34% of global e-commerce transactions with that figure expected to rise to 40% by the year's end (Criteo 2015). A key output of the proliferation in mobile infrastructure has been the emergence of the app economy. Rooted in iTunes App Store of 2008, the accessibility of app-making tools means that creation is essentially democratised, irrespective of status or location as barriers are minimal. This latter factor is perhaps best epitomised by the fact that the geographically peripheral Nordic region is home to some highly successful app companies such as Rovio (Angry Birds), Supercell (Candy Crush) and King.com (Clash of Clans). Additionally, all three have their headquarters in geographically marginal areas (Helsinki, Helsinki and Dublin). Breslin et al. (2014) in their study of the app economy estimate that EU developers took in €17.5 billion in revenue in 2013 with a total workforce (including marketing and support staff) of 1.8 million. Moreover, they forecast these figures to increase to €63 billion and 4.8 million, respectively, by 2018. Other studies have reported analogous findings with Vision Mobile (2015) suggesting that the app industry has created spillover employment of almost 850,000. Similarly, they argue that revenue and workforce figures are only going to rise as enhanced smartphone penetration fuels enormous demand for skilled app developers.

Furthermore, enhanced worldwide internet penetration exerts a fundamental role in the democratisation of access to creative and cultural content. It is crucial that this penetration extends to rural and peripheral areas, thus mitigating the digital divide. ICT has been posited as a solution to the problems faced by rural businesses due to its ability to transcend space (Warren and Evitt 2010). LaRose et al. (2007) suggest that the provision of internet connectivity fosters social interactions that increase attachment to rural areas, thus alleviating out-migration. Similarly, McGranahan et al. (2011) contend that the spread of broadband appeared to have facilitated movement out of cities. By extension, the provision of a quality internet connection would allow rural and peripheral areas to retain already present intraregional creatives while also allowing them to attract extraregional individuals. In a similar vein, Whitacre et al. (2013) noted a direct correlation between high-quality broadband provision in rural areas and the presence of creative individuals.

The provision of broadband has been disseminated on a much wider basis, epitomised by the sheer amount of fixed and mobile subscriptions around the world. It is crucial that this extends further into rural areas as it is a crucial factor in alleviating the 'rural penalty' (Malecki 2003); problems inherently associated with a low population density, geographical isolation and the distance from markets. Anderson et al. (2015) tentatively argue that ICT proffers a new rural geography: the creative countryside which is culturally inspired and entrepreneurially driven and in which place increasingly supersedes space in terms of importance.

The socialisation of technology reflects a wider, ever-increasing pattern by which individuals' patterns of consumption are being fundamentally altered, subsuming the way they access media and culture. Jones et al. (2015) argue that technology transforms the material base of creative products, altering processes of production and consumption. Hence, technology has disrupted industry business models and industry structures by altering cost, accessibility, reproducibility and scalability. These changes in material base have vastly expanded those who have access to creative content, connecting producers and consumers in novel ways and altering industry economics and structure

(Hirsch and Gruber 2015). Mangematin et al. (2014) contend that our news supply, the selection of occupation environments, how we connect with clientele, how goods are consumed, our professional and private-sphere lives are transfigured by digital technology. One of the primary transfigurations is how technology has fundamentally shaken traditional music, publishing and film industry structures (Andersen et al. 2007; Currah 2007), which hitherto had monopolised their respective industries, restricting access and controlling production. In the following section we will take a look at how particular creative industries have responded to the advance practice of digital production and highlight how new responses to the original decline of (physical music sales and newspaper circulation) are driving the rise of the digital Creative Economy.

1.4.2 Changing the Ways We Produce and Consume: Digitalisation and Prosumers

1.4.2.1 Digitalisation

The creative industries have had a very unique relationship with the rise of the digitalisation of content. Best understood by the advent of peer-to-peer file sharing, facilitated by sites such as Napster and Pirate Bay, many marque industries within the creative economy from music to audiovisual have been the first to witness the digitalisation of their produce. At first look, many statistics point to a devastating effect on industry earnings: music revenues plummeting from $38 billion to $15 billion over the period 1999–2014 (IFPI 2015); in 2013, total revenue within the newspaper industry decreased by 2.6%, representing over a billion dollars in deficits (Saperstein 2014). To illustrate the changing ways we produce and consumer and how digitalisation is changing industry norms and reshaping industries, we focus on two sectors – the music and newspaper industries. In particular these two illustrative examples highlight the many consequences not just for the consumption of culture, but crucially for its production as well.

The Music Industry

From Napster to iTunes to Spotify it will come as little surprise that in 2014 the International Federation of the Phonographic Industry (IFPI 2015) noted that the same proportion of revenues was derived from digital mediums as physical format sales. The growth rates are impressive, digital revenues increased 65% between 2014 and 2015 (BMI 2015), while the RIAA (2015) note how total streaming revenue has overtaken total physical sales revenue in 2014. As already eluded too, these figures are in the context of the massive shock suffered by the industry with the advent of digitalisation. Here we note how new modes of consumption and production of this innately cultural product has helped to undermine the monopoly of 'the big 5' music companies and usher in a new age of more equal access. Benghozi et al. (2015) highlight the emergence of Spotify in this regard, citing its ambition to 'make all the world's music available instantly to everyone, wherever and whenever they want it' (Benghozi et al. 2015). These streaming services increase the possibility for marginalised artists to connect with a worldwide audience or at the very least garner some income for their work (DiMaggio 2014).

With the shift away from the 'Big 5' Wikström (2014) argues that the integrated multinational music companies created opportunities for small firms and indie record companies that have more than compensated in the quantity of album production induced by this shift. Waldfogel (2012) argues that between 1998 and 2010, albums released by major labels decreased by roughly 40% and releases by independent record companies accelerated dramatically, passing the majors in 2001 and peaking in 2005, at which point their numbers decline. This decline was subsequently compensated by the number of self-released albums. One of the more successful self-released albums has been Macklemore and Ryan Lewis' 'The Heist' (2012). The album was independently produced, recorded and self-released with no mainstream promotion or support as it was marketed through social media, YouTube and touring. The album debuted at number two in the Billboard charts and one of its songs 'Thrift Shop' experienced international success, reaching top spot in 17 countries' music charts and 83% of the first-week sales derived from digital downloads (total, 78,000). Indeed, platforms in the ilk of Spotify and YouTube bring local artists to the fore, with the vast majority (80% +) of top ten albums in Denmark, France, the Netherlands, Spain, Italy and Sweden in 2013 by locally signed artists (Ernst and Young 2014). Moreover, Mortimer et al. (2012) noted that although file sharing reduces album sales to an extent, it has the opposite effect on demand for live concerts, especially for artists who have not reached stardom.

This illustrative case of the music industry demonstrates how streaming models and lower costs of production and dissemination have decentralised the music industry, facilitating the access of artists who heretofore had been marginalised. It also highlights how digitalisation coupled with the growth of new online music platforms has changed both the production and consumption of music. This has meant that technology, production and new consumption business models have undermined the traditional big label music model's competitive dominance. This illustrative example also highlights how the scope of participation can be scaled globally and the cost of participation of both artists (producers) and consumers (buyers) can be lowered, as well as providing consumers with more choice that reflects their individual rather than mass market tastes and preferences.

The Newspaper Industry

The newspaper industry has also witnessed some fundamental changes to its structure as increasing quantities of readers migrate to digital readership. It reflects a trend that originated with the desktop, and subsequently the laptop, and that has been hastened by the emergence and the popularity of mobile devices, such as smartphones and tablets. According to Rothmann and Koch (2014) changes in the newspaper industry have been as significant as those discernible in other traditional media industries. While we see evidence of similarities in the impacts, again, we are concerned with the response to the shock of digitalisation pursued by the print media and the role it plays in driving the Creative Economy.

While technological progress has disrupted the traditional business model of the newspaper industry, it has concurrently democratised the wider sector, with bloggers now a key fulcrum of many people's digital activities and purchases. Technological progress has been key in facilitating access to a sector that in the twentieth century was dominated by media conglomerates (Leurdijk and Nieuwenhuis 2014). With the rise of social media sites (Twitter, Facebook and Instagram) credence must be given to the claim that we have entered an age in which news must be conveyed in less than 140 characters (Saperstein 2014). Indeed, sites of this denomination represent mediums that embrace a phenomenon that has become known as 'citizen journalism' or 'participatory journalism', a process which is epitomised by public citizens 'playing an active role in the process of collecting, reporting, analysing, and disseminating news and information' (Bowman and Willis 2003, p. 9).

For example, Reuters' (2015) analysis demonstrates that social media is considered more important than print in the USA, Ireland, Brazil, Italy, France, Spain and Australia, in terms of accessing news. An OFCOM report of July 2014 demonstrated that 59% of active internet users in the UK visited blogging sites during the month, spending an average of 23.8 minutes on such websites. In a separate study (OFCOM 2014) noted that 23% of people contributed or commented on other people's blogs. The Open-Source Foundation (OSF 2014) contends that the emergence of digital media has given minority voice in media circles. For instance Guatemala and Thailand report the increment of hyper-local media in rural areas, examining contentions otherwise disregarded by traditional media. Furthermore, in countries with authoritarian regimes, bottom-up citizen journalism initiatives are democratising the public sphere. In Pakistan, citizen media was integral in organising protests against the emergency rule of General Pervez Musharraf in 2007 (OSF 2014), while interesting work has been carried out on the role of social media in the Arab Spring movement (Howard et al. 2011).
Citizen reporters are using modern technology to blur the previously unique role of the journalist by interviewing, recording, writing and publishing their own content. Social media has facilitated citizen journalism in news production, distribution and consumption. The OSF (2014) also cites the importance of microbloggers such as Twitter users who disseminate emerging events much quicker than traditional media, the 2008 Sichuan earthquake providing a case in point. Moreover, the OSF study contends that Twitter and domestic microblogs often distribute information not reported by traditional media, creating an alternative network of news, challenging established media which may be biased (some might say leading to fake news or what has been termed post-truthism). In this sense, it has developed into a type of regulator system, redressing inaccuracies and acts of corruption which otherwise would not be brought to the public eye.

The importance of social media as a news outlet was further highlighted in survey by PEW (2015) in which they reported that nearly half of adults (34 or younger) who get news from Facebook or Twitter say the services are 'the most or an important way they get news'. A survey in Germany acknowledged that journalists understand that they can no longer assume an attitude of passivity on the part of their audience with over 50% stating that social media have a high or very high relevance for journalistic work (Schroder and Steeg Larsen 2010). Similarly, in Ireland, 99% of journalists interviewed used at least one social media tool professionally (Heravi et al. 2014) with 92% using Twitter on a weekly basis, the most popular platform. Interestingly, despite the almost ubiquitous adoption of social media by Irish journalists, 55% agree or strongly agree that these tools are undermining 'traditional journalistic values' (Heravi et al. 2014). Alternatives to social media as mediums for news have also proliferated. One of the main platforms in this regard has been Storyful, an Irish-based new media organisation that 'uses proprietary technology (...) to find, verify, and share tweets, photos, and videos from social media' (Greenberg 2015).

Essentially, these examples (Facebook, Twitter, Storyful) represent opportunities for the vast majority to become both creators and users. Digitalisation is reducing or eliminating barriers to entry and also increasing the power of buyer. Users have the freedom to generate content and can monetise their participation. For such companies this has significantly and irrecoverably changed industry norms and status quo. Similar to their counterparts in music, the result of the digitalisation of content, while in the first instance a negative shock, has more latterly opened up new possibilities for individuals as producers. The illustrative examples highlight industrial change in the face of a technological and digital imperative and provide an interesting perspective not alone on the current state but of future possibilities for the creative economy.[2]

1.4.2.2 Prosumers

Much of that which has been identified above and in many other analyses of creative industry business models embodies the changing patterns that Toffler (1980) termed the rise of the *prosumer*. In its most simplistic definition, the prosumer constitutes a marriage between production and consumption or production by consumers. As a result of the proliferation of Web 2.0, studies have more recently taken a focus on prosumer and prosumption (see Ritzer and Jurgenson 2010; Ritzer et al. 2012; Rifkin 2014a; Ritzer 2015) or synonymous terms such as produser and produsage (Bruns 2007) or co-creation (Prahalad and Ramaswamy 2004; Ramaswamy and Ozcan 2014). Thus, studies have tended to focus on differentiated means of prosumption through social media sites such as Facebook (Boyd 2006, 2008a, 2008b) and Wikipedia (Konieczny 2007, 2009a, b, 2012). Others have argued

[2] In Chapter 3 we will have the opportunity to explore these further in the context of our case-study regions.

that it was not a novel concept given its ingrained nature within human society (Ritzer 2015). Ritzer (2009) argued that the Industrial Age separated production and consumption but that even at its height prosumption was discernible to a certain degree (producers consumed raw materials; consumers produced their meals).

This prosumption-induced freedom is epitomised by the propagation of user-generated content (UGC), most visible on sites of cultural consumption such as Pinterest, YouTube, Wikipedia and Tumblr. UGC is published content that may be individually or collaboratively produced, modified, shared and consumed, and 'can be seen as the sum of all ways in which people make use of social media' (Kaplan and Haenlein 2010: 61). This is citizen journalism, authors self-publishing books, musicians distributing their own albums and the audio visual producers on YouTube lending to a massive increase in cultural content available for consumption. As such people are bypassing conventional intermediaries and supply chains, creating and distributing their own produce. BOP Consulting (2009) cite examples of a 20,000 person co-created open-source movie, the fact that 13 hours of content is uploaded to YouTube every minute as some evidence of technological influence in changing creative and cultural production. Such expressions of mass creative collaboration are redefining the ways in which we organise ourselves with the explosion of collaborative innovation, a phenomenon facilitated by the internet's ability to link audience and artist. Cultural products are now highly democratised, no longer solely unique to the elites' milieu (see Rothler and Wenzlaff 2011; Collins et al. 2013). As Mann (2000: 41) contends 'every scrap of human culture transcribed, no matter how obscure or commercially successful will be available to all'. Thus, owing to technological developments, mass participation and mass creativity are enhanced and are changing the landscape of creative and cultural production. Prosumers and prosumption open up potentially significant opportunities for all stakeholders in peripheral regions. As prosumers search and seek difference in terms of content etc., this provides peripheral creative industries with a distinct advantage that is centred on place and authenticity.

The potential future of a more creative economy where goods and services are more tailored to individual tastes, where choices are made on the basis of customer needs and wants rather than at the behest of an all-powerful board of executives is a compelling one. In the following section we explore these drivers and test them against more critical perspective on the rise of the creative economy. An economy that while full of potential for different growth trajectories is also one that suffers from extreme precariousness an exploitation.

1.5 Some Creative Economy Critiques

In the eighteenth century the novel term was 'industrial', more recently we have moved through 'post-industrial' to 'information' and 'knowledge' economies. Admittedly the term *creative economy* is one in a long line of efforts to better describe current and future developments in the ways we work, interact and consume. The usual mode of filtration of these adjectives are from a start point in research (commercial and/or academic) where interested parties recognise new patterns emerging, and on that basis proffer future growth trajectories. Depending on the cogency of that argument many filter into the policymaking forum via a recognition on behalf of governments as to the possible gains from pursuing these emerging patterns. This path of filtration is rarely pure, asides from vested interest and the game of politics, the emerging nature of these trends are wrought with unknown and lack of certainty.

This is as true for the creative adjective as any that went before. Indeed, looking to Scott's (2010) argument that we simply do not have the metrics or the instruments to gauge the true impact of the production of culture, a lack of certainty in creative economy discourse can be taken as a given. Before we consider this distinction in greater depth in Chapter 2, we first examine some of criticisms being labelled at the creative industries in general. In keeping with the purpose of this monograph we divide this literature into two parts: the first looks at the general concept critique and issues relating to larger scale creative economy activity. The second, is more focussed on criticisms that relate to the nature of creative work on a smaller scale, issues of individualisation and romanticisation of labour.

1.5.1 The Concept and Precarity

The term creative economy has not been universally welcomed into the literature. A coherent argument emanating from writers associated with a political economy viewpoint is loosely bound by a belief that there is little new about the creative economy. For Donald (2004: 255) the creative economy is simply 'the old wolf of capitalism in designer clothing'. Garnham (2005) critically interrogates the concept and argues that the media/content industry sectors are increasingly central to the dynamism of contemporary capitalist economies. Rossiter (2004: 26) denounces creative industries as being driven by "'market populism'... defined by delirious faith in entrepreneurial culture and the capacity for new ICTs... to function as a policy panacea". Others view the creative economy as a marketing ploy, at the cutting edge of capitalism by placing ever more value on that which is ultimately ephemeral. So what Pine and Gilmore (1999) term the experience, others see as another example of commercialising that which had previously been free. The analogous rise of branding seems far from inconsequential in this light. For Flew (2012) creative industries began not as a concept but as a neo-liberalist tactical manoeuvre. Where the role advertising plays in the success or failure of a product of service is fully determining.

Other criticisms are that the creative economy is far too incoherent as a concept as creativity is far too vague to characterise the particular industry (ibid.). For Rossiter (2004: 98), the recent emphasis placed upon creativity in contemporary policy discourse that stems from the 'new economy dynamics' should not be read as dealing with 'creativity in the artistic or cultural sense'. Cunninghman (2009: 375) sees creative industries as a type of 'Trojan Horse, secreting the intellectual heritage of the information society and its technocratic baggage into the realm of cultural practice, suborning the latter's proper claims on the public purse and aligning it with inappropriate bedfellows such as business services', telecommunication etc.

In terms of gaining a greater understanding of the work of creative industries, some critics contend this new development model is reactionary insofar that it reinforces the status quo of labour relations within a neo-liberal paradigm. From low value add work in large multinational organisations, to the project-based nature of the working existence and hard to predict commissions, the precarious nature of employment is in evidence across most industries on the creative economy. Risk and uncertainty are not just markers of the outset of a career or the start of a new enterprise in the creative and cultural sectors; they are persistently at the core (De Beukelaer 2015).

Others raise concerns over the pursuit of the creative economy as a development tool. Key to their criticisms is the nature of work and how working practices in certain industries bring with them some serious ethical questions. Investigative journalism as well as academic work has gone to great lengths to uncover practices tantamount to sweatshops in the fashion industry (see Ross 2007). Similarly, the work of Yoon (2015) makes it clear that the ever-expanding value chains in the animation industry are pushing questionable work practices in less-developed economies that are far from the image that creative economy advocates like to invoke. At the larger creative industry scale it is clear that there are a number of examples of low value-added work moving into less developed regions following a similar route to those of more traditional industries like electronics and the automotive. The result is that many of these 'new industries' are reliant on traditional modes of exploitation and can therefore be subject to the same criticisms of their capitalistic forbearers.

Related to this is the notion of cultural imperialism, Flew (2013), contends that there is a mismatch between the global nature of the creative economy debate and the engagement with the term in particular places and that most framing of this debate remains confined within western social theory. This relates not just to the produce of the large-scale creative industries (i.e. the cultural monopoly of Hollywood and its representation of the idealised western consumer-led lifestyle) but the practices and policies that have accompanied its development. Oakley (2004: 72–73) talks of the danger of creative economy discourses as applied in the policy domain generating 'cookie-cutter' approaches to cultural development strategies: 'the sense that these are sectors that can be replicated and developed pretty much anywhere, without regards for the specifics of place (. . .) we currently seem hellbent on trying to replicate a single creative industries model across the country. It appears everywhere needs a university, some incubators and a "creative hub" with or without a café, galleries and fancy shops'.

1.5.2 Individualised and Romanticised Ideas of Small-Scale Creative Work

We have a long history of ascribing invention to individuals (see Isaacson 2014). Take the recent case of Steve Jobs, this has, on some occasion, transferred into the area of idolisation. The reality is that Steve Jobs did not invent the MP3 player or the smartphone, a fact that Stern and Seifert (2008) refer to as the misperception of culture and creativity as a product of individual genius rather than collective activity. The perceived individualisation of creative economy pursuits can have very negative effects on the support of the creative economy. For Christopherson (2008: 92) it is the conventional understanding of creative work as an individualised, project-based activity that demands originality of expression that begets intensely competitive, gatekeeper mediated environments. In this, creative workers are perceived as exceptional, their work processes are then treated as 'idiosyncratic' and their 'goals and strategies are depicted as driven by personal and internal motives rather than influenced by the political and economic context within which they work' (see also Bain and McLean 2013). In our case studies below, we will see how many of these creatives suffer from the perception, that 'we will do this anyway, regardless of any kind of support structure' (Interview 47 Audio Visual Worker, West of Ireland).

Individualisation of working practices in the creative economy through misconceptions of working practice or via policy and funding supports happens at the expense of social relations that make both individual and collective activities possible. As we will see further on, it is the collective activities of the creative industries that help push the creative economy on to greater stages of development. This individualisation also feeds directly into the precariousness of work in the creative industries. Miller (2010) contends that an increasing number of cultural workers are subject to flexible exploitation characterised by low pay, lack of security, intermittent income and high risk of social exclusion because of low incomes, welfare cuts and high cost of living. In order to combat this precarity inherent within the cultural and creative industries/the creative economy, it is suggested that collective action is needed to challenge precarious work conditions, rather than the individual nature currently dominant (MacRobbie 2002; Ross 2007).

In the more peripheral context, this individualisation also feeds into the romanticisation of creative work. The perception of individuals 'tuning out from the rat race' in pursuit of a more fulfilling career in creativity dominates not just the rhetoric, but policy to support the development of the creative economy in rural areas. For Cunninghman (2013), this perception has its roots in early writings that overly romanticise the notions of creative labour. As we will make clear below, this serves to do a disservice to the enterprise in evidence in more peripheral locations. The following section serves to start by making the case for creative economies in peripheral areas.

1.6 Making the Case for Peripheral Creative Economies

Since it began to enter the policy and academic debate, the creative economy has been considered an urban-based activity. The term creative economy and indeed creative industries brings with it images of young, hip, diverse people situated in the trendy cultural quarters of the world's leading cities. Here we do not wish to deny the urban leaning of much of the creative work, rather we intend to make the case that the creative economy and its industries also exist in more peripheral/non-urban contexts. Doing this puts us in line with a small but growing literature on the vitality of creative industries in more rural settings. One crucial starting point is to move away from assumptions about the rural urban divide in the creative economy. While early writings on the creative economy did not ignore rural areas, there was a tendency to assume the kind of creativity was markedly different from their urban counterpart. Where the urban was about innovation and dynamism, the non-urban tended to be cast as loners, escaping the 'rat race' to produce their more 'artistic content'.

Indeed, much of the policy invoked in promoting the creative economy tends to fall fowl of these generalisations. We shall deal more with this in the final chapter, but for now we are concerned with exploring the growing literature on non-urban creative economies in an effort to better understand the peripheral context of our findings.

1.6.1 The Importance of Place

Much work has tended to focus on the demographic differences of creatives in their place. Those located in the cities tend to be younger than those in the countryside (see Andersen 2010; Bennett et al. 2015). From relevant research, it appears that the rural creatives are attracted more by the area's soft factors, rather than the hard factors. For this reason, quality of life, natural amenities, a strong, close-knit community and peace are all important elements. These sit in contrast to the 'buzz', employment, opportunity and infrastructure-based attraction of the metropolis. Verdich (2010) cite outdoor amenities, downshifting, increased family time, the proximity to the natural environment and a strong sense of community as vital to attracting creative workers to Launceston. Bennett et al. (2015) parallel a similar situation in relation to rural Welsh craftspeople. Similarly, Daniel (2014) cites the collaborative and tight-knit communities of Cairns and Townsville as key to fostering a strong sense of belonging amongst inhabitants and in-migrants. Likewise, other research has further emphasised the importance of lifestyle features as of paramount importance in attracting and retaining creative individuals in rural areas (Andersen 2010; Herslund 2012) and general ex-metropolis areas (Collis et al. 2013; Felton and Collis 2012; Felton et al. 2010 Denis-Jacob 2012). Hence, it is arguable that the reasons for migrating or staying within rural creative economies are much more prosaic and modest than those of urban creative economies.

Another related feature is the connection to place in the rural creative economy. The rural creative economy has a more intimate connection with place, when compared with its urban equivalent. While in the latter, infrastructure and buzz are oft seen as highly important, the surrounding natural environment and landscape are seen as key facilitators of rural creative work. In this sense, Luckman (2012: 3) argues that for non-urban creative workers 'an awareness of place is central to their creative practice and provides a profound practical and emotive link between their lives and their work'. Indeed, in an earlier study she argued that a return to the emotions associated with place is one way of counteracting the problematic imposition of 'one-size-fits-all' policy strategy to rural areas that obscures vernacular creativity, local strengths and community wishes (Luckman et al. 2009). Moreover, Daniel (2014) notes a strong connection to place and explicitly the natural environment amongst creatives in the remote regional cities of Townville and Cairns. He contends that this connection is a key source of creative strength for these practitioners as it allows them personal and creative freedom. Andersen (2010) notes how this same type of freedom had attracted in-migrants into rural Broken Hill. Furthermore, these in-migrants were inspired by the qualities of place associated with the local desert and mining landscapes. Curtis (2010) comments on the success of rural festivals in marketing their location as an appealing physical, cultural and social landscape. She argues that 'rural towns have used their mountains, forests, beaches and cliffs to create a sense of distinctiveness and attract people to a particular location to experience jazz and other localised cultural activities' (103). While physical location of place may be a burden, it is also conceptualised as an enabler by many rural creatives, affording them creative freedom away as Andersen (2010: 84) notes from the 'city-based art fads, stress and busyness' of the urban creative economy.

Researching urban contexts Brown (2015) showed that the migration decisions of Birmingham's creatives are dictated by a diverse range of factors other than quality of place or diversity; typically related to higher education and personal and career development opportunities. Borén and Young (2013) noted a similar attraction amongst Stockholm's creative in-migrants. In the case of Western Australia, studying the migration of artists Bennett (2010) found that employment opportunities do play a key role in attracting them to Sydney and Melbourne. In the UK, Comunian and Faggian (2014) suggested that the provision of creative university courses is highly concentrated in the Greater London Area (24%) and the South East (13%). By contrast, more peripheral regions like Northern Ireland have the lowest percentages. Additionally, they argue that urban areas provide greater job opportunities and contracts for young graduates, which enhance opportunities to earn a living.

In Dublin Murphy et al. (2015) conclude that for computer game and media companies, 'hard' factors are of primary importance in choosing a location but that 'soft' factors play quite an important role when 'hard' factors are satisfied in multiple locations. Furthermore, Hansen and Niedomysl (2008) argued that the Swedish creative class predominantly migrate to cities with a lower 'people climate', because this decision happens during the job search following higher education. The 'buzz' of cities, a somewhat softer factor is also of interest to younger creatives. Dublin's 'cosmopolitan' atmosphere played some role in creative migration dynamics (Boyle 2006), but respondents said that it appealed to them while they were young and was less attractive when thinking of starting a family. Studies in the USA of those in creative occupations, artists engineers and the highly skilled showed that the young tended to move to city regions (Wojan et al. 2007, Scott 2010). Comunian and Faggian (2014) argue, in agreement with Pratt (2004), that the urban environment with its 'buzz' is vital for artists (Pratt 2004) and the city environment offers a wider cultural infrastructure as well as creative networks and informal learning environment for creative practitioners. Finally, Clare (2013) describes how London's creatives seek out not only agglomeration, but also a social milieu through increased interactions, learning and advancing career opportunities.

1.6.2 More Traditional Creativity: Hybridisation

One contention is that the rural creative economy consists of a mix of craft-based and traditional local culture (both material and symbolic) and new creative industries (see Bennett et al. 2015; Thomas et al. 2013). Moreover, Banks (2007, p123) suggested 'the revival of craft production amongst amateurs, artisans, small firms and enterprises is becoming a prominent feature of late-modern life'. According to Luckman (2012), this is increasingly enabled and sought after by rural, regional and remote cultural workers. An analysis of the Italian craft industry, Bertacchini and Borrione (2013) define such industries as having a tendency to locate in rural and non-metropolitan areas. The study of the Australian rural creative economy in Victoria demonstrated similar findings with job provision generally more focussed on traditional creative and cultural activities (libraries, visual and performing arts, printing, libraries). This stands in contrast to Metropolitan Melbourne where Creative Sector job provision is largely dependent on IT, telecommunications and advertising (Rural Councils Victoria 2013).

There are growing interfaces between the creative industry and other industries in rural or peripheral settings. For example, Woodward and Bremner (2015) coin the term 'agri-tivity' to describe the productive interface between agriculture and creative industries commonly found in rural and regional communities. Agri-tivity recognises that innovation is already present in many forms and identifies the services and products that fall outside current metropolitan based definitions of creative industries (agri-tourism, cultural tourism, festivals, new food movements). All this points to some new hybridisation within the creative economy and between creative industries and other industry sectors. While Comunian et al. (2011) cite how while UK creative technology and architecture students are concentrated in the Greater London area, craft courses are almost non-existent, instead clustering in the South West and East Midlands. Moreover they noted that the more 'traditional' conceptualisations of creativity are flagships of more peripheral areas (Crafts – South West, East Midlands, West Midlands; Writing and Publishing – Wales and Northern Ireland).

1.6.3 Beyond the Economic?

While there is a natural tendency for the larger IT or telecoms companies to locate in urban creative economies, rural creative economies will be occupied by small to medium-sized companies or individual endeavours. In the next chapter we will have to opportunity to discuss in greater detail the nature of the creative economies of our peripheral areas, but here we wish to focus on the different kind of positive externalities exuded by urban and non-urban creative economies. We will see that rural creatives are often inspired by 'extra-economic' incentives (see Collins Forthcoming). Many cite their love for the work or their desire to benefit the wider community. Hence, cultural and social goals are seen to take precedence over economic motivations.

Mayes' (2010) study of postcard production in Ravensthorpe provides a case in point. Residents are motivated by symbolic contribution to the town's identity rather than economic gains, facilitating social cohesion and a general sense of community.

Based on their analysis of rural Australian festivals Connell and Gibson (2013) concluded that while some were motivated by capital returns, most began for no other reason than for entertainment and because local authorities wanted to enhance local cultural life or promote particular music genres (see also Curtis (2010) on rural jazz festivals). Much of this work in the rural context points to the value placed on social returns, where social cohesion and community spirit was fortified through non-compensated volunteer work (see Collins Forthcoming for similar conclusions in the Irish context). In a study on Victoria's rural creative economy, the conclusion was reached that there were much higher levels of volunteerism in rural Victoria when compared with the metropolis (Rural Councils Victoria 2013). Herslund (2012) presents a similar conclusion in their work on the rural Danish context. This is part of a growing body of work that see the contribution of the rural creative practitioner as lying well beyond their economic returns. These are variably summarised as 'other advantages' such as providing 'organisational energy' (Herslund 2012: 253) to the region as a whole and (p. 253) using their 'skills for the betterment of the area' (Herslund 2012: 251).

Bringing this further, Daniel (2014) argues that regional creatives lack of engagement with policy may represent their lack of interest in growth and economic gains. In a similar argument, McDonald and Mason (2015) contend that the economic outcomes of regional creative practice are usurped by the social outcomes such as social cohesion and community spirit. Furthermore, Anwar McHenry (2011) noted that the arts were key in fortifying resilience via the strengthening of a sense of place amongst rural Mid-West Australians due to their capacity to explore community identity. The arts were viewed as a means for encouraging and enabling civic participation, thus enabling the identification and resolution of local problems. Indeed, the arts here were also seen as a means for facilitating understanding between opposite groups, a vital process in efforts relating to common objectives.

In essence, creativity in rural and remote regions has a different significance to the cutting edge creativity often associated with the city. Warren and Evitt (2010) elucidate how creativity represented a medium of self-determination and political expression for young Aboriginal musicians otherwise marginalised. Felton et al. (2010) describe the value of artisan social networks in outer suburbs, there, creativity is less about civic 'buzz' and mirrors more the hard slog and passion of key individuals. Gibson (2010: 7–8) argues that such examples 'suggest new ways in which creative industries research can be enlivened and made social, by not assuming a capitalist-orientated language of firms, growth, employment and export and instead valuing the communitarian purposes to which creativity can be put'. Hence, distinct but active rural creative industries emerge, highlighting a different, perhaps more united and collaborative form of creative economy than in the urban metropolis.

1.7 Conclusion

We have begun the chapter by expanding the scale and scope of the creative economy and industries in a global context. We then focussed our attention on defining what is meant by the creative economy and industries and the varied approached that have been taken to date. This has highlighted some key challenging in measuring this sector and the likelihood that existing measures underestimate the potential economic contribution of creative industries. Our focus on creative economies in peripheral regions taking inspiration from Oxford Economies we categorised the creative economy as consisting of, creative application, creative expression and creative technology subsectors, which we will explore in more depth in the next chapter. Increasing demand for creative produce and the changes in the way we produce and consume (digitalisation and prosumers) are key drivers influencing the future growth and development of the creative economy and industries. We then turned our attention to making the case for the creative economy and industries in peripheral regions as well as examining some critical perspectives of the creative economy. In examining the nuanced differences about the creative economy in peripheral regions we focussed on the importance of place, the potential hybridisation between creative industry sectors and other sectors in peripheral settings and the benefits of this sector and economy beyond the economic ones.

Bibliography

Americans for the Arts. 2004. *Creative Industries Study*. Washington, DC.

Andersen, B., R. Kozul-Wright, and Z. Kozul-Wright. 2007. Rents, rights n'rhythm: Cooperation, conflict and capabilities in the music industry. *Industry & Innovation* 14(5): 513–540.

Andersen, L. 2010. Magic light, silver city: The business of culture in Broken Hill. *Australian Geographer* 41(1): 71–85.

Anderson, A. R., Wallace, C., and Townsend, L. 2015. Great expectations or small country living? Enabling small rural creative businesses with ICT. *Sociologia Ruralis* 36(3): 450–468.

Anwar McHenry, J. 2011. Rural empowerment through the arts: The role of the arts in civic and social participation in the Mid West region of Western Australia. *Journal of Rural Studies* 27(3): 245–253.

Bain, A., and H. McLean. 2013. The artistic precariat. *Cambridge Journal of Regions, Economy and Society* 6(1): 93–111.

Bakhshi, H., A. Freeman, and P. Higgs. 2013. *A dynamic mapping of the UK's creative industries*. London: NESTA.

Bakhshi, H., and G. Windsor. 2015. *The creative economy and the future of employment*. London: Nesta.

Banks, M. 2007. *The politics of cultural work*. Basingstoke: Palgrave Macmillan.

Belk, Russell W., and Ronald Groves. 1999. Marketing and the multiple meanings of Australian aboriginal art. *Journal of Macromarketing* 19(1): 20–33.

Bell, D. and Jayne, M. 2006. *Small cities: Urban experience beyond the metropolis*. London: Routledge.

Benghozi, P.J, E. Salvador, and J. P. Simon. 2015. *Models of ICT innovation: A focus on the cinema sector*. Brussels: JRC Science and Policy Report.

Bennett, D. 2010. Creative migration: A Western Australian case study of creative artists. *Australian Geographer* 41(1): 117–128.

Bennett, S., S. McGuire, and R. Rahman. 2015. Living hand to mouth: Why the Bohemian lifestyle does not lead to wealth creation in peripheral regions? *European Planning Studies* 23(12): 2390–2403.

Bertacchini, E., and P. Borrione. 2013. The geography of the Italian creative economy: The special role of the design and craft based industries. *Regional Studies* 47(2): 135–147.

BOP Consulting. 2009. *Creative clusters 2008 conference report*. London: BOP Consulting.

Borén, T., and C. Young. 2013. Getting creative with the 'Creative City'? Towards new perspectives on creativity in urban policy. *International Journal of Urban and Regional Research* 37(5): 1799–1815.

Bourdieu, Pierre. 1984. *Distinction: A social critique of the judgement of taste*. Cambridge, MA: Harvard University Press.

Bowman, S., and C. Willis. 2003. We media. API Media Center paper. Retrieved 15 September 2015, from http://www.hypergene.net/wemedia/download/we_media.pdf.

Boyd, D. 2006. Friends, friendsters, and top 8: Writing community into being on social network sites. *First Monday* 11(12).

Boyd, D. 2008a. Facebook's privacy trainwreck: Exposure, invasion, and social convergence. *Convergence* 14(1),13–20.

Boyd, D. 2008b. *Taken out of context: American teen sociality in networked publics*. Berkeley: University of California.

Boyle, M. 2006. Culture in the rise of tiger economies: Scottish expatriates in Dublin and the 'creative class' thesis. *International Journal of Urban and Regional Research* 30(2): 403–426.

Breslin, J. G., Card, D., Dabrowski, M. and Mulligan, M. 2014. *Sizing the EU App Economy: Eurapp Final Report*, Directorate-General for Communications Networks, Content and Technology, European Commission.

Broadcast Music Incorporated. 2015. BMI reports record-breaking revenues of over $1 Billion. Retrieved 14 September 2015, from http://www.bmi.com/press/entry/572180.

Brown, J. 2015. Home from home? Locational choices of international 'Creative Class' workers. *European Planning Studies* 23(12): 2336–2355.

Bruns, A. 2007. *Produsage*. Proceedings of the 6th ACM SIGCHI conference on Creativity & cognition – C&C '07.

Caves, R. E. 2000. *Creative industries: Contracts between art and commerce*. London: Harvard University Press.

CCI. 2013. *Creative industries statistical analysis for Western Australia (Report for Department of Culture and Arts)*. Queensland: CCI.

Christen, K. 2006. Tracking properness: Repackaging culture in a remote Australian town. *Cultural Anthropology* 21(3): 416–446.

Clare, K. 2013. The essential role of place within the creative industries: Boundaries, networks and play. *Cities 34*, 52–57.

Christopherson, S. 2008. Beyond the self-expressive creative worker: An industry perspective on entertainment media. *Theory, Culture & Society December* 25(7): 73–95.

Clark, D. 2009. Crunching creativity: An attempt to measure creative employment. *Creative Industries Journal* 2(3): 217–230.

Clifton, N., and P. Cooke. 2009. Creative knowledge workers and location in Europe and North America: A comparative review. *Creative Industries Journal* 2(1): 73–89.

Collins, P. 2007. Information age Ireland: The attraction, the reality and never ending geography. *European Planning Studies* 15(1): 67–86.

Collins. Forthcoming. Measuring the extra economic impacts of festivals and event. *European Urban and Regional Studies.*

Collins, P, Cunningham, J and Murtagh, A. 2013. *The creative edge policy toolkit: Supporting the Development of the Creative Economy in Europe's Northern Periphery.* Galway: Creative Edge.

Collis, C., S. Freebody, and T. Flew. 2013. Seeing the outer suburbs: Addressing the urban bias in creative place thinking. *Regional Studies* 47(2): 148–160.

Comunian, R., and A. Faggian. 2014. creative graduates and creative cities: exploring the geography of creative education in the UK. *International Journal of Cultural and Creative Industries* 1(2): 18–34.

Comunian, R., Faggian, A. and Jewell, S. 2011. Winning and losing in the creative industries: An analysis of creative graduates' career opportunities across creative disciplines. *Cultural Trends* 20(3–4): 291–308.

Connell, J., and C. Gibson. 2013. Mobilizing music festivals for rural transformation: Opportunities and ambiguities. In *The globalization of musics in transit: Music migration and tourism,* eds. S. Kruger and R. Trandafoiu, 115–134. New York: Routledge.

Criteo. 2015. *State of mobile commerce: Growing like a weed.* Criteo. Available at: http://www.criteo.com/media/1894/criteo-state-of-mobile-commerce-q1-2015-ppt.pdf (Accessed June 2016).

Cunningham, S. 2002. From cultural to creative industries: Theory, industry, and policy implications. *Media International Australia Incorporating Culture and Policy: Quarterly Journal of Media Research and Resources* 102: 54–65.

Cunninghman, S. 2009. Trojan horse or Rorschach blot? Creative industries discourse around the world. *International Journal of Cultural Policy* 15(4): 375–386.

Cunninghman, S. 2013. *Hidden innovation: Policy, industry and the creative sector*. Queensland: University of Queensland Press.
Currah, A. 2007. Hollywood, the internet and the world: A geography of disruptive innovation. *Industry & Innovation* 14(4): 359–384.
Curran, D, and C. Van Egeraat. 2010. *Defining and valuing dublin's creative industries*. Dublin: Office of International Relations and Research, Dublin City Council.
Curtis, R. A. 2010. Australia's Capital of Jazz? The (re)creation of place, music and community at the Wangaratta Jazz Festival. *Australian Geographer* 41(1): 101–116.
Daniel, R. 2014a. Building the northern Australia vision through creative industries: The case of Cairns in far north Queensland. *Creative Industries Journal* 7(2): 134–147.
De Beukelaer, C. 2015. *Developing cultural industries: Learning from the palimpsest of practice*. Amsterdam: European Cultural Foundation.
De Propris, L., C. Chapain, P. Cooke, S. MacNeill, and J. Mateos-García. 2009. *The geography of creativity*. London: NESTA.
Denis-Jacob, J. 2012. Cultural industries in small-sized Canadian cities dream or reality? *Urban Studies* 49(1): 97–114.
Department of Culture Media and Sport (DCMS). 1998. *Creative industries mapping document*. London: DCMS.
Department of Culture Media and Sport. 2001. *Creative industries mapping document*. London: DCMS.
Department of Culture Media and Sport. 2005. *Creative industries economic estimates statistical bulletin*. London: Department for Culture, Media and Sport.
Department of Culture Media and Sport. 2010. December 2011 Creative Industries Economic Estimates (Experimental). http://www.culture.gov.uk/publications/7634.aspx
Department of Culture Media and Sport. 2015. *Creative industries: Focus on employment, June 2015*. London: DCMS.
DiMaggio, P. 2014. the internet's influence on the production and consumption of culture: Creative destruction and new opportunities. In Francisco Gonzalez (Ed.), *19 key essays on how internet is changing our lives*, 359–396. Madrid: BBVA.
Donald, J. 2004. What's new? A letter to Terry Flew. *Continuum* 18(2): 235–246.
Ernst and Young. 2014. *Measuring cultural and creative markets in the EU*. Brussels: European Grouping of Societies of Authors and Composers.

Ernst and Young. 2015. *Cultural times: The first global map of cultural and creative industries*. Paris: CISAC.

European Commission. 2010. *Unlocking the potential of cultural and creative industries*. Brussels: European Commission.

EUROSTAT. 2015. Information society statistics - households and individuals. Retrieved 14 September 2015, from http://ec.europa.eu/eurostat/statistics-explained/index.php/Information_society_statistics_-_households_and_individuals (Accessed July 2016).

Felton, E., and C. Collis. 2012. Creativity and the Australian suburbs: The appeal of suburban localities for the creative industries workforce. *Journal of Australian Studies* 36(2): 177–190.

Felton, E., C. Collis, and P. Graham. 2010. Making connections: Creative industries networks in outer-suburban locations. *Australian Geographer* 41(1): 57–70.

Fletcher, K. 2010. Slow Fashion: An invitation for Systems change. *Fashion Practice* 2(2): 259–266.

Flew, T. 2012. *The Creative industries: Culture and policy*. London: SAGE.

Flew, T. 2013. *Global creative industries*. Cambridge; Malden, MA: Polity Press.

Freeman, A. 2004. *London's creative sector. 2004 update*. London: Greater London Authority.

Garnham, N. 2005. From cultural to creative industries. *International Journal of Cultural Policy* 11(1): 15–29.

Gibson, C. 2010. Guest Editorial – Creative Geographies tales from the margins. *Australian Geographer* 41(1): 1–10.

Gibson, C., and J. Connell. 2004. Cultural industry production in remote places: Indigenous popular music in Australia. In *Cultural Industries and the Production of Culture*, eds. D. Power and A. Scott, 243–258. London and New York: Routledge.

Gibson, C., and L. Kong. 2005. Cultural economy: A critical review. *Progress in Human Geography* 29(5): 541–561.

Greenberg, J. 2015. Humans are Tech's next big thing—and that could be risky, *Wired Magazine* 24th of June 2015. https://www.wired.com/2015/06/apple-news-twitter-facebook/

Hansen, H. K., and T. Niedomysl. 2008. Migration of the creative class: Evidence from Sweden. *Journal of Economic Geography* 9(2): 191–206.

Heravi, B. R., N. Harrower, and M. Boran. 2014. *Social journalism survey: First national study on Irish journalists' use of social media*. HuJo, Insight Centre for Data Analytics, National University of Ireland, Galway.

Herslund, L. 2012. The rural creative class: Counterurbanisation and entrepreneurship in the Danish countryside. *Sociologia Ruralis* 52(2): 235–255.

Hesmondhalgh, D. 2002. *The cultural industries*. London: Sage.

Higgs, P., and S. Cunningham. 2008. Creative industries mapping: Where have we come from and where are we going? *Creative Industries Journal* 1(1): 7–30.

Hirsch, P., and D. Gruber. 2015. Digitizing fads and fashions: Disintermediation and glocalized markets in creative industries. In *The oxford handbook of creative industries*, eds. C. Jones, M. Lorenzen, and J. Sapsed, 421–438. Oxford: Oxford University Press.

Hirschman, E. C., and Holbrook, M. B. 1982. Hedonic consumption: emerging concepts, methods and propositions. *The Journal of Marketing*, July 92–101.

Horkheimer, M., and T. W. Adorno. 2001: 2009. The culture industry: Enlightenment as mass deception. In *Media and Cultural Studies: Keywords,* 41. Oxford: Blackwell Publishing.

Howard, P. N., A. Duffy, D. Freelon, M. M. Hussain, W. Mari, and M. Maziad. 2011. Opening closed regimes: What was the role of social media during the Arab Spring? *Available at SSRN 2595096.*

IHS. 2015. Smartphones and tablets transforming the audio market landscape, IHS Says. Retrieved 21 September 2015, from https://technology.ihs.com/546320/smartphones-and-tablets-transforming-the-audio-market-landscape-ihs-says.

Ii, B. J. P., and J. H. Gilmore. 1999. *Experience economy-work is theatre & every business a stage*. Cambridge, MA: Harvard business school press.

Interactive Media in Retail Group (IMRG). 2015. Has mobile penetration plateaued? Retrieved 22 September 2015, from http://www.imrg.org/index.php?catalog=2272.

International Federation of the Phonographic Industry (IFPI). 2015. *IFPI Digital Music Report: Charting the path to Sustainable Growth*. London: IFPI.

Isaacson, W. 2014. *The innovators: How a group of hackers, geniuses, and geeks created the digital revolution*. New York: Simon and Schuster.

Jones, C., Lorenzen, M. and Sapsed, J. 2015. *Creative Industries: A typology of change. The Handbook of Creative Industries*, 3–32. Oxford: Oxford University Press.

Kaplan, A., and M. Haenlein. 2010. Users of the world, unite! The challenges and opportunities of Social Media. *Business Horizons* 53: 59–68.

KEA. 2006. *The economy of culture in Europe*. Brussels: KEA European Affairs.

Konieczny, P. 2007. Wikis and Wikipedia as a teaching tool. *International Journal of Instructional Technology and Distance Education*, January 4(1): 15–34.

Konieczny, P. 2009a. Governance, organization, and democracy on the internet: The iron law and the evolution of wikipedia. *Sociological Forum* 24: 162–192.

Konieczny, P. 2009b. Wikipedia: Community or social movement? *Interface: A Journal for and about Social Movements* 1(2): 212–232.

Konieczny, P. 2012. Wikis and Wikipedia as a teaching tool: Five years later. *First Monday* Volume 17, Number 9 – 3 September 2012 available at http://firstmonday.org/ojs/index.php/fm/article/view/3583/3313?utm_source=dlvr.it&utm_medium=feed.

LaRose, R., J. Gregg, S. Strover, J. Straubhaar, and S. Carpenter. 2007. Closing the rural broadband gap: Promoting adoption of the Internet in rural America. *Telecommunications Policy* 31: 359–373.

LaSalle, D., and T. Britton. 2003. *Priceless: Turning ordinary products into extraordinary experiences*. Cambridge, MA: Harvard Business Press.

Lazzaretti, L., N. Innocenti, and F. Capone. 2015. Does related variety matter for creative industries? *Papers in Evolutionary Economic Geography* 15(10): 1–17.

Lazzaretti, L., and F. Capone. 2015. Narrow or broad definition of cultural and creative industries: some evidence from Tuscany, Italy. *International Journal of Cultural and Creative Industries* 2(2): 4–19.

Leslie, D., T. Brydges, and S. Brail. 2015. Qualifying aesthetic values in the experience economy. In Lorentzen, A., Larsen, K., and Schroder, L. (Eds.,) *Spatial dynamics of the Experience Economy*, 88–102. London: Routledge.

Leurdijk, A., and O. Nieuwenhuis. 2014. The newspaper industry. In *Digital Media Worlds; The new media economy*, eds. G. De Prato, E. Sanz, and J. P Simon, 147–162. Oxford: Palgrave.

Luckman, S., C. Gibson, and T. Lea. 2009. Mosquitoes in the mix: How transferable is creative city thinking? *Singapore Journal of Tropical Geography* 30(1): 70–85.

Luckman, S. 2012. *Locating cultural work: The politics and poetics of rural, regional and remote creativity*. New York: Palgrave MacMillan.

Macklemore and Lewis, R. 2012. "The Heist" Alternative Distribution Alliance and Macklemore LLC.

MacRobbie, A. 2002. Clubs to companies: Notes on the decline of political culture in speeded up creative worlds. *Cultural Studies* 16(4): 516–531.

Malecki, E. 2003. Digital development in rural areas: Potentials and pitfalls. *Journal of Rural Studies* 19: 201–214.

Mangematin, V., J. Sapsed, and E. Schußler. 2014. Disassembly and reassembly: An introduction to the Special Issue on digital technology and creative industries. *Technological Forecasting and Social Change* 83: 1–9.

Mann, C. 2000. The heavenly jukebox. *Atlantic Monthly*, September (41).

Markusen, A., G. Wassall, D. DeNatale, and R. Cohen. 2008. Defining the creative economy: Industry and occupational approaches. *Economic Development Quarterly* 22(1): 24–45.

Mayes, R. 2010. Postcards from Somewhere: 'Marginal' cultural production, creativity and community. *Australian Geographer* 41(1): 11–23.

McDonald, J., and R. Mason. 2015. *Creative communities: Regional inclusion & the arts*. Bristol: Intellect.

McGranahan, D., and T. Wojan. 2007. Recasting the creative class to examine growth processes in rural and urban countries. *Regional Studies* 41(2): 197–216.

McGranahan, D. A., T. R. Wojan, and D. M. Lambert. 2011. The rural growth trifecta: Outdoor amenities, creative class and entrepreneurial context. *Journal of Economic Geography* 11(3): 529–557.

McRobbie, A. 2003. Settling accounts with subcultures: A feminist critique. In *Culture: Critical Concepts in Sociology, Volume 3*, ed. C. Jenks, 246–258. London: Routledge.

Miller, T. 2010. Culture+Labour=Precariat. *Communication and Critical/ Cultural Studies* 7(1): 96–99.

Mortimer, J., C. Nosko, and A. Sorensen. 2012. Supply responses to digital distribution: Recorded music and live performances. *Information Economics and Policy* 24(1): 3–14.

Murphy, E., L. Fox-Rodgers, and D. Redmond. 2015. Location decision making of 'creative industries': The media and computer game sectors in Dublin, Ireland. *Growth and Change* 46(1): 97–113.

Myers, F. R. 2002. *Painting culture: The making of an Aboriginal High Art*. London: Duke University Press.

Nathan, M., A. Pratt, and A. Rincon-Azner. 2015. *Creative economy employment in the EU and UK: A comparative analysis*. London: Nesta.

NESTA. 2006. *Creating Growth-How the UK can develop world class creative business*. London: NESTA Research Report.

Novak-Leonard, J. 2014. *Measuring Chicago's (Artistically) creative economy*. Chicago: Cultural Policy Centre at the University of Chicago.

O'Connor, J. 2010. *The cultural and creative industries: A literature review.* Second Edition. London: Creativity, Culture and Education.

Oakley, K. 2004. Not so cool Britannia: The role of the creative industries in economic development. *International Journal of Cultural Studies* 7(1): 67–77.

OECD. 2015. OECD broadband statistics update. Retrieved 26 October 2015, from http://www.oecd.org/sti/broadband/broadband-statistics-update.htm.

Office of Communications. 2014. *Internet Citizens 2014: Use of selected citizen-related online content and services.* London: OFCOM.

Open Source Foundation. 2014. *Mapping digital media: Global findings.* London: OSF.

Pew Research Center. 2015. *The evolving role of news on Twitter and Facebook.* Washington, DC: PEW.

Pine, B. J., and J. H. Gilmore. 1999. *The experience economy: Work is theatre & every business a stage.* Cambridge, MA: Harvard Business Press.

Pizam, A. 2010. Creating memorable experiences. *International Journal of Hospitality Management* 29(3): 343.

Pookulangara, S., and A. Shephard. 2013. Slow fashion movement: Understanding consumer perceptions—An exploratory study. *Journal of Retailing and Consumer Services* 20(2): 200–206.

Potts, J., Cunningham, S., Hartley, J., and Ormerod, P. 2008. Social network markets: A new definition of the creative industries. *Journal of Cultural Economics* 32(3),167–185.

Power, D. 2002. 'Cultural industries' in Sweden: An assessment of their place in the Swedish economy. *Economic Geography* 78(2): 103–127.

Prahalad, K., and V. Ramaswamy. 2004. Co Creating unique value with customers. *Strategy & Leadership* 32(3): 4–9.

Pratt, A. C. 2004. The cultural economy a call for spatialized 'Production of Culture' perspectives. *International Journal of Cultural Studies* 7(1): 117–128.

Pratt, A. C. 2005. Cultural industries and public policy: An oxymoron? *International Journal of Cultural Policy* 11(1): 31–44.

PWC. 2015. *Global entertainment and media outlook 2015–2019.* New York: PWC.

Ramaswamy, V., and K. Ozcan. 2014. *The co-creation paradigm.* Stanford: Stanford University Press.

Recording Industry Association of America. 2015. *News and notes on 2014 RIAA music industry shipment and revenue statistics.* Washington, DC: RIAA.

Reuters. 2015. *Reuters Institute Digital News Report 2015.* Oxford: Reuters.

Rifkin, J. 2014. *The zero marginal cost society; The internet of things, the collaborative commons, and the collapse of capitalism.* New York: Palgrave Macmillan.

Ritzer, G. 2009. Keynote address: Correcting an historical error. *Conference on Prosumption,* Frankfurt, Germany, 26–27 March, 2009.

Ritzer, G. 2015. Prosumer capitalism. *The Sociological Quarterly* 56(3): 413–445.

Ritzer, G., and N. Jurgenson. 2010. Production, consumption, prosumption: The nature of capitalism in the age of the digital 'prosumer'. *Journal of Consumer Culture* 10(1): 13–36.

Ritzer, G., Dean, P., and Jurgenson, N. 2012. The coming of age of the prosumer. *American Behavioral Scientist* 56(4),379–398.

Ross, A. 2007. Nice work if you can get it: The mercurial career of creative industries policy. In *my creativity reader: A critique of creative industries*, eds. G. Lovink and N. Rossiter, 17–40. Amsterdam: Institute of Network Cultures.

Rossiter, N. 2004. Creative industries, comparative media theory and the limits of critique from within. *Topia: A Canadian Journal of Cultural Studies* 11: 21–48.

Rothler, D., and K. Wenzlaff. 2011. *Crowdfunding schemes in Europe.* Brussels: European Expert Network on Culture.

Rothmann, W., and J. Koch. 2014. Creativity in strategic lock-ins: The newspaper industry and the digital revolution. *Technological Forecasting and Social Change* 83: 66–83.

Rural Councils Victoria. 2013. *Creative industry in rural Victoria.* Melbourne: Rural Councils Victoria.

Santos Cruz, S., and A. A. C. Teixeira. 2015. The magnitude of creative industries in Portugal: What do the distinct industry-based approaches tell us? *Creative Industries Journal* 8(1): 85–102.

Saperstein, T. 2014. *The future of print: Newspapers struggle to survive in the age of technology.* Harvard: Harvard Political Review.

Schrøder, K. C., and B. Steeg Larsen. 2010. The shifting cross-media news landscape: Challenges for news producers. *Journalism Studies* 11(4): 524–534.

Scott, A. 2001. Capitalism, cities, and the production of symbolic forms. *Transactions Institute British Geog* 26(1): 11–23.

Scott, A. 2004. Cultural-Products industries and urban economic development: Prospects for growth and market contestation in global context. *Urban Affairs Review* 39(4): 461–490.

Scott, A. J. 2010. The cultural economy of landscape and prospects for peripheral development in the twenty-first century: The case of the English Lake District. *European Planning Studies* 18(10): 1567–1589.

Siegel, A., M. Burnside, C. Kester, T. Howes, and K. Robertson. 2012. Retail sustainability report: Successes, challenges, and a vision for the future. Retail Industry Leaders Association.

Steiner, M., and F. Prettenthler. 2015. Creativity reconsidered – so your firm is creative, but how much? A trans-sectoral and continuous approach to creative industries. *Regional Studies* 2(1): 274–288.

Stern, M., and S. Seifert. 2008. *From creative economy to creative society.* Philadelphia: University of Pennsylvania, Social Impact of the Arts Project.

Thomas, N., D. Harvey, and H. Hawkins. 2013. Crafting the region: Creative industries and practices of regional space. *Regional Studies* 47(1): 75–88.

Throsby, D. 2001. Defining the artistic workforce: The Australian experience. *Poetics* 28(4): 255–271.

Throsby, D. 2008. The concentric circles model of the cultural industries. *Cultural Trends* 17(3): 147–164.

Toffler, A. 1980. *The third wave: The classic study of tomorrow.* New York: Bantam.

Townley, B., and N. Beech. 2010. *Managing creativity: Exploring the paradox.* Cambridge: Cambridge University Press.

UNCTAD. 2010. *The creative economy report. Creative economy, a feasible development option.* Geneva/New York: UNCTAD/UNDP.

Van Der Ploeg, F. 2006. The making of cultural policy: A European perspective. In *handbook of the economics of art and culture,* 1183–1221. Amsterdam: Elsevier BV.

Van Der Ploeg, R. 2002. In art we trust. *De Economist* 150(4): 333–362.

Verdich, M. 2010. Creative migration? The attraction and retention of the creative class in Launceston, Tasmania. *Australian Geographer* 41(1): 129–140.

Visa Europe. 2015. *Visa Europe Consumer Spending Index* online, Available at www.visa.com/spendingindex.html (Accessed February 2016).

VisionMobile. 2015. *European app economy: Creating jobs and driving economic growth in Europe.* London: VisionMobile.

Waldfogel, J. 2012. copyright protection, technological change, and the quality of new products: Evidence from recorded music since Napster. *Journal of Law and Economics, University of Chicago* 55(4): 715–740.

Warren, A., and R. Evitt. 2010. Indigenous hip-hop: Overcoming marginality, encountering constraints. *Australian Geographer* 41(1): 141–158.

Western Development Commission Ireland. 2009. *Creative west: The creative sector in the Western Region*. Ballaghaderreen: WDC.

Whitacre, B., R. Gallardo, and S. Strover. 2013. Broadband's contribution to economic health in rural areas: A causal analysis and an assessment of the 'Connected Nation' program. *Telecommunications Policy Research Conference*, Arlington, VA. September 27-29, 2013.

Wikström, P. 2014. The Music industry in an age of digital distribution. In *19 key essays on how internet is changing our lives*, eds. F. Gonzalez, 423–444. Madrid: BBVA.

Wojan, T. R., Lambert, D. M., and McGranahan, D. A. 2007. Emoting with their feet: Bohemian attraction to creative milieu. *Journal of Economic Geography* 7(6), 711–736.

Woodward, M., and C. Bremner. 2015. Learning from Inland: Redefining regional creativity. In *Creative communities: Regional inclusion & the arts*, eds. J. McDonald and R. Mason, 63–78. Bristol: Intellect.

World Intellectual Property Organization. 2003. *Guide on surveying the economic contribution of the copyright based industries*. Geneva: WIPO.

Yoon, H. 2015. Globalization of the animation industry: Multiscalar linkages of six animation production centers. *International Journal of Cultural Policy*, September 1–18.

2
The Role of Culture and Its Consumption

2.1 Introduction

Cultural expression and the production of culture is how human beings have marked our place on earth. For centuries, we have expressed ourselves in unique ways, leaving behind us cultural artefacts and norms that would give those that came after us an insight into the way we lived. Throughout this long history, from scribbles on the walls of caves, through renaissance art and up to Pokemon Go, the way we have consumed this culture has directly informed how it has been produced.

In this chapter we explore the sometimes overlooked area of cultural consumption and question how it is that our demand for cultural expression is shaped by and helps shape the way we produce culture. Over the past 200 years we have witnessed the industrialisation of culture (Adorno and Horkheimer 2002; O'Connor 2015); production has been subject to a process of commercialisation and commodification that has sometimes led to the cheapening of its offer, and other times led to the democratisation of its appreciation (McKee 2013). In looking at this evolution we will pay particular attention to the role played by technology and how it is affecting both the ways we produce and consume.

P. Collins, J.A. Cunningham, *Creative Economies in Peripheral Regions*, DOI 10.1007/978-3-319-52165-7_2

How we consume culture also gives us a different perspective of how it is that we consume more generally. The increasing pervasiveness of cultural facets from branding to design across a greater number of products and services has radically altered how it is that they are both consumed and produced. The expressive values of products and services, from symbolism to a search for authenticity, have impacted production techniques far beyond the realm of cultural and creative industries. For creative industries in peripheral regions this creates opportunities and challenges.

After examining the more general traits in the rising demand for cultural produce we will explore the celebration of culture in our case study regions. Differentiating types of cultural consumption based on place, will lend to a better understanding on the types of culture produced in those places (the subject of the subsequent chapter). In more peripheral settings different types of expressive value are demanded, this has obvious impacts not just in how firms set themselves up to meet this demand but also helps us better understand the creative economy. These cases also highlight the importance of place and some of the non-economic benefits we discussed in the previous chapter.

2.2 The Evolution of Consumption

Cultural artefacts have helped us navigate our past. Most of our understanding of human history is based on surviving pieces of culture from stone implements to scripts and visual art that define the key epochs of human evolution. In today's world of mass-produced goods we can often fall into the trap of romanticising the past and how our forbearers lived in what were perceived as more cultural times. Artefacts such as the great works of fine artists from the Middle Ages give us a skewed sense of the cultural past. We know that a very small segment of the world's elite consumed the high art that has survived. The Renaissance in fifteenth-century Europe portrays a cultured people enjoying the visual art and the production of culture, not a human race that was struggling to survive in the face of pestilence, famine and other adversities.

The evolution of consumption and the evolution of our consumption of culture are in direct correlation. When we look beneath the surface we quickly see that this relationship moves beyond that of a hierarchy of needs (that we can only afford to consume culture once our basic needs are taken care of). Over the past two centuries, with an acceleration over the last 60 years, the cultural endowment of all goods have increased at an increasing rate. Much of this has to do with the rise of marketing and advertisement agencies and their capacity to create narratives behind the goods and services that we consume. Once these goods become imbued with the less tangible exchange values denoted by fashion, tastes and branding, their overall value changes. As this trend grew, the 'culture' of products and indeed 'cultural products' themselves moved beyond the traditional realm of Art and Artistic expression to infiltrate many different economies from coffee and beer to sunglasses and travel.

Within the sectors seen as more traditionally artistic the increasing pervasiveness of the cultural product has been the subject of much debate. Much of this has taken the dichotomous form of either High Art versus Low Art or Art versus Entertainment (Levine 1988). Framed in different discourses, much of the debate revolves around increased culturalisation. For some this is a positive, in that it brings art out of the 'reserve of the privileged' so that it can be appreciated by a greater percentage of the world's population than heretofore. For others increased culturalisation has led to the marketisation of culture with artistic value being replaced by commercial value (see Napoli 2011).

Starting in the late nineteenth century, this debate has been inspired by changes in the markets for cultural produce. A number of factors such as increased education, increased leisure time, greater wealth (distribution) all contributed to an increased demand for culture. Innovations in technology and practice, broadly termed industrialisation placed cultural producers in a better position to respond to these market changes. The employment of industrial practices in making culture has remained a contested topic to this very day.

The debate that started with the scaling up of printing presses and the invention of phonographs was ratcheted up by the employment of industrial-scale production in the Film and television industries in the early half of the twentieth century, and was given a new lease of life with the advent of the internet in the early twenty-first century (O'Connor 2007, 2015; Potts et al., 2008). Through each of these stages and changes in the modes of production, more people had access to culture, but more and more were inspired to question the value of the kind of culture people had access to. At the heart of the debate has to be the role played by technology.

2.2.1 Cultural Consumption: Role of Technology in Creating Experiences

From the choice of plants and the methods behind mixing their colours through parchment and the printing press, all the way up to televisions and the smartphones, technology has always played a role in how we make and appreciate culture. Here we are concerned with more recent advances in technology (namely digital ones) and how they have brought the consumption of culture to the fore. Parallels between the printing press and the internet have been drawn by many (Standage 1998), and there are a multitude of similarities from increased access to texts through to increased ability to express. The most compelling comparison has to be about how both these technological advances led to the increased democratisation of cultural production. The printing press brought literature, science and many other forms of cultural expression from cooking to religion out of the libraries and institutions of the elites and helped place them in the hands of many.

The advent of the internet did the same, but we see the scale of its impact being much larger. This is because as well as making text available, the internet made free many other forms of cultural expression, from music to games and audiovisual produce. We also contend that the increased access brought about by the internet (most obviously through Web 2.0) has had a greater effect on a greater percentage of the world's population (the printed word could only be accessed by the literate – or those within earshot of them) thereby dwarfing the relative impact of Gutenberg's invention.

2.2.2 Technological Advance in the Industrial Age

While the publishing industry had helped people consume the thoughts and expressions of writers far from their point of origin, other forms of cultural consumption remained stubborn in their geographic fixity. Advances in science and technology over the course of the industrial revolution filtered through to the cultural sector. The first of these to make an impact was the phonograph. Invented by Thomas Edison in 1877 this mechanical method of recording and reproducing sound was the seed from which today's multi-billion-dollar music industry grew. Some met this invention with dismay, claiming that the proliferation of recorded music would sound the death knell for innate musical talents (Lemley 2012).

Fears of these *first-stage cultural technologies* warrant some reflection as they remain pertinent today, albeit for very different reasons. For John Philip Sousa (1906) and other sceptics, new technologies would be the ruin of artistic creation, they highlighted the fact that music would now only be consumed. In the place of traditions of handing down songs to younger generations, our children would instead just go out and purchase music, they would no longer be active participants in its creation. For Lessig (2002), Sousa's predictions have rung true. Lessig (2002) describes how these first-stage cultural technologies were pivotal in moving artistic creation from a 'read-write' culture to a 'read-only' culture. Under 'read-write' conditions we were part of the making of culture, songs were sung, handed down from generation to generation, learned and modified over the course of time. Under read-only culture, the increased professionalisation of culture practice made consumers passive in the culture creation process and concentrated the capacity to produce in fewer and fewer hands.

In terms of cultural consumption new technologies radically altered how people engaged with culture. That said, this alteration was not immediate. First stage cultural technologies took much longer to have the kind of impact that later technologies (Personal Computers, mobile phone) had. Indeed, while wealth accumulation was rising over the first part of the twentieth century, it was more concentrated, and the vast majority's consumption spend was on basic needs. Post-war-developed economies from the USA to Australia were markedly different from their pre-war guises. The boom in consumer spending changed the shape of our modern societies (Ritzer and Jurgenson 2010). In the midst of these changes culture and its consumption was operant and operand (Halliday 2016).

The *second-stage cultural technologies* brought with them cultural consumption into almost every household in the developed world. Patterns of consuming culture were also impacted by the advent of technologies such as the television and video recorder. Culture came into the living rooms of the middle classes; it no longer required going to a site of cultural celebration (theatre or opera house) but could be enjoyed in the comfort of one's own home.

The effects of the change are noted by many (see Baudillard 1970; Fontanelle 2015; Planells 2015; O'Connor 2007; Toffler 1980), but here we reflect on two key facets. The first is that with the proliferation of second stage cultural technologies, consuming culture became, at least on the face of it, a much more private pursuit. It could be done by oneself or in the company of family and friends, but usually in a private setting. This division of the market, the consideration of a more splintered audience helped the proliferation of the production of different cultures. This brought with a change in the market type for cultural producers. Something we see as more akin to oligopolistic competition (most recognisable in the TV and music entertainment sectors). Under this form of market structure, competitiveness relies not just on the quality of the product /service but on market regulations. With the industrialisation of cultural production in these forms, the protection of copyright and application of patenting laws became central. This form of cultural consumption was more akin to the pacifying of audiences as predicted by the likes of Sousa a century earlier than the democratisation of culture and how we engaged with it.

The second has more to do with particular technologies and how they would pave the way for the third stage of cultural consumption and production. As video recorders, tape recorders, video cameras and the turntable became more prevalent tools in our cultural consumption they enabled a different form of engagement with the product. Consumers could now record and retransmit material in a way that they could never have done before (Lessig 2002; Ritzer and Jurgenson 2010). This brought with it many court cases that scrutinised copyright and patenting laws, but it also changed the way we consumed culture. Home videos, mix tapes and the birth of movements such as Hip Hop and pirate radio stations signified a more active form of cultural consumption. One that would truly come into its own with the advent of the digital era.

The *third-stage cultural technologies* came into being with the advent of the digital era. Personal Computers, mobile phones and the increasing pervasiveness of the internet has fundamentally altered the way we all engage with culture. Examples from Chapter 1 highlight that they not only brought with them seismic alterations to specific industries but whole new industries as well. Computer gaming rose from nothing to a $75billion revenue generating industry in 2015 (DFC Intelligence 2015). The app development sector went from zero to 1.64 million jobs in Europe alone in the space of eight years (Breslin et al., 2014).

The development of these technologies is replete with stories of small ventures, often times started in the bedrooms and basements of private homes that have shot to international success at eye-watering speed. While the technologies differ, we recognise a commonality in their inception that we explore further in the next section. From computer programming to hacking, from digital downloads to file sharing, there is a recognisable appetite for active participation in the formation of cultural produce. We argue that the technologies of the third stage affect the way we interact with culture in a wholly unique way. We see these technologies as the true democratisation of culture that was predicted by some over 100 years ago. We see the active consumption of culture through the use of these technologies as blurring the lines between consumption and production. Similarly, we recognise a different kind of market structure emerging through this new form of consumption – one that has an ethos of sharing at its heart. One that makes use of cutting-edge technologies to resurrect the ways we used to engage with technology prior to the advent of the Industrial Age.

2.2.3 Back to the Future: Technology Enhanced Sharing

Sharing, like the prosuming that we discussed in Chapter 1, is a phenomenon that was previously ubiquitous, then overshadowed by the rise of market economies and capitalist practices only to see a reprisal with the advent of digital technology. In its original guise, the World Wide Web as invented by Tim Berners-Lee and colleagues at CERN, was dominated by hyperlinked textual structures. Ability to affect that structure or indeed upload to that web required a level of technological proficiency that only a very small percentage of the population had. Web 1.0 provided information without much interaction. With the advent of Web 2.0 we all became creators of the content available on the web. Social networking sites and file sharing sites boosted the traffic across the internet as the barriers to entry in terms of technical proficiency fell away.

Existing under many different terms from collaborative consumption (Botsman and Rogers 2010) to the commercial sharing systems and co-creation (Lamberton and Rose 2012) the sharing phenomenon is likely best understood in how it is enacted through service providers and websites such as AirBnB, Flickr, YouTube, Zipcar, Wikipedia etc. The Sharing Economy is set to reach a valuation of $335billion by 2025 (valued at $15billion in 2013; PWC 2015) as we move according to Belk (2014) from 'you are what you own' to the newer wisdom of 'you are what you share'. We see this of relevance because sharing has been instrumental in the growth of the creative economy. We contend that it has been patterns of cultural consumption, or indeed, prosumption that have inspired the growth of the sharing economy. This offers great opportunities for creative industries in peripheral regions, while noting, however one major constraint will be the availability of telecommunications and mobile network infrastructure.

Sharing, be it music (in the form of MP3s, knowledge – lyrics or cords) or video (in digital forms from MP4s to Gifs), has been revolutionised by the advent of Web 2.0. Similar to the invention of the phonograph, it has its supporters and its detractors. Rather interesting in comparing the two is the role played by copyright. The nineteenth-century invention spurred the formation of new laws around copyright and patenting, while Web 2.0 has brought about a circumvention of those same laws at a level never before seen. Sousa's fear that the phonograph would lead to a read-only culture where power would be concentrated in the hands of the few, and commercial/capitalistic interest would dominate, have been replaced 100 years later by genuine worries on behalf of those interests that their models are being undone by the sharing and prosumption of culture.

2.2.4 Cultural Consumption: Distribution and Communication

Cultural consumption through sharing can be seen in two ways – *distribution* and *communication*. One of the most famous example of distributing culture was the file-sharing site Napster. Over the course of a few months in the early 2000s, the website brought a multibillion-dollar industry to its knees. Peer-2-Peer file sharing on websites like Napster and gomusic.ru brought music out of the market economy and replaced it with the gift economy. Once the technology allowed, larger audiovisual content was shared through sites like LimeWire and Pirate Bay. More recently we have seen industry response in the guise of content streaming. Sites like Spotify and Netflix have brought sharing back into the marketplace by centralised distribution. That said, sites like Napster existed prior to the recent revival of the sharing economy term. It was with the arrival of more socially oriented sites like Facebook and Twitter that the term share in its new guise began to take hold. More relevant here are sites that encourage us to share and distribute our own creativity. Primary among these are sites/apps like Flickr, bandcamp, Instagram, Vimeo and YouTube. For Planells (2015), the dichotomy in terms of what they mean for cultural production remain.

The second aspect of the sharing economy and how it relies on third-stage cultural technologies are the communicative aspects embedded in them. Technologies, from the World Wide Web, as a search tool, to online market places such as eBay and Etsy are helping buyers and sellers communicate in a way they have never done before. This world-wide communication is allowing sellers to access buyers and buyers access sellers in more and more refined and targeted ways. Underlying this was the provision of information, it's provision at the global level has helped bring some markets to a level nearing perfect information. Goods and services that were previously seen as niche could find greater market shares in different jurisdictions. For example, new rules in the Irish sport of hurling making it mandatory to wear protective head gear brought one Canadian sports equipment company that sold ice hockey helmets back from the brink of closure through online sales.

Communication and its effect on the sharing economy is likely best seen in the rise of new companies and their online presence such as Airbnb, Uber and crowd funding sites such as Kickstarter and Fundit (see Planells 2015). The most recognisable of these exploit information and help users bring to the market under used resources such as idle automobiles and empty bedrooms. This aspect of the sharing economy can be seen as aiding the process of market clearing and generally adding efficiencies. Zipcar cites the fact that cars are on average only in use for

8% of their lifetime to make the case that car sharing can lead to greater efficiencies. Communicating the stock of unfulfilled assets makes a great deal of practical and economic sense for the consumer, the environment and in the case of the true sharing sites (non-monetary exchange) the community (ibid.).

Provision of information with respect to funding potential are particularly relevant to the creative economy. Kickstarter (and its Irish equivalent Fundit) are impacting the way we consume culture from theatre to film and computer gaming. This is a new way of making consumers active in the development and production of the product. Becoming a funder involves participating in decision-making structures at the highest level. The collective financing model replaces the top-down culture of business with bottom-up participation allowing the funder freedom to contribute to development; be that changes to the script, advice on gameplay or backstage access on opening night.

2.3 Values in Consuming

So far we have argued how the methods by which we consume culture are unique, and in some cases signatory of new patterns of consumption that could affect change beyond the creative and cultural economies. Before moving on to look at the experience of cultural consumption in our study regions we first consider what it is that makes the products and services of the this economy unique. By understanding this we will gain a better insight into how the consumption and production of these products differ across different spaces.

In Chapter 1 we made clear the sectors that together comprise of the creative economy. There we made reference to the fact that the broad range and the diversity of their offerings make a holistic understanding difficult to pin down. We know that they stretch across different industrial sectors and offer different products and services within the same sub sector. In this section we approach each of our distinct sectors and consider the products and services that they offer and examine them through the lens of their unique value. After this we attempt to further our understanding by considering the different types of markets evident in each of the sectors.

2.3.1 Expressive Values

Consumption patterns and the produce of the creative industries are unique. The products and the services that make up the creative economy inhabit different markets and show very different traits to products that are usually analysed in the social sciences. One of the best known economic analysis of the sector is put forth by David Throsby (2001) who distinguishes the output of the creative economy on their 'expressive values'. These can be seen across the many different sectors in the creative economy as noted by the Work Foundation (2007: 97): 'In the first decade of the twenty-first century, expressive value is no longer confined to traditional artforms. Expressive value (in the sense of symbolic value) is represented in software programmes and video games such as the Grand Theft Auto and Metal Gear series where engrossing narratives combine with performance-driven play and increasingly naturalistic graphics.'

We know that creative industries generate the larger part of their revenues by commercialising 'expressive value'. Throsby's (2008a) use of the term expressive value refers to the cultural meaning and understanding imbued in the products and services of the creative economy. From original art works to graphic design, what binds them together and sets them apart from others sectors of the broader economy is that innate in each is a narrative of cultural interpretation. These products and services are expressive, they have a story that speaks to a broader cultural understanding of its time and place.

Understanding the nuances of the particular stories of particular cultural offerings is key to understanding how the creative economy exists differently across different places. In an attempt to get a better grasp we make use of Throsby's (2001) taxanomy of expressive values and cross reference it with the sub-sectors of the creative economy we laid out in Chapter 1. Doing this will go some way towards providing a better understanding as to how the creative economy exists differently in different sectors. Later on we will use a similar method to compare how different the market types and modes of consumption across different sectors are, in an attempt to provide a more complete picture.

The expressive values (aesthetic, spiritual, social, historical, symbolic and authenticity) are said to be what distinguishes the produce of the creative industries from others. David Throsby (2001; 2008a, 2008b) has deftly highlighted the different nuances among these values. For him, aesthetic values relate to the beauty of a product, appreciated in its form and how well it appeals to our senses. Spiritual value, does not solely refer to the religiosity of a product, but rather imbues a metaphysical connection we can have to a product. Social and historical values are more contextual. The former value is in how a product reflects a societal issue or can act as a social glue, the latter value is seen in how it reflects on issues of the past and how they relate to the present. Symbolic value expresses a meaning beyond the physical nature of the production, it is intrinsic in the work of artists, while authenticity value, offers a comparative difference to cultural produce by relating a sense of being real, original and of a place.

Taking our creative industries categorises from Chapter 1 of creative expression, creative application and creative technologies we apply and discuss the expressive values against these categories. Historical and social values in peripheral and rural regions are very distinctive. Such expressive values are a cumulative reflection of how these regions dealt with and coped with the challenges and opportunities they faced.

2.3.2 Creative Expression

The outputs of this sector of the creative economy are likely those that could be best described as culture imbued. They range from visual art pieces that are traded in auction houses to one-off pieces of jewellery sold out of small studios. The range of commercial value is breathtaking, from album sales in the millions, to theatre performances to an audience of 10, the commercial success of this sector is unpredictable. Such is the variety of creative offering, and the fact that success is difficult to predict (think of viral sensations) the creatives that produce these goods laden with expressive values find it difficult to anticipate market value. For the purposes of classification of core cultural industries we include Visual Art; Performing Art; Music Performance; Photography (Artistic); Video and Film; Radio and TV Production and Festivals.

The consumption of these products are a unique form of consumption in that the produce are uniquely identity forming. The expressive value of the goods and services in this sector are what we use to pit ourselves relative to our peers. Be it the types of movies we like to watch or the music that we listen to, we see these are key parts of our own unique make up. This is the sector that most closely abides to the traditional/core creative industries and therefore scores highest on the expressive value scale. For this, reason as depicted below, creative expression goods and services score highest overall across all of the values associated with expression (see Fig. 2.1).

Art, in particular visual art (through many different mediums from paint to video) has a high aesthetic value associated with its output. Many different factors are associated with how we consume this, from the role of gatekeepers (art critics) to cascade effects (word of mouth) this is content that chimes most with a visual connection (Peltoniemi 2015). For similar reasons the symbolic value of the produce of this sector is high. Art, from music to theatre, provide an opportunity to us as consumers to interpret it, to recognise meanings and values in different pieces. Related to this is the perceived authenticity of the produce of these creatives, for certain pieces of art, this is the highest of all expressive values (think of the world's most famous works of visual art) for others, the patterns by which we consume it is undermining this aspect of expression (think of the markets for forgery). The historical and spiritual values of creative expression goods and services are the highest of the three sectors of the creative economy. The rationale here is the ingrained heritage in the production of craft and art pieces. The production of religious icons and reproduction of historical artefacts reflect this. The social value of these goods relate in part to the identity forming aspects of the produce but also to the socialisation of those identities into collectives as seen most easily through fandom associated with different art forms.

How these goods are consumed is of particular relevance to our work. We will explore this further in the following sections but recognise that the modes of consumption are influenced by many different factors from advancing technologies (see above) to the pursuit of consumer experiences

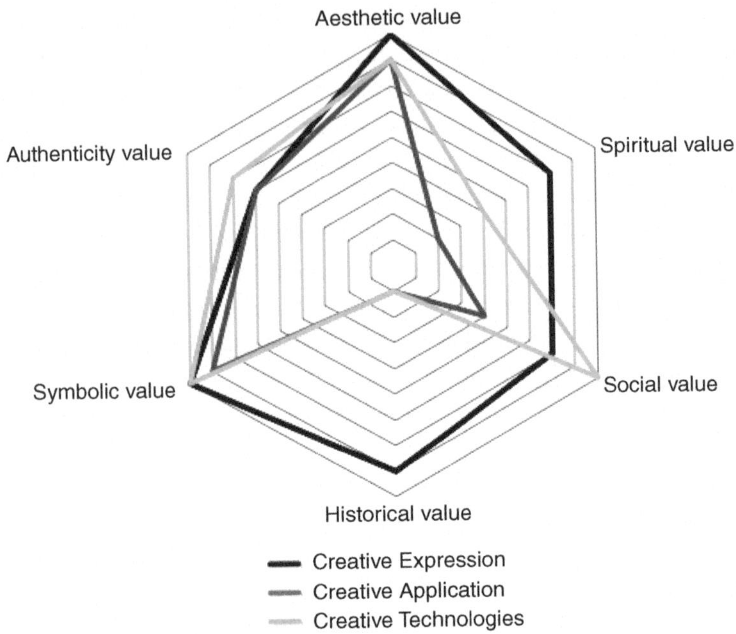

Fig. 2.1 Expressive values across the creative industries
Source: Authors calculations based on Throsby (2001)

(the growing market for festivals and events as a way to consume expressive cultural produce).

2.3.3 Creative Application

The creative application sector is primarily concerned with meeting market demand. Typical sub categories of this sector include architecture, fashion, publishing, advertising, art and antique trade. Natural overlap exists between all sectors of the creative economy, but this sector shares much with the creative expression sector. This is due in part to the fact that much of the activity of this sector is the commercialisation of the produce of the creative expression industries. This is most true for antiques and art trade that organise new and existing markets for cultural produce. Similarly for the publishing industry, it relies on the writers and authors in the creative expression sector to for their content. Some refer to this sector as the 'content industries' (Hartley 2009) in which virtually all the produce is creative and relies heavily on copyright to sustain their competitive offering. Others such as the Work Foundation (2007) might consider the application sector as the 'creative industries' sector that are more market-oriented.

The produce of the application sector is immediately recognisable as creative. From fashion to books and branding to blueprints, these products are established features of the consumer market. As such they abide by sometimes very different market rules. Some of the produce that might be deemed as the most successful in this sector, take for instance mass produced high street fashion, would also be considered as that which had the least 'expressive value'. The application sector, more than the other two sectors of the economy as defined here depicts most starkly the artistic value versus commercial value dichotomy.

This sector is the most commercial of all three sectors and as such less reliant on the public purse relative to the creative expression sector. Yet application requires the output of the expressive arts to make it commercially viable. Other works such as (Throsby 2001; Work Foundation 2007) have shown the degree of porosity between the sectors and how both require each other to function.

As a result, the expressive values of the produce of the creative application sector are lower than those of the other two sectors in the creative economy. The aesthetic and symbolic values of high fashion and architectural services are pitted against the questionable authenticity of mass produced fashion and the biographies of celebrities. The sector scores lowest in values associated with historical or spiritual meaning due mainly to their commercial orientation. Social values according to Durkheim (2014) are imbued in any product, but the nature of massification in the industries associated with this sector means that identity formation values are less prevalent than with the other sectors of the creative economy.

2.3.4 Creative Technology

The creative technology sector is at the cutting edge of product and service innovation as well as being at the forefront of changing patterns of consumption. Industries that make up this sector bleed into other creative economy sectors, through aspects of new media, the production of creative expression and the area of new design and how it inhabits the area of creative application. Sub sectors include app development, gaming, animation and internet services. Creative technology industries are those that rely on digital media for their delivery and for their core functioning. What marks these industries out is their novelty, they are young industries targeting younger consumers with a high rate of turnover, both in terms of revenue, company formation and product delivery.

The internet enables the delivery of these items, as such, their markets are skewed by a number of key influencers:

- Increased levels of prosumption
- Open source innovation
- Decreased or near-minimal laws of marginal cost of production
- Collaborative consumption
- Markets of near perfect information

Such is the nature of these products, new to market, new market forming and brim full of artistic expression and application, they traverse the dichotomy of cultural goods and display elements of both commercial and artistic values. In the following chapters we will see how this sector has come to dominate the debate on the promotion of the creative economy, we will see also that any promotion of it, in isolation, does little to support the creative economy as a whole.

Within the sector there exits and large range of diversity, from graphic design and web development to app development and delivering new media art online. The prevalence of prosumption in the sectors means that any real appreciation of how we understand the sector is stymied by traditional accounting metrics. That said, the sector is at the leading edge of new economy developments and any inquiry into how it is the produce is consumed or the produced is worthy.

The expressive value of this produce is what differentiates it from other tech products. Games, applications and new media are laden with narratives and identity forming characteristics. While the aesthetic value of the produce is difficult to decipher across the whole sector (some games and animation being tantamount to the finest artistic expression of our age) the symbolic value cannot be doubted. Such is the interactive and connected nature by which we consume creative technologies, the social value of these products and services are high. The more time we spend online, the more we socialise in that medium and more social value is ascribed to the produce of this sector. The level of fandom and the experiential nature of their offering adds to the spiritual values, while the historical value (save games and applications based on historical events) is among the least of the expressive values on display. While new and emerging, the commercial aspect of this sector can dwarf the performance of the other sectors that make up the creative economy.

2.4 Consumption: Market Types and Modes

The nature of the types of value consumed in the creative economy has been the subject of much work (McKee 2013; Peltoniemi 2015). What we see when we examine the nature of expressive values in the different sectors of the creative economy is the separation between values that chime more with commercial sentiment and those with artistic sentiment. For McKee (2013) this is best described as the consumption of entertainment versus the consumption of art. In the latter, text has power over its consumers, affecting them on a spiritual level, whereas the entertainment model is almost consumed unknowingly.

The dichotomous nature of the market for cultural produce has been summarised as the 'higher the aesthetic value, the lower the utilitarian value' (Hirsch 2000). This fact helps determine the nature of the market demand for these goods and services. The market for aesthetic, social and symbolic laden produce is, according to Peltoniemi (2015), heavily influenced by *taste, popularity* and *gatekeepers*. Assumptions underlying these influences relate to the desire for novelty, the law of increasing returns (marginal costs of selling extra units of an album or movie approaching zero) and the variance of sales/unpredictability of demand (hits and misses) (Caves 2000; Hesmonddalgh 2002; Holbrook and Hisrschman 1982).

Much of the work of on tastes and hedonic consumption relates to social class and refers to the work of Bourdieu (2000) on higher tastes (Art) among the upper classes and more popular tastes (Entertainment) among the lower classes. Taste is seen as forming cumulatively through consumption (people who like Jazz, listen to Jazz), while other factors at play include nostalgia effects (Holbrook and Hirschman 1982) and genre preferences (Miesen 2004).

In Fig. 2.2 we see how the high art versus commodification/entertainment dichotomy exists in the separate sectors of the creative economy. This is captured best by the comparison between creative expression and creative application sectors. We know that there exists a degree of overlap between the two sectors, namely in the areas of craft and audiovisual production. The presence of these subsectors serve to lessen the tension between the high art and commercial focus of creative expression and creative application, respectively. Produce of the creative application sector fair better in commercial settings but a challenge for them relates to artistic merit. While those of the creative expression sector are assured in their artistic value, something that only sometimes translates into a marketable good or service, the produce of the creative technology sector is notable for its ability to contain artistic value that translates well into commodified produce. This goes some way to explaining the nature of the production and the success of the industry in last ten years.

Fig. 2.2 also depicts how cultural produce uses new modes of consumption to access its market. As described above, the rise of prosumption and the sharing economy are two processes that affect and are affected by the growing creative economy. Collaborative consumption has been the subject of much intellectual endeavour in recent years. Employing a Marxists dialectical approach, Fontenelle (2015) highlights the restructuring of the organisational practices and norms in the 1980s as a key point in the rise of consumer management informing production. From here the boundaries between work and consumption started to become more fuzzy. For Pine and Gilmore (1999) that organisational change had to come about to enable the rise of the experience economy. Here we highlight the knock-on effects of prosumption and sharing as something that has been heralded by the advance in the creative economy. While this is likely best understood

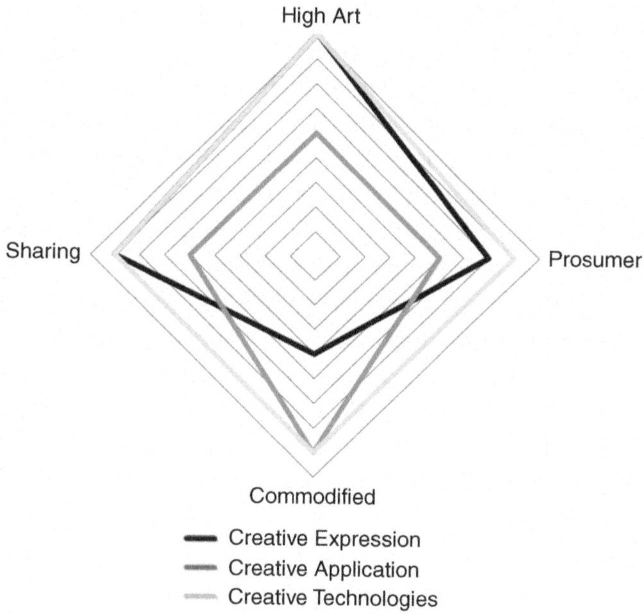

Fig. 2.2 Market types across the creative sectors

with reference to peer-to-peer file sharing we contend that the relationship runs deeper than that.

In his 2012 study of British radio Chapman (2012) found that the BBC had an initial monopoly on radio in the 1950s. The Corporation acted under the 'public service remit' to produce cultural offering that audiences should, not they necessarily did, want. In it's early guise, Rock and Roll was deemed inappropriate to the public services (Chapman 2012). More informed audiences, expressing a desire to fulfil many of the values we see have discussed here, from identity formation to a spiritual connection of types, defected to illegal pirate radio stations. These practices were consumer-led, run from bedrooms and ships in an effort to avoid sanction, they operated in both the informal and formal economy and were examples of how culture has unique sharing and prosumption qualities.

Taking the BBC example of how creative produce is shared and consumer produced, it is no surprise that we see the majority of our creative economy sectors score high in both these modes of consumption. Indeed the example of Pirate Radio resonates loudly with many of the new and emerging markets in creative technology. From the hacker phenomenon to YouTube the anti-establishment ethos burns bright in this sector. We know that collective action and distributed production was behind many of best examples of cultural prosumption from Linux to Soundcloud. We can see YouTube users as a co-creative community where the value of individual videos is collectively produced via the consumption, evaluation and entrepreneurial activities of users en masse, not by top down programming (Potts et al. 2008). Such is the expressive nature of much of this content, we see that the produce of this sector also scores highly in both modes of consumption. The commercial, and indeed established/formal market nature of much of the produce of creative application sector sees it score the lowest in sharing economy and prosumption modes of consumption.[1]

So what are the implications for the creative economy and industries in peripheral regions of market types and modes of consumption? The drivers shaping this economy particularly the growth in sharing and prosumption means that peripheral regions are not precluded from participation and the move from mass production can play to their natural strengths. Peripherally based companies can be upstream and down stream selectors as Peltoniemi (2015) posits and can influence and shape the sector. In particular we argue such companies in these regions are even better placed to exploit the overlaps between creative expression and applications sectors. For peripheral companies expressive values particularly rooted in historical, authenticity, social values can easily transcend these markets types and modes of consumption.

[1] Such is the nature of these modes of consumption, they sit outside of usual metrics for quantifying and analysing these produce. This is part of the reason why many efforts to truly gauge the nature of creative economy activity fail to grasp the full impact.

2.5 Cultural Participation and Opportunities for Cultural Consumption in Europe's Periphery

Nearly half of all Europeans aged 25–64 years declared having participated in cultural activities such as going to the cinema, attending live performances and visiting cultural sites at least once in 2006 (EUROSTAT 2011). The geography of participation differed across the member states with northern countries showing a higher rate of cultural consumption than their southern counterparts. Statistics for cinema attendance act as an interesting proxy for cultural consumption. There exists a high and positive correlation between infrastructure provision and consumption. Iceland, Sweden and Ireland have the highest density of cinema screens per capita, these countries also rank the highest in number of cinema trips per person in 2010.

Though somewhat dated, Eurostat figures on cultural consumption online provide some interesting indicators. In 2008, 38% of internet users in the EU–27 downloaded or listened to music, 29% downloaded or watched films and 33% listened to the radio. Using the internet for leisure activities mainly concerned young people, students and more men than women. Also in 2009, 32% of European internet users purchased films, music, books, newspapers, magazines, e-learning material or computer software online. This form of purchase is particularly frequent in the UK, Luxembourg, Germany, Denmark and Norway. More and more consumers are using the internet as a mode of access and a mode of delivery of cultural produce.

Perhaps the time of the year that most people are willing to engage in cultural participation are those couple of weeks spent on holidays and thereby usually consuming a different culture. According to the 2009 Eurobarometer survey, cultural attractiveness is the second motivation for Europeans (after value for money) when deciding on a holiday destination. The report highlighted the rate of demand inelasticity in the outlook of Europeans on holiday with regard to cultural activities. While seemingly obvious as an observation this can have massive effects on the creative economies of particular places, both in their make up and in their sustainability.

2.5.1 Spaces and Places for Celebrating Culture in Europe's Periphery

Organising, hosting and staging festivals and events is a growth industry. Relatively recession proof, it now seems that every town and village has something to celebrate at certain times of the year. For instance, the music festival business has grown from almost nothing a few decades ago to account for roughly $1.36 billion in Britain alone in 2010 (Grose 2011). According to Prentice and Andersen (2003) there are many reasons for the growth of the festival machine; tourism development and civic re-positioning on the supply side, and, increased leisure time, lifestyle sampling and the search for the 'authentic' on the demand side.

The process of 'festivalisation' is not wholly reactionary. Indeed, the supply side is sometimes driven by very different rationales. Such is their place-based nature, a considerable amount of festivals are organised (partly or wholly) by civic representatives. Local authorities in many countries have realised that culture and festivals have great promotional potential. They can act as a shop window for cities to display their unique traits. At the core of the celebration is the culture that is unique to the place of its hosting. They also generate new jobs and income from festival tourism providing a clear rationale for cities to subsidise them. The impacts of staging events stretch far beyond the economic, to areas such as identity, civic pride and increased social capital (Quinn 2005). This relates to some of our discussion in Chapter 1 about the non-economic benefits of this sector.

'Festivalisation' has a unique relationship with the broader process of globalisation. Getz (2008) points out that in an era of globalisation, cities and regions make use of festivals and events to stand out in an effort at what others term 'place branding'. Mega events have become integral to the entrepreneurial strategies of places seeking to gain a competitive advantage in the global economy (Hall 2006). The growth of festivals is also the result of the globalisation process itself which sees many regions feeling the need to stage festivals in an attempt to remain competitive vis-à-vis competitor locations, in what Kotler et al. (1993) snappily term 'place wars'.

In essence, festivals can be thought of as experiential products sold by their hosts under differing brands from music to art to sport and religion. These products are used to attract visitors and residents of different kinds (mainly middle class according to Waitt 2008; Zimmerman 2008) to consume that experience in different ways in the 'hope' that a positive experience will forever then be associated with that place (see Westerbeek et al. 2002).

Over the course of two years we set about auditing the festival offering of each of our case study regions. In terms of better understanding the culture and in particular the celebration of culture in our regions we see it as a unique contribution to defining the creative economies of our case study regions. Taken in isolation, they provide a picture of the cultural offering of their place, they also give an insight in to the kinds of culture produced in that place, but seen relative to the creative industries of those places (Chapter 3) we see a potential of understanding the lifecycle of cultural offerings in places.

2.5.2 The West of Ireland – Sites, Spaces and Places of Cultural Celebration[2]

Ireland's western region is a particularly rural place, with 64.9% of people living outside of towns of a population of 1,500 or more. Small towns of between 1,500 and 2,999 in population are where 16.4% of the region's population live (Western Development Commission Ireland 2012). This adds to the region's distinctive and attractive nature, with clustered small settlements in villages and small towns existing alongside a more dispersed population in rural areas.

Arts and culture in the western region of Ireland are strong. For example, counties Donegal, Galway and Mayo have extensive Gaeltacht areas, where Irish is the main language spoken by large numbers in the community. The largest Gaeltacht area in Ireland is in county Galway. It is concentrated in the west of the county, and is particularly strong in An Spidéal and An Cheathrú Rua (Údarás na Gaeltachta 2013). Ireland is well known for its strong literary tradition. A number of highly acclaimed writers including John McGahern are associated with the western region, and playwrights Brian Friel and Tom Murphy are from the region. The landscape of county Sligo is

[2] This extract was originally published as part of the Creative Edge Policy Toolkit (2013) (see http://www.creative-edge.eu/wp-content/uploads/2014/01/Creative-Edge-Policy-ToolKit-web.pdf)

closely associated with the poetry of William Butler Yeats. Internationally renowned and award-winning theatre companies such as Macnas and Druid are based in Galway. Traditional Irish music is also strong in the west of Ireland – there are vibrant musical traditions for example in counties such as Clare, Donegal and Sligo (Bayliss 2004).

The western region's landscape is composed of a diverse mix of agricultural lands, mountains, bogs, lakes, rivers and coastline. Cultural heritage is embedded in the natural landscape, observed in distinctive cultural landscapes such as the Burren in county Clare, Neolithic sites such as the Céide Fields in county Mayo, as well as ancient sites such as Rathcroghan in county Roscommon. The region boasts four of Ireland's six national parks – Glenveagh in county Donegal, Connemara in county Galway and the Burren and Ballycroy in county Clare. Despite its peripheral location, the region is a popular tourist destination. Much of the region's tourism is driven by its strong culture. Two of Ireland's top ten tourist attractions are located in the region in county Clare: the Cliffs of Moher Visitor Experience and Bunratty Castle and Folk Park (Failte Ireland 2012). Galway, one of Ireland's main cities, is located in Ireland's western region, was recently designated the European Capital of Culture for 2020. With its wealth of cultural activities, Galway city has been referred to as the 'city of festivals'.

A wide variety of festivals exist, such as local fairs, arts, theatre, food, music, film and literary festivals (see Fig. 2.3). Local fairs are often rooted in agriculture, e.g. livestock shows, but also provide an opportunity for local celebrations around music, dance and markets. Music festivals cover a range of musical genres, from blues, bluegrass, baroque, rock, jazz and electronic music, but most often focus on traditional Irish music. Traditional Irish music festivals can also focus on celebrating particular musicians, and particular aspects of Irish music and dance such as sean-nós and set-dancing, or particular instruments such as the fiddle or bodhrán. A significant number of literary festivals are also identified in the western region, some with a broad focus on contemporary literature and literary traditions, with others focussing on particular aspects of literature such as books or poetry. Some literary festivals focus on celebrating the work of particular writers who had an

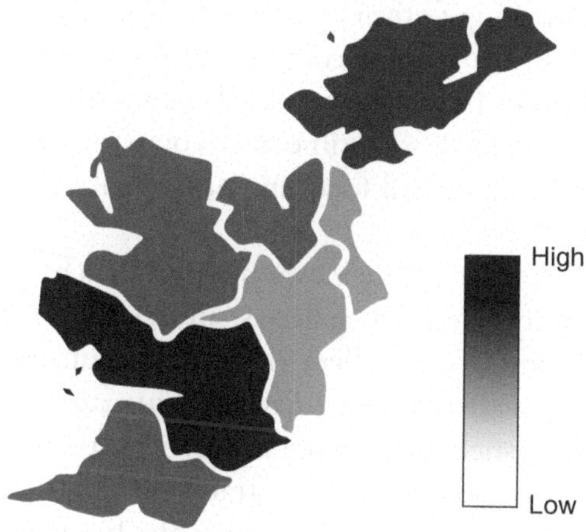

Cultural Infrastructure

	West of Ireland
Art Galleries	49
Cinemas	15
Studios (Art, Design)	18
Studios (Sound)	23
Studios (Film and TV)	32
Heritage/Visitor centre	64
Libraries and Archives	106
Museums	44
Music venues	35
Theatres	50

Fig. 2.3 Cultural infrastructure of the west of Ireland

association with, or were from, the particular place, such as William Butler Years in county Sligo, John McGahern in county Leitrim and J.R. R. Tolkien in County Clare. Storytelling is a theme incorporated in some literary festivals, and festivals devoted to storytelling are also found. Film festivals with a particular focus, from the highly successful Galway Film Fleadh, acting as an official Oscar selector for short films to a documentary film festival in county Donegal.

Distinct festivals include celebrations of film and television associated with the region. Two festivals celebrating Father Ted are identified. Father Ted is a comedy series based around three priests and their housekeeper living on an island off the Irish west coast, which was made in the mid–1990s by Hat Trick Productions and first broadcast on the British television station Channel 4. The 1950s film directed by John Ford, the Quiet Man, was filmed in the western region. Some filming was carried out in Cong, county Mayo, and the Quiet Man features in the Cong annual festival. Parts of the west coast of Ireland have become popular surfing destinations, and this wider attraction of place is represented in festivals, with surfing festivals identified in counties Clare and Sligo. Long established festivals are also found, which have become iconic and closely associated with the place they originate. For example, Lisdoonvarna in county Clare and matchmaking are closely associated, the annual matchmaking festival reputed to be the largest of its kind in Europe. Halloween festivals are also common in the west of Ireland, reflecting the strong tradition in Ireland of holding bonfires on the Celtic festival of Samhain. Halloween festivals sometimes focus on particular themes, such as a Halloween festival in Donegal focussing on Dracula and marking the death of Bram Stoker.

A diverse range of cultural spaces exist in the western region, such as libraries, heritage centres, tour companies, art galleries, museums and theatres. Museums and heritage centres can reflect the general culture and traditions of the region, but also its distinct nature. This can be industrial and agricultural traditions, such as the wool industry that once thrived around Leenane in county Galway. The tradition of the Connemara pony in the county is preserved by the presence of a heritage centre in the county. Historical figures and events of significance are also represented through these cultural spaces. For example, there are museums and heritage centres marking important nineteenth-century political figures such as Michael Cusack, a founder of the Gaelic Athletic Association, who was born in county Clare; Michael Davitt, founder of the Land League, who was born in county Mayo; and Isaac Butt, who was born in county Donegal and prominent in the Home Rule movement. The Irish famine of the 1840s and the Battle of Aughrim of 1691 are two significant events in Ireland's history marked by the presence of cultural spaces based around them.

At the level of community cultural organisations, local writers' groups, amateur theatre groups, film clubs, local historical societies and local genealogical societies are observed across the western region, showing the existence of cultural production and consumption at the grassroots, voluntary level within communities in the western region. Community arts organisations with a broad focus, and organisations focussing on engaging children or people with disabilities with the arts are also identified.

There is a web of theatres, arts centres and community centres in the western region for the production and consumption of performing arts. Pubs are also identified as an important space for 'live' music performances. Art galleries and design studios are identified for the presence and consumption of visual arts. Cinemas, sound recording studios, film and TV studios are also found, again showing the diversity in the cultural products and consumption of culture in the region.

Broad creative industry organisations are not found in the western region; however a number of organisations in sub-sectors of creative industries focussing their activities in specific counties are identified, such as the audio visual, craft, visual art and information technology sectors. For example, the Film Commission is a division within the Irish Film Board (Ireland's national development agency for film, television and animation) and a network of film commissions at local county level support filmmaking. Non-profit organisations support the audiovisual sector in county Galway, such as the Galway Picture Palace, (the as yet to be finished arthouse cinema) in Galway city. The Galway Film Centre is another non-profit body: it acts as a resource centre for film in the west of Ireland. The Galway Film Centre operates Screenwest, which supports the production of audiovisual content in the west of Ireland. There is a network organisation, the Galway Film Partnership, for film organisations in Galway, and operates in conjunction with Galway County Council. In the craft sector, the presence of local, county level, business networks of craft entrepreneurs working together is identified. These networks are often members of the national umbrella body supporting craft in Ireland, the Craft Council of Ireland.

2.5.3 SEED Northern Ireland – Sites, Spaces and Places

Formed in the 1990s, SEED is a group of local authorities that work together to promote economic development in south–eastern Northern Ireland. The South East Economic Development Economic Development strategy highlights how the economy of the SEED area differs depending on the local authority area of focus. For example, agriculture is particularly important in Armagh and Banbridge, fishing in Ards and Down, and Craigavon has an important industrial base. Retail is also an important sector identified across the local authority areas. The SEED area has a growing population, forecast as growing at a faster rate than the Northern

Ireland average. The SEED member councils face diverse economic and social challenges. However, significant overlap exists and the SEED consortium works across areas where collaborative work can be undertaken, specifically business development, education and skills development and rural development. The SEED development strategy outlines common issues for action to realise its vision of creating a skilled and flexible workforce supporting a diverse and competitive economy. The SEED area has been affected by the decline in manufacturing in Northern Ireland, with a loss of around 8,000 jobs in the area over the last decade, with further job losses predicted, however at a declining rate. Other vulnerable sectors identified in the action plan are agriculture and fishing. One of the business objectives of the action plan is to develop regionally significant business sectors, with craft one of the sectors identified (FGS McClure Watters and Regional Forecasts 2008). SEED's work has also focussed specifically on creative industries e.g. through its Craft Development Programme and Creative Industries Programme (Newry and Mourne district council 2013).

A diversity of festivals occur in the SEED area, including local fairs, music, arts, theatre, craft, food and film festivals (see Fig. 2.4). Long-established festivals exist alongside newer festivals. Music festivals most often focus on traditional Irish music, but also celebrate modern reinventions of traditional Irish music, such as Celtic fusion, as well as other types of music and musical performance, such as guitar music and busking. Local fairs are rooted in agriculture, such as livestock shows, but are also of a more general nature, as a celebration for the community. One distinct pattern is that a number of festivals in the SEED area had an automotive theme, and displayed vintage cars or tractors. Other festivals are clearly rooted in cultural heritage, preserving and continuing traditions, such as the Apple Blossom Fair in Armagh that celebrates the heritage of the apple in county Armagh, which is known as the Orchard County. Longer running festivals have also become admired and valued, such as the Bard of Armagh Festival of Humorous Verse.

A diverse range of cultural spaces exist in the SEED area, such as libraries, theatres, music venues, tour companies and heritage centres. A network of performance spaces exist, such as theatres, art centres and

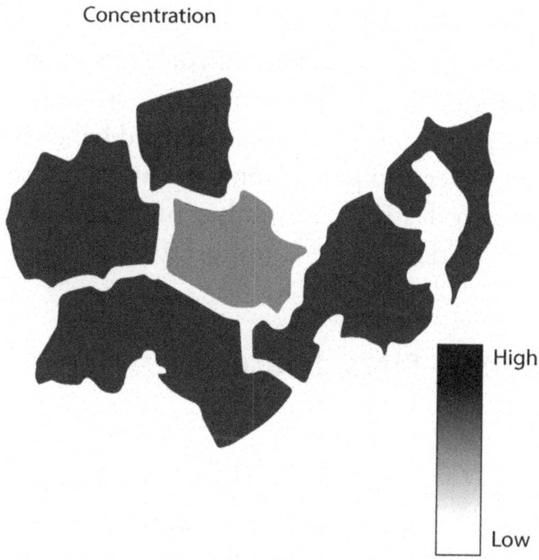

Cultural Infrastructure

	Northern Ireland
Art Galleries	7
Cinemas	5
Studios (Art, Design)	8
Studios (Sound)	0
Studios (Film and TV)	0
Heritage/Visitor centre	9
Libraries and Archives	27
Museums	5
Music venues	13
Theatres	13

Fig. 2.4 Cultural infrastructure of the southeast of Northern Ireland

multipurpose buildings such as town halls and community centres. Public houses are also performance spaces and are important as music venues. The cultural heritage displayed at museums could be of general interest, and associated with a local area, but also focussed on particular artefacts and aspects of history. For example, the Royal Irish Fusiliers Museum displays militaria from the Armagh, Cavan and Monaghan militias; and the Ballywalter Mini Collection is a private museum collection of 30 Minis. Heritage and cultural centres are also important cultural spaces that preserve locally rooted traditions, such as the Brontë Homeland Interpretive Centre in county Down that focuses on the heritage surrounding the homeplace of Patrick Brontë, father of the Brontë sisters of literary fame. Another example is Navan Fort in county Armagh – in Irish mythology, the seat of the ancient Kings of Ulster.

The presence of culture and the arts in broader society and community is found in the SEED area. Community arts organisations are identified, along with organisations that promote engagement with the arts among children and people with disabilities. Broader community level organisations demonstrate the diversity of local people's cultural interests. Writers groups, amateur drama groups, film clubs and local history societies exist at the local community level highlighting the importance of voluntary efforts in communities in local cultural production and consumption. Distinctive features of community level organisations are choral societies and bands of musicians playing a range of brass, silver and percussion instruments. Also linked to the presence of automotive festivals, a number of automotive societies, such as car clubs, are also evident at the community level.

2.5.4 Västerbotten, Sweden – Sites, Spaces and Places

Covering one-eighth of the total land area of Sweden, Västerbotten county is the second largest county in Sweden and described as a region of diversity and contrasts. A distinguishing characteristic of Västerbotten is its level of afforestation. Over half of the county, 56%, is either forested or subalpine woodland. Just 1% is agricultural land and 1% covered by built-up areas (County Administrative Board of Västerbotten & Region Västerbotten 2010). The three most densely populated municipalities in Västerbotten county are Umeå (117,524), Skellefteå (71,831) and Lycksele (12,348), with the remaining municipalities having populations of less than 10,000. Its total population is just over 260,000 and it has a low population density of 4.7 per km^2 (Statistics Sweden 2013).

Important industries in the county are mining, forestry and hydropower. Mining has been carried out since the 1920s, focussed in an area called the Skellefteå field. Forestry is very important in the county, as well as being a nationally important industry. The county produces 20% of Sweden's hydroelectric power and there are hydropower plants on the Skellefte, Ume and Ångerman rivers. Biofuels and wind power are also sources of energy generation. The nature and landscape of the county are an important resource for Västerbotten. The largest nature reserve in Europe, Vindelfjällen, is located in the northwest of Västerbotten county, and there are 236 nature reserves in the county. Reindeer herding occurs throughout Västerbotten county in reindeer-herding districts or 'čearrus', of which there are seven (County Administrative Board of Västerbotten and Region Västerbotten 2010).

Västerbotten also has a rich and diverse culture and heritage. Mining towns, church towns and mountain homesteads form an important part of the cultural heritage landscape. Known as the 'land of storytelling', Västerbotten has a tradition of storytelling that exists to the present. Umeå, the largest city in the region, is an important cultural hub, and has become known as the art capital of Northern Sweden, because of, for example, the good population of artists and art galleries in the city. Umeå was the 2014 European Capital of Culture (County Administrative Board of Vaästerbotten and Region Vaästerbotten 2010).

From fashion to film and dance to arts, a diversity of festivals are evident. Looking at different types of festival, there is variety among each type. For example, different types of music festivals include jazz, country, metal, folk and sixties music. Across Västerbotten county, a common theme among local festivals is the celebration of Midsummer. Festivities traditionally take place on Midsummer's Eve, which occurs each year between June 21st and 25th, and includes feasting on herring, the season's first potatoes, and dancing around a maypole decorated with flowers. Film festivals in Västerbotten county often display themes, such as focussing on short film or documentaries. Film festivals can target particular groups. For example, the School Cinema Festival 'Tjugo5' takes place alongside the MOVE film festival in Umeå, focussing on education and film, and is targeted towards school children of all ages, from kindergarten to high school.

Distinct aspects of Swedish culture are identified through the presence of festivals. Festivals celebrating Sami culture are one example, where traditions around food, craft, music and art of the Sami people, indigenous to northern parts of Scandinavia, are celebrated. Other multicultural celebrations are identified, such as Chinese culture day. Cultural organisations display a multicultural theme, with a Russian–Swedish Culture Association in Umeå that promotes Russian–Swedish culture, the Bangladeshi Society based in Umeå and the Sweden–Asia Association located in Wilhelmina (Fig. 2.5).

Cultural spaces offer insights on Västerbotten county's cultural infrastructure. Museums offer a window on traditions relating to industrial and economic heritage. The Masonite Museum in Rundvik focusses on the history of masonite (a hardboard made from wood fibres) production in

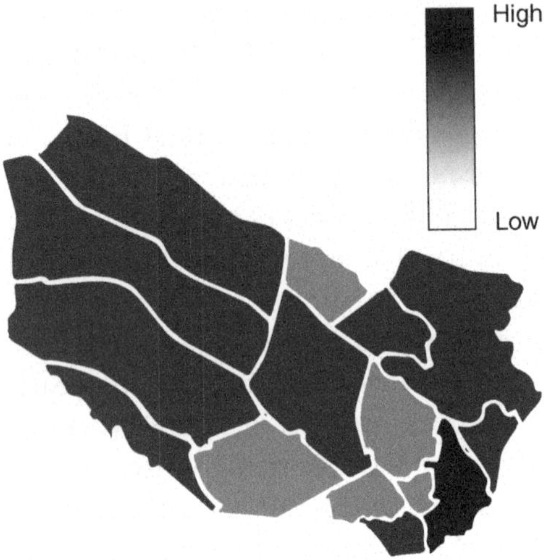

Cultural Infrastructure

	Vasterbotten
Art Galleries	2
Cinemas	12
Studios (Art, Design)	0
Studios (Sound)	16
Studios (Film and TV)	7
Heritage/Visitor centre	1
Libraries and Archives	45
Museums	32
Music venues	0
Theatres	1

Fig. 2.5 Cultural infrastructure of the Vasterbotten, Sweden

the area, and displays a variety of artefacts. The Forestry Museum showcases the history and heritage of forestry activities in Sweden, such as manual logging and the introduction of machines. Museums also display artefacts reflecting Sweden's climate, and people's attempts to deal with the sometimes harsh conditions, such as the Snowmobile museum in Storuman.

Strong cultural participation and consumption is also evident in Västerbotten county, because of the presence of different kinds of spaces for culture. Theatres, libraries, galleries and community centres exist alongside local clubs focussing on special interests such as art, dance, photography and amateur drama. Different types of musical organisations are identified, such as folk, rock, jazz and choir groups. Local historical societies also exist, showing efforts at community level to preserve heritage and culture.

Cultural spaces also reflect the strong audiovisual industry in Västerbotten county, with production spaces such as film and television studios and sound recording studios existing alongside cinemas and local film clubs. A distinctive organisation identified is the People's Cinema, a non-commercial film distribution organisation that supports a network of locally-based cinemas operating on a non-commercial basis. A local branch of the People's Cinema is based in Umeå. A number of local 'Film Studios' or film clubs are also identified, which are affiliated to the national non-profit organisation, the Swedish Federation of Film Studios, that distributes film to its local member groups.

Creative industry organisations are identified in Västerbotten county, such as the Umeå Creative Industries Association and the Lodge, a network of film, gaming and internet companies based around Skellefteå. Alongside this are support organisations for the development of particular skills such as Media Centre, a multimedia education centre, and creative industry sub-sectors such as the regional film resource centre Film i Västerbotten. Craft and design non-profit organisations are also identified. The Swedish Society of Craft and Design and the National Association of Handicraft Societies, both non-profit umbrella organisations, each have regional organisations based in Västerbotten county. To be affiliated with the National Association of Handicraft Societies, members must meet a set of standards. The Västerbotten group operate a retail outlet selling members' handicrafts in Umeå. At the municipality and local levels, craft producer associations, for specific crafts or sometimes with a variety of different types of craftspeople, are also identified.

2.5.5 Kemi-Tornio's, Finland: Sites, Spaces and Places

Located in Lapland province in northern Finland, Kemi-Tornio is a small region made up of five municipalities: Tornio, Kemi, Tervola, Keminmaa and Simo. The Lapland Regional Council describes the province as having rich natural landscape, distinct culture and strong creativity. The province has a population of 195,000 and 59,847 of the total population is located in the Kemi-Tornio region (Regional council of lapland 2012; Statistics Finland 2013). The Kemi-Tornio region accounts for the second largest number of people employed in the Lapland province, with the highest number employed in the Rovaniemi region (Regional council of lapland

2012). The region is classed as a regional centre in Lapland province and is served by Kemi-Tornio airport. The area is also known as Sea Lapland and has developed a tourism experience around its climate of ice, snow and frozen seas in wintertime. Industry in the region includes forestry, mining and agriculture.

Located on the Bothnian Arc, Kemi and Tornio are two cities in the region and Tornio is twined with the Swedish city Haparanda. Tervola is a mainly rural area and important industries are agriculture, forestry and the mining of rock and metal. Based in Bothnian Bay, Keminmaa is located on the mouth of the Kemijoki River. Processing of wood and plastics are important industries in Keminmaa. Simo is known for salmon fishing, which is a long tradition because of rich stocks along the coast and in the Simojoki river. Fishing tourism is important to the area, as well as forestry and agriculture (Regional Council of Lapland 2013).

A broad scope of festivals exists with music, dance, arts, film, food and comedy festivals (see Fig. 2.6). Jazz, blues, rock, country and sixties are among the music festivals in Kemi-Tornio. Two themes are identified as distinct among sports events in Kemi-Tornio. One is motoring events, reflecting the popularity of motorsports in Finland. The second is skiing, reflecting the climate and landscape. Traditions also emerge through festival celebrations, such as the annual whitefish festival that is celebrated in July of each year in Kukkolankoski, a place where whitefish have long been caught.

A range of cultural spaces exist in Kemi-Tornio. Museums, galleries, theatres, libraries, cinemas and music venues are among those identified in the database. Distinct aspects of Finnish culture showcased through museums include the heritage of hairdressing at the Finnish Hairdressers' Museum that displays artefacts of hairdressing from the 1850s onwards. Ways of life are preserved at the Kemi Workers' Museum, where living conditions of different classes of workers who worked in sawmills and other industries around Kemi are displayed. The Kemi Snowcastle, built from snow each year, and which houses a snow chapel, show hotel and snow restaurant, shows how cultural spaces are connected with specific aspects of place, such as climate. Community cultural organisations also exist in the region, such as amateur drama groups, local history societies and book clubs.

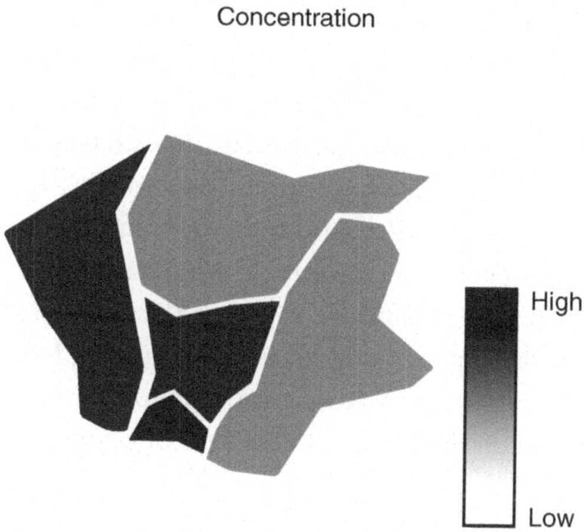

Cultural Infrastructure

	Kemi Tornio
Art Galleries	6
Cinemas	2
Studios (Art, Design)	0
Studios (Sound)	5
Studios (Film and TV)	1
Heritage/Visitor centre	1
Libraries and Archives	4
Museums	16
Music venues	7
Theatres	3

Fig. 2.6 Cultural infrastructure of the Kemi-Tornio, Finland

2.6 Consuming the Periphery

Through an analysis of the cultural infrastructure in the case-study regions we get a better understanding of how the periphery itself is consumed. Knowing the extent and type of infrastructure in these places is of the utmost importance in understanding how the creative economy exists there. The types and variety of infrastructure in peripheral regions matters and shapes how the creative economy survives and thrives. As we will highlight in the following chapter, cultural production does not occur aspatially, what is produced, how it is produced and by whom relates directly to the place they inhabit. This, we argue is more true for the creative industries of peripheral areas than any other emerging sector in the contemporary economy. As such, culture and creativity are place based entities. This embeddedness results from how creatives use their environs (be it inspiration, geographic remove, reflection) as an active agent of production. This trend runs in direct contrast to the increasing placelessness of production in this hyper-globalised era. More and more of that which we consume have vast and lengthy geographical biographies, the local nature of cultural production lies in stark contrast.

For these reasons a better understanding of how we consume culture is required. In an age of that could be arguably described as peak consumption (environmental consequences of global production, increased awareness of unsavoury practices involved in mass production) greater emphasis has to be put on how we understand the changing ways we consume. Recognising the fact that increased symbolic content is more in demand than previously is not enough to plan for the growth of the creative economy. Understanding the how different values are imbued in different produce is key to the successful planning of creative economy growth in peripheral areas. Recognising how talents innate to the peripheral can match the increased appetite for 'authenticity' or social meaning in goods will be the key to the success of peripheral regions.

Matching the types of value ascribed to cultural products with a reflection on the innate cultural qualities of a place is the key to deciding on the best way for producers in that place to reap the most from a growing creative economy. Reflecting on the types of market that the creative produce inhabit is also of importance for understanding future growth trajectories. The emergence or indeed, reemergence of forms of prosumption and sharing will be of increasing importance to peripheral areas. Because it is these regions that were the most recent converts to the market economy model. As we will see in the final chapter of this book, there are examples of collaborative approaches to business that hark back to a pre-industrial modes of production, techniques that for many peripheral regions not so far removed in time.

2.7 Conclusion

In this chapter we focussed on the key themes of consumption that have significant implications for the creative economy and industry as whole, but in particular for peripheral regions. The role of technology in creative experiences has open up new opportunities for this sector in peripheral regions and potentially gives peripheral regions the platform to shape and lead different sub-sectors of this industry. As prosumers are seeking uniqueness and difference in their consumption this also provides opportunities that peripheral regions can exploit effectively. Where we see peripheral regions having a distinct advantage is through expressive values. In our overviews of the sites, spaces and places of peripheral regions on this island of Ireland, in Sweden and Finland it is evident that expressive values are different and are shaped by local environment, culture and economic contexts. The social and historic values are distinctly different and are firmly rooted in place. We suggest that there is a commonality of authenticity value that is bound by sense of place and originality. There is also a vibrancy evident in our cases studies and it is quiet clear that some of these peripheral regions have a broad range of sectoral activity but there is a focus or strength in one of two particular sub-sectors. Moreover, two of these peripheral regions have been awarded European Capital of Culture that further reflects on the strengths and vibrancy of these sectors in peripheral regions. What is also remarkable from these case studies is the diversity of activities which may go against the myth that peripheral regions have limited activities due to constraints such as infrastructure, population, remoteness etc.

Our overview also gives rise to a number of challenges. How sustainable is it for peripheral regions to maintain such diversity of activities and sites? What is the appropriate balance between maintain exploiting expressive values such as authenticity and exploiting it to meet the growing demands of prosumers? Is such diversity of activities necessary to meet both the economic and social needs of peripheral regions? How can the competing economic and social needs be balanced through creative industries sub-sectors? These and other questions raise some systematic issues for the creative economy and industries in peripheral regions. The expressive values of peripheral regions if exploited too much can eventually undermine growth and opportunities. Exploited too little can mean the diversity that we have unearthed in these peripheral regions is difficult and challenging to sustain and maintain over the longer term. A fine and delicate balance has to be achieved that meets competing economic, social and cultural needs of peripheral regions.

Bibliography

Adorno, T., and M. Horkheimer. 2002. *Dialectic of Enlightenment*. Stanford: Stanford University Press.

Baudrillard, J. 1970. *The Consumer Society: Myths and Structures*, trans by C. Turner. London: Sage.

Bayliss, D. 2004. Creative Planning in Ireland: The Role of Culture-led Development in Irish Planning. *European Planning Studies* 12(4): 497–515.
Belk, R. 2014. You are what you can access: Sharing and collaborative consumption online. *Journal of Business Research* 67: 1595–600.
Botsman, R., and R. Rogers. 2010. *What's mine is yours: The rise of collaborative consumption*. New York: Harper Collins.
Bourdieu, P. 2000. *The production of belief: Contribution to an economy of symbolic goods*. Media, culture & society: A critical reader.
Breslin, J. G., Card, D., Dabrowski, M. and Mulligan, M. 2014. *Sizing the EU App economy: Eurapp final report*, Directorate-General for Communications Networks, Content and Technology, European Commission.
Caves, R. E. 2000. *Creative industries: Contracts between art and commerce*. London: Harvard University Press.
Chapman, R. 2012. *Selling the sixties: The pirates and pop music radio*. Routledge.
County Administrative Board of Västerbotten and Region Vaästerbotten. 2010. Facts about Västerbotten 2010. Available at: helsinkidesignlab.org/files/601/original.pdf
DFC Intelligence. 2015. Worldwide Video Game Market Forecasts. San Diego: DFC Intelligence. Available at: http://www.dfcint.com/wp/product/worldwide-video-gamemarket-forecasts/
Durkheim, E. 2014. *The division of labor in society*. New York: Simon and Schuster.
Eurobarometer. 2009. *European cultural values*. Brussels, Belgium: European Commission Directorate.
EUROSTAT. 2011. Cultural Statistics, EUROSTAT.
Failte Ireland. 2012. Tourism Facts. Available at: http://wwwfailteireland.ie/Failteireland/media/WebsiteStructure/Documents/3_Research_insights/3_General_ SurveysReports/Tourism_Facts_2011_V3.pdf?ext=.pdf.
FGS McClure Watters and Regional Forecasts. 2008. South East Economic development: Economic Development Strategy. Available at: http://www.newryandmourne.gov.uk/documents/SEED_Report.pdf
Fontenelle, I. 2015. Organisations as producers of consumers. *Organization* 22(5): 644–60.
Getz, D. 2008. Event tourism: Definition, evolution, and research. *Tourism Management* 29: 403–28.
Grose, T.K. 2011, 14 November. Live, at a Field Near You: Why the Music Industry Is Singing a Happy Tune. Time. Retrieved from http://content.time.com/time/magazine/article/0,9171,2098639,00.html

Hall, C. M. 2006. Urban entrepreneurship, corporate interests and sports mega-events: The thin policies of competitiveness within the hard outcomes of neoliberalism. *The Sociological Review* 54(s2): 59–70.

Halliday, S. V. 2016. User-generated content about brands: Understanding its creators and consumers. *Journal of Business Research* 69(1): 137–44.

Hartley, J. 2009. From the consciousness industry to the creative industries: Consumer-created content, social network markets, & the growth of knowledge. In Holt, J. and Perren, A. (Eds.), *Media Industries: History, Theory & Method*, 231–44.

Hesmondhalgh, D. 2002. *The Cultural Industries*. London: SAGE.

Hirsch, P. M. 2000. Cultural industries revisited. *Organization Science* 11(3): 356–61.

Holbrook, M. B., and E. C. Hirschman. 1982. The experiential aspects of consumption: Consumer fantasies, feelings, and fun. *Journal of Consumer Research* 9(2): 132–40. http://www.udaras.ie/en/an-ghaeilge-an-ghaeltacht/an- ghaeltacht/.

Kotler, P., Haider, D.H. and Rein, I.J. 1993. *Marketing places: Attracting investment, industry, and tourism to cities, states and nations*. New York: Free Press.

Lamberton, C. P., and R. L. Rose. 2012. When is ours better than mine? A framework for understanding and altering participation in commercial sharing systems. *Journal of Marketing* 76(4): 109–25.

Lemley, M. A. 2012. The myth of the sole inventor. *Michigan Law Review*: 709–60.

Lessig, L. 2002. *The future of ideas: The fate of the commons in a connected world*. London: Vintage.

Levine, L. W. 1988. *Highbrow/lowbrow*, Vol. 1986. Cambridge, MA: Harvard University Press.

McKee, A. 2013. The power of art, the power of entertainment. *Media, Culture & Society* 35(6): 759–70.

Miesen, H. 2004. Fiction readers' appreciation of text attributes in literary and popular novels: Some empirical findings. *International Journal of Arts Management* 7(1): 45–56.

Napoli, P. M. 2011. *Audience evolution: New technologies and the transformation of media audiences*. Columbia: Columbia University Press.

Newry and Mourne district council. 2013. South East Economic Development. Available at: http://www.newryandmourne.gov.uk/business/SEED.aspx

O'Connor, J. 2007. *The cultural and creative industries: A review of the literature (Report for Creative Partnerships)*. London: Arts Council.

O'Connor, J. 2015. Intermediaries and imaginaries in the cultural and creative industries. *Regional Studies* 49(3): 374–87.

Peltoniemi, M. 2015. Cultural Industries: Product–Market Characteristics, Management Challenges and Industry Dynamics. *International Journal of Management Reviews* 17(1): 41–68.

Pine, B. J., and J. H. Gilmore. 1999. *The experience economy: Work is theatre & every business a stage*. Cambridge, MA: Harvard Business Press.

Planells, A. J. 2015. Video games and the crowdfunding ideology: From the gamer-buyer to the prosumer-investor. *Journal of Consumer Culture* 0(0): 1–19.

Potts, J., J. Hartley, J. Banks, J. Burgess, R. Cobcroft, S. Cunningham, and L. Montgomery. 2008. Consumer Co-creation and Situated Creativity. *Industry and Innovation* 15(5): 459–74.

Prentice, R., and Vivien Andersen. 2003. Festival as Creative Destination. *Annals of Tourism Research* 30(1): 7–30.

PWC. 2015. Global entertainment and media outlook 2015–2019, PWC.

Quinn, B. 2005. Changing festival places: Insights from Galway. *Social & Cultural Geography* 6(2): 237–52.

Regional council of lapland. 2012. Lapland in Figures 2012–2013. Available at: http://www.lapland.fi/en/lapinliitto/c/document_library/get_file?folderid=931431&name=Dl FE-16378.pdf

Regional council of lapland. 2013. Lapland in Figures 2012–2013. Available at: http://www.lapland.fi/en/lapinliitto/c/document_library/get_file?folderid=931431&name=Dl FE-16378.pdf

Ritzer, G., and N. Jurgenson. 2010. Production, Consumption, Prosumption The nature of capitalism in the age of the digital 'prosumer'. *Journal of Consumer Culture* 10(1): 13–36.

Standage, T. 1998. *The Victorian Internet: The remarkable story of the telegraph and the nineteenth century's online pioneers*. London: Weidenfeld & Nicolson.

Statistics Finland. 2013. Population Structure. Available at: http://www.stat.fi/til/vaerak/tau_en.html

Statistics Sweden. 2013. Population Statistics. Stockholm. Available at http://www.scb.se/en/finding-statistics/statistics-by-subject-area/population/population-composition/population-statistics/

Throsby, D. 2001. *Economics and Culture*. Cambridge: Cambridge University Press.

Throsby, D. 2008a. Modelling the cultural industries. *International Journal of Cultural Policy* 14(3): 217–32.

Throsby, D. 2008b. The Concentric Circles Model of the Cultural Industries. *Cultural Trends* 17(3): 147–64.

Toffler, A. 1980. *The Third Wave: The classic study of tomorrow*. New York: Bantam.

Údaraás na gaeltachta. 2013. The gaeltacht. Available at: http://www.udaras.ie/en/an-ghaeilge-an-ghaeltacht/an- ghaeltacht/

Waitt, G. 2008. Urban Festivals: Geographies of Hype, Helplessness and Hope. *Geography Compass* 2(2): 513–37.

Westerbeek, H, M., P Turene, and L. Ingerson. 2002. Key Success Factors in bidding to hallmark sporting events. *International Marketing Review* 19(3): 303–22.

Western Development Commission. 2012. This is Ireland: Highlights from census 2011. Part 1, Pro le 1: Town and country overview of the Western Region. Western development commission: Roscommon.

Work Foundation. 2007. *Staying Ahead: The Economic Performance of the UK's Creative Industries*. London: The Work Foundation.

Zimmerman, J. 2008. From brew town to cool town: Neoliberalism and the creative city development strategy in Milwaukee. *Cities* 25(4): 230–42.

3

Producing Culture by Creative Means: A View from the Periphery

3.1 Introduction

Culture production and consumption, has marked the key milestones in the development of the human race. As more attention has been drawn to it, we understand more and more about how important culture is becoming as an agent of economic change. Previously, we made the case that the consumption of culture can be seen in context of how consumption itself has evolved. In this chapter we make a similar case on the supply/production side of the creative economy. How creative industries have embraced, battled with and exploited technology demonstrates their capacity to cope with change. Here, we focus on their guise as agents of change in the peripheral economics of the developed world.

Taking a more global view in the first instance, culture has always been produced, but of late (last two centuries), it has been produced more and more for economic returns (see Table 3.1). This practice has seen the creative economy grow to what it is today. Contemporary production of culture, relies on industrial techniques and makes use of commodification to reach an ever greater number of customers. Going back to the invention of the phonograph we see it as important as it could be considered as the first step

P. Collins, J.A. Cunningham, *Creative Economies in Peripheral Regions*, DOI 10.1007/978-3-319-52165-7_3

Table 3.1 Creative economy figures

Creative Economy	Revenue	Employment
Creative Application		
Advertising	285	2
Architecture	222	1.7
Books	143	3.7
Other publishing	354	2.9
Creative Technology		
Gaming	99	0.6
Audiovisual A	77	2.5
Creative Expression		
Music	65	4
Audiovisual B	477	3.5
Performing Arts	127	3.5
Visual Arts	391	6.7
Radio	46	0.5

Source: Adopted from PWC, 2015

towards the industrialisation of cultural production. There are two different schools of thought on the industrialisation of culture, some see it as democratising, others see it as antithetical to the very nature of artistic production.

We can see the industrialisation of culture with the application of industrial techniques in emergent industries of the mid-twentieth century like film and television heralding the mass reproduction of culture. This brought with it the separation of high and low art or the art versus entertainment duality noted by McKee (2013) and others. The application of industrial techniques brought with it mass production that allowed for initial investments to be reproduced by volume sales of copies. Referred to in Chapter 2 as second-stage cultural technologies, the effect of a massive upswing in cultural consumption, is that cultural produce which began to become more prevalent in everyday life (Ritzer and Juregenson 2010). What Ardorno and Horkheimer term the rise of the Culture Industry in the 1950s laid the ground work for the development of the creative economy and the creative industries that we focus on here.

Theorists like O'Connor (2007, 2010, 2015) and Pratt (2004, 2012) are adept at drawing a clear lineage for the rise of the contemporary creative economy, going as far back as the 1970s to describe its inception. They look to the work of Markusen (1996) and Piore and Sabel (1984) that depicted the shift from mass production to flexible specialisation and post-fordism. Daniel Bell's contribution on the *Rise of a Post Industrial Society* (1976) pointed to a radical departure from the past in terms of economic and industrial growth. Add to this the change in consumer markets as demand shifted towards smaller, niche markets and goods and services that offered a 'narrative' and were full of 'symbolic content' (Hesmondalgh 2013), and we begin to see more clearly the seeds from which the creative economy has grown (O'Connor 2010; Pratt 2007, 2008).

The identity-forming traits of goods imbued with symbolic content had a profound effect on the organisation of production (Lash and Urry 1994). For Castells' (1996) flows of people, money, goods and information was added to objects (texts, images, sounds and experiences), which helped the position of the cultural industries vis-à-vis, the rest of the economy. The growth of symbolic consumption meant that the tensions and difficulties of producing for such a market had become central to many different businesses. As a result, the cultural industries were no longer seen as a strange remnant of an older production system but became the cutting edge, a template for the others to follow into a new economy of 'signs and space' (Lash and Urry 1994; O'Connor 2010).

Economic geography provides an ideal lens through which we can observe the evolution of the creative economy over the past 40 years. Turning their back on modernist economic geography in the late 1980s, economic geographers began to highlight social space as a crucial factor in economic understanding. This ran in close parallel to the 'cultural turn' in geography and the social sciences more broadly (see Crang 1997). As a direct result the early 1990s saw the rise of a body of work that reignited Alfred Marshall's theories from a century previous to tell us about the importance of place in an increasingly globalised world. In the USA, the work of the Californian school (Storper and Walker 1989) began to highlight the fact that not all economic transactions were based on 'rational' calculations of profit and loss and that untraded externalities could provide huge benefits. In Europe, building on the template formed by Piore and Sabel (1984), economic geographers were looking at institutional thickness and dissecting the anatomy of successful regional systems of innovation at the same time that the UK's Department for Culture, Media and Sport (DCMS) was publishing its oft-quoted definition of the creative industries (Cooke and Morgan 2001; Boschma 2005).

The academic and policy recognition of the creative economy can be appreciated in the context of a refocussing of economic development at the subnational level and a spatial turn away from the nation scale towards multilayered spatial scales (Castells 1996). This coincides with the more global move away from the products of fordist production techniques towards, specialised, symbol-laden products that creative economy industries specialised in. In many ways then, the creative economy itself is a natural test bed for spatial economic development theory. As a set of industries it shows a tendency to cluster, it is also extremely flexible in its production processes and methods, and, crucially for us, it has a vibrant incarnation beyond the limits of cities. As an example, audiovisual (AV) output is generally the result of projects where teams, partnerships and alliances dissolve and re-form constantly (Bilton 2010). Output in that sector is also contingent on dense flows of information and goods and services that benefit from economies of scale in skills-sourcing and know-how (Kerr and Cawley 2012). AV clusters tend to involve complex divisions of labour while exploiting new ICT developments that help them transcend space barriers. The demonstrated ability of the AV sector to work across different spatial scales, and indeed in diverse (sometimes remote) geographies, while being tightly clustered makes it an ideal analytic focal point for economic geographers (see Scott 2001; Turok 2004).

3.2 The Creative Economy

Classifying and measuring the scale and scope of the creative economy is challenging as we have discussed in Chapter 1. Ernst and Young provide first attempt to map the creative and cultural industries across the globe. The headline statistics are impressive, one of the least expected results was that the largest revenue was generated in the Asia Pacific region (Ernst and Young 2015). That said, this could have been predicted with the help of trends identified in the most recent UNCTAD report on the creative economy in developing countries (UNCTAD 2013). The definition of the creative economy used by Ernst and Young differs from our by point of fact that they exclude internet and software companies. Their estimation of the revenues of the global creative economy reaching $2,250 billion, we suggest undervalues it considerably (we would estimate by as much as one third). E&Y (2015) estimate creative applications (advertising, architectures, books and other publishing) is worth $804 billion, creative technology (gaming and audiovisual a) is worth 176 billion and creative expression is worth (music, audiovisual, performing arts, visual arts and radio) 1,106 billion in 2015. In terms of employment, PWC estimate that audiovisual and performing arts employ 3.5 million respectively, visual arts employs 6.7 million and books employ 3.7 million

Considering that one sector was under-represented, we can still see some interesting patterns from the above schema. From Chapter 2 we can understand that the creative application, the sector that is most commercial market oriented, is indeed the sector responsible for a significant share of revenues in the global creative economy. At the sub-sectoral level, television is responsible for the greatest share at $477billion in 2013. In terms of numbers employed, creative expression has the highest number of employees, accounting for 14.7 million jobs in the same year. Within that, Ernst and Young (2015) estimate 6.7 million people as employed in the visual arts sub-sector. The Ernst and Young (2015) analysis estimates Europe as the second largest regional economy (32% of global revenues and 26% of global employment). The main traits of the European creative economy are:

- It is young (employing 19.1% of all 15–29-year olds)
- It is creative (Europe is some to more creators than any other global region – 1 million musicians)
- It is rooted in history (the unique concentration of heritage and art institutions in a well-structured and supported cultural ecosystem)
- High level of creative education
- A trendsetter in key creative areas from Art to advertising.

NESTA have also reflected on the state of the European creative economy in a recent report comparing employment in the UK and EU creative industries. Using the DCMS classification theirs is a definition of the creative economy that better reflects our own (Nathan et al. 2015). They estimate employment at circa 11.3 million while the Enrst and Young estimate was closer to 8 million. Crucially NESTA estimate employment numbers in the IT and software services sub-sector just over 3 million, making for a more comparable understanding between both reports. In terms of the breakdown of figures at the sectoral level, it is no surprise to see a much higher percentage of the workforce employed in the creative technology sector. Most surprising is the difference (even accounting for different methods and definitions employed in both reports) of the relative numbers employed in the core creative areas of creative expression. In Europe only one-fifth of the creative workforce is employed in the creative expression sector, while close to half are employed in the creative application sector (1.9 million employed in advertising and marketing alone). The largest sub-sector for employment is the one all but ignored by Ernst and Young, employment in IT and Software services across the continent reaching close to 3.1 million people.

More recently again, a NESTA report on the geography of the UK's creative economy provides for more interesting insights (Mateos-Garcia and Bakshi 2016). Following on from previous work exploring the development of creative clusters in and near some of the UK's largest cities, this report pushes the level of analysis further and identifies 47 creative clusters across the UK. Obviously, London and the South East dominate, this report points to emerging clusters in less urban regions, in the North of England, Scotland, Wales and Northern Ireland. It was estimated that these clusters grew their creative employment by 28% between 2007 and 2014 (ibid.). These analyses further highlight the growth of the sector, but also provide evidence of creative clusters emerging in less urban areas and regions.

3.2.1 Beyond the Urban: the Local Level

Only so much can be understood from the supranational scale of enquiry. In what follows we probe deep down, beyond the national or city level to consider the types of creative economies (industries) that exist at the local level. By doing this we are contributing to a small but growing literature that is focussing on the creative industries of rural/more peripheral regions (see for example Asheim and Hansen 2009; Collins et al. 2014; Connel and Rugendyke 2010; Faggian et al. 2013; Hansen and Niedomysl 2008; Mayes 2010; Scott 2010). The urban bias of the literature heretofore is completely understandable. We do not contend that the following case studies rival what is going on in the larger cities of the nation states to which these regions belong. We seek instead to better understand what it is that is going on in these regions and how it is different.

It was Richard Florida's 'Creative Class' thesis (2002) that led to a proliferation of studies with a common focus on the urban metropolis as the prime or sole stimulator of the creative economy (Brown et al. 2000; Casellas and Pallares-Barbera 2009; Johnson 2009; MacLeod 2002). Limitations of Florida's approach have been well-documented (see for example, Peck 2005). While it is not the intention of this review to contest the aforementioned thesis, it is worth indicating briefly that it has been labelled as what Oakley (2009: 404) as 'more focused on high-tech growth than on creative and cultural industries', lacking empirical evidence (Asheim and Hansen 2009) and as being synonymous with the previously well-established concept of human capital in economies and regional studies (Glaeser et al. 2010).

Despite these limitations, the thesis led to a distinct urban–rural divide in the context of creative economy studies thus ignoring the presence and potential of creative economies in non-urban areas (Woods 2015). Bell and Jayne (2006) contend that existing policy is urban-centric and that when studies have been conducted on other areas, they have followed an urban script, which imposes the urban values and qualities on the rural, oppressing 'their own breed of creative economy'. Furthermore, Banks et al. (2000) categorised creative economies as being quintessentially urban while Glaeser et al. (2010) attributed entrepreneurship with the same quality. Similarly, Freire-Gibb and Nelsein (2014) assert that entrepreneurship studies in Denmark have been urban-centric. Hence, a divide emerges in a sector which has tended to prioritise economic growth while excluding those unable to participate (Atkinson and Easthope 2009) even though socially it pledged to effectuate the exact opposite (Banks 2007: 71).

Studies in Dutch and Nordic regions, respectively, have highlighted a significant rural–urban divide in terms of innovation (see Hansen 2007 and Stam et al. 2008). This urban focus has been eagerly embraced by politicians and stakeholders which has induced 'urban concentric models' (Felton et al. 2010). Consequently, uncertainties exist about what will happen to less favoured or 'ordinary' areas (Asheim and Hansen 2008;

Hardhill et al. 2006). Therefore, this confirms the need to further study these 'ordinary' places and their creative economies, further highlighting the value of research of this nature.

In assessments of Sweden's regional creative industries Power (2002) and Strom and Nelson (2010), found them to be more drawn towards urban areas but still exerting a sizeable impact in more peripheral locales. Similarly, Huggins and Clifton (2011) and Woods (2015) acknowledged the same phenomenon in the UK. Furthermore, research in rural Australia found that creative activity is increasing in ex-urban locations (Felton et al. 2010) with larger rural towns attracting more creative individuals (McGranahan and Wojan 2007). A report on Donegal's (West of Ireland) cultural activities also exhibits an urban concentration (Donegal County Council 2009). A similar disproportionate distribution is seen in literature demonstrating that outer-suburban locations exhibited 'hidden' creative networks (Bennett 2010; Felton et al. 2010) due to application of unsuitable data and methodological instruments.

Location quotients have been common in many studies (Currid 2006; Florida 2002; Pratt 1997) but the majority display an inherent limitation in that when used to measure creative industries employment they systematically favour those localities with a larger workforce (Collis et al. 2013; De Propris et al. 2009; Lazaretti et al. 2016). Similarly, use of census or federal databases in such studies implicate certain limitations as they are premised on notions of singular workspace, a view which is not valid in relation to creative individuals (Brennan-Horley and Gibson 2009). Moreover, Throsby and Hollister (2003) and Throsby (2008) exemplify this, believing Australian census data to have underestimated the artist population by 50%. Hence, there is a gap for different analytical methods that do not privilege inner cities and unfounded views of creatives as static which only serve to increase the already prevalent divide.

Given such an analytical and empirical bias, it is well overdue 'to break out of the mould of thinking about creativity as a bohemian inner city phenomenon' (Gibson and Brennan-Horley 2006: 469). Furthermore, creativity is highly democratic (Schelsinger 2007) and is found everywhere in the world and is an inexhaustible resource (UNCTAD 2010). Gibson and Kong (2005) and Jayne et al. (2010) highlight the need for more refined and exploratory theoretical and empirical research with the prevalent metropolitan focus incapable of encapsulating the authenticity and intricacy of cultural production and consumption in smaller areas. The findings of several researchers corroborate the belief that there exists a vibrant, creative economy in peripheral areas (Asheim and Hansen 2009; Connell and Rugendyke 2010; Collins et al. 2014; Drake 2003; Faggian et al. 2013; Mayes 2010; McGranahan and Wojan. 2007; Warren and Evitt 2010; Scott 2010; Woods 2011). The next section focusses on the changing patterns of cultural consumption, which have a profound effect on the cultural and creative industries.

3.3 Peripheral Creative Economies: Distinctive Aspects

The creative economy and industries in peripheral regions have some distinct dimensions. We have distilled them in to five dimensions that pervade across the sub-sectors of the creative economy in peripheral regions. These centre around product and place, uniqueness and authenticity of rural, remoteness, non-economic motivations and the allure of rural.

3.3.1 Product and Place

Relating to the earlier discussion of increased desire for cultural content (Chapter 2), Currid and Wiliams (2010) contend that a brand or product acquires value from the geographical location of its production site, citing the examples of French wine and New York art. Products such as these are immediately imbued with values that are too dynamic to be simply seen in economic terms. This parallels Molotch's (2002, 2003) concept of product in place. For him, place is fundamental to the production of creative content and is intricately linked to culture and tradition. What offers creative industries operating out of rural and peripheral areas a competitive advantage is their ability to exploit place and its link to culture and tradition. Highly relevant here is the notion of authenticity, something that is increasingly demanded by that are consumers weary of mass-produced goods (Collins et al. 2014). This is furthered by Scott's (2005) perspective that historic infrastructure has a key role in place branding. The work of Munoz et al. (2006) on the West of Ireland and perceived authenticity of the Irish Pub is interesting here. For them authentic infrastructure can exert a considerable role in place branding.

Places can become products themselves (Currid and Williams 2010) and can be consumed as such. Moreover, Molotch (2002, 2003) extends his role through his contention that by associating themselves with certain places, products can gain higher value. An example of this is provided by the Swedish jewellery company JohannaN, which has 'based a lot of the brand around Norrland and Umeå, both in the spirit of the company and the design itself. There's a certain amount of exoticism around northern Sweden in countries like the Netherlands and Belgium'.[1] In this way, the product attains more value as it is based on elements unique to the surrounding area. This higher value is similar to the concept of buzz that motivates consumption as people consume cultural goods socially (Caves 2000). The social milieu in which people generate buzz plays a key role in the production, consumption and valorisation of cultural goods (Currid and Williams 2010) by establishing connections for appraising art (Becker 1982), facilitating the establishment of taste and genre classification (Cave 2000; Di Maggio 1987) and allowing access to gatekeepers (Blau 1989; Crane 1989). Moreover, the role of media and new media highlighted previously is also important here as media creates simulacrums of areas, in the process cultivating an image of place (Brooks 2000; Clark 2009; Florida 2002; Glaeser et al. 2010). Thus, this image of place is essential in attracting creative individuals, such as artists who seek buzz in the metropolis or other creative individuals who want a better quality of life, away from the urban rat race (Hoey 2005; Woods 2011). Therefore place branding is not limited to the urban metropolis but can also be used to great effect in the peripheral region. This is seen through projects such as Look West (www.lookwest.ie) which attempts to attract more migrants and businesses to the Western Region of Ireland. Such place branding is of vital

[1] See (http://www.mycreativeedge.eu/johannan/ – Accessed 04/08/2015).

importance as people desire to live in an authentic location with unique characters and as such can be used as a local economic development tool (AuthentiCity 2009).

Intertwined into the consumption of place are notions of intangible assets (Gibson and Connell 2004; Myers 2002; Stratton 2008; Andersen 2010). Intangible cultural resources includes the history of a community unique and defining traditions and customs images and perceptions of place (AuthentiCity 2009). Thus, the product inherits an expressive value, an immaterial attribute that represents the desire to produce and consume products whose value is not purely practical (British Council 2010). Referring back to the story element, it has been argued that our brains are 'hard-wired' for stories and help us make sense of place and our relationships as part of a community. Powerful stories bring the invisible and abstract to life, making them effective containers of rich information that people can quickly transmit to others (AuthentiCity 2010). In essence, stories represent authenticity in one of its purest forms. The importance of intangible assets to place has been previously noted by several authors (Bouchard 2009; Dos Santos 1991) who suggest that heritage narratives can act as a tool for social cohesion.

As opposed to other industries, value is much more uncertain, dynamic and taste-driven in the creative and cultural industries. However, among many creative individuals, such as engineers, (Asheim and Hansen 2009) a desire or taste for a better quality of life exists. Rural and peripheral areas can offer an authenticity or remoteness and this is a key factor in the development of creative economies in these places.

3.3.2 Uniqueness and Authenticity of Rural

Several studies have stated that there have been many attempts to directly transcribe successful urban legislation onto a rural context (Bell and Jayne 2010; Mossig 2011; Strom and Nelson 2010). We argue that such a notion is problematic and shift the focus to the value of landscape and other general quality of life factors in our analysis.

Place is intricately linked to culture and tradition. A creative individual's subjective, personal or emotional reaction to place determines the manner in which they employ the characteristics of that place for aesthetic inspiration, and that response will be formed by personal identities, perceptions and philosophies. Furthermore, in the process of responding to place individuals and groups construct place (Drake 2003). As Lippard (1997: 9) argues, 'Our personal relationships to history and place form us, as individuals and groups, and in reciprocal ways we form them.' This is evident in Drake's (2003) Australian study in which it is clear that links between place and creativity were pivotal in the creative process. One interviewee, a film producer contended that using the outback or badlands myth in art was a big part of the identity. Indeed, the same author echoes Molotch's (2002, 2003) place in product in theorising that the local branding of a place based on reputation and inspiration was key to craft metalworkers.

Similarly, Andersen (2010) noted that since the 1960s more than 60 feature films have been shot in the scenic surroundings of Broken Hill. Indeed, this iconic landscape has been fundamental in the emergence of a lively visual arts industry in Broken Hill. The colonial frontier context was noted to be a source of local inspiration in a study in Darwin, Australia (Gibson et al. 2010). Moreover, a study in Cumbria advocated the use of bigger narratives of place which could act as 'cultural glue' holding together the heritage industry which is thought to be crucial for rural regions (Cabras and Bosworth 2014). An example of this is the previously referenced construction of Celtic standing stones in order to create a narrative of place wrapped up in an 'inauthentic' cultural heritage (Connell and Rugendyke 2010). Perhaps another example of this 'inauthentic' narrative of place is seen in Wangaratta's Jazz Festival (Curtis 2010). Albeit lacking in any previous connection to Jazz, Wangarrata has managed to attain a reputation of the place where Jazz belongs.

Festivals such as this are key to the creative economy as those with the greatest authenticity and deepest roots within a community's or a place's cultural identity are best positioned to help weather the economic shocks (BOP Consulting 2009). However, a discussion on place and peripherality cannot exclude a discussion on the influence of isolation or remoteness which is considered as one of the main sources of authenticity.

3.3.3 Benefits of Remoteness

Although remoteness has been considered to be a negative influence on creativity (Florida 2002, 2005; Landry 2000) various studies have shown that it can in fact have the opposite effect (Andersen 2010; Dunbar-Hall and Gibson 2004; McGranahan and Wojan 2007; Warren and Evitt 2010). Furthermore it is argued that in the creative industry, remoteness from the metropolis exerts less of an influence than in other sectors (DKM Consultants 2009). Gibson et al. (2010) argues that it is in the tourism industry especially, that tourism, remoteness, marginality and distinctiveness can be brought together to fashion a prosperous industry base.

Furthermore, Gibson et al. (2010) highlighted that remoteness was a 'boon' for some allowing them to develop creatively, freedom to pursue their own vision, unencumbered by the demands of city inclinations and tastes. The same 'haven' away from the rat race concept is paralleled by Waitt and Gibson (2009) as well as Bell and Jayne (2006) and Verdich (2010). Gibson et al. (2010) contend that creatives and visual artists relished the opportunity of laissez-faire creative expression. Moreover, several academics claim that remoteness is paramount in securing the authenticity required to successfully market products (Gibson and Connell 2004; Myers 2002). Furthermore, albeit not in an equally remote context, Felton et al. (2010) argues that remoteness is encouraging new forms of networking and interconnectivity, phenomenon also present in Bennett's (2010) popular music observations.

Following on from our previous discussion on authenticity of rural, Florida (2002: 228) in the original creative class thesis considered authenticity to be vital in attracting creative individuals to a place, encompassing 'historic buildings, established neighbourhoods, a music scene or specific cultural attributes'. Moreover, Prideaux (2002) postulates that peripheral uniqueness or authenticity is the most significant catalyst in raising the interest needed to prevail against issues of remoteness. Indeed, festivals have been shown to be more authentic given the dearth of international influence. A prime example of this is the authentic nature of the festival in Ballingup (Kenyon and Black 2001) which has managed to attract an influx of creative individuals who brought entrepreneurial and enterprise skills with them, thus benefitting the local economy. Similar cases have been noted in Gibson et al. (2010: 36) as 'Remoteness matters for everyone in Darwin but is also a state of being in which people unevenly invest and believe.'

3.3.3.1 Disadvantages of Remoteness

Remoteness is a double-edged sword and can also have negative implications which affect the development of the peripheral creative economy. Warren and Evitt (2010) assert that despite the digitisation impacts of new media such as YouTube, sheer physical geographic distance exerts its influence as paid performances are few and far between. Compounding this, they see themselves obligated to perform at national indigenous festivals where there performances are shaped by prevailing, often tourist 'patron' discourses, Irish dance and traditional music.

Furthermore Gibson et al. (2010) argue that this physical distance also inhibits access to traditional gatekeepers whilst for others it was a type of professional isolation, deficient of professional environment stimulation. Correspondingly, isolation was found to be the main locational disadvantage amongst creatives in Broken Hill (Andersen 2010) and a similar problem was uncovered by others (Curtis 2010; Connell and Rugendyke 2010). Therefore, referring back to Gibson, not investing and believing in remoteness as a catalyst for authenticity is also observable. In addition, it challenges the 'death of distance' notion (Cairncross 2001) as distance, to some of these creative individuals, exerts its considerable restrictive capacity.

3.3.4 Non-Economic Motivations

The fact that products are imbued with place and authenticity suggests that the importance of creative products and creative industries is much further-reaching than acknowledged by the majority of the literature. Indeed, the British British Council (2010) highlight that the creative industries are demarcated by an aspiration to create things that are attributed with an expressive value. As such, they represent a desire to make products characterised by a quintessence that is not purely practical including beautiful products, commodities that communicate cultural value through music, drama entertainment and visual arts. Prime examples of such social, political and cultural motivation – as opposed to economic – have been noted in several peripheral areas. Mayes (2010: 20) noted that in the production of postcards, the main aim was to foster a sense of community and that creative production had 'a clear social role in the production of a sense of community' with creativity emphasised here as socially and politically motivated. In addition, an analogous incentive was apparent in Connel and Rugendyke's (2010) study.

A social impetus was also key in Warren and Evitt's (2010) study in which hip-hop artists helped give young people something to do in order to keep them out of trouble. Local artisan groups also indicated the importance of sociality in other studies (Banks et al. 2000; Kong 2005). Several academics have noted the importance of cultural heritage that promotes social cohesion (Bouchard 2009). Banks (2007) albeit in a more urban context, acknowledged that Manchester's creative workers esteemed more intrinsic awards with moral and ethical principles considered more meaningful than their economic counterpart. Moreover, Dunphy (2009) contended that artists viewed the creation of art itself as more significant than economic revenue. Markusen (2010) argues that the size of the creative economy is under-represented if non-profit organisations are not included. Therefore, considering that the creative economy in the peripheral area may be less about economic goals, Hesmondhalgh and Pratt (2005) have argued that creative and cultural policy should not be considered merely in monetary terms but ought to augment social unity and local community growth. Thus, creativity in peripheral areas is less about civic buzz and more about the passion of key individuals and collectives they form (Andersen 2010; Connell and Rugendyke 2010; Curtis 2010).

3.3.5 Allure of the Rural

The allure of the periphery to creative individuals has been accepted as having an influential role in regional prosperity (Comunian and Faggian 2011; Jayne et al. 2010). Moreover, Rutten (2016) contend that the place of residence of the creatives and not that of the industries is an important factor in this prosperity. Therefore, it is of utmost importance that peripheral areas are capable of attracting, and subsequently retaining, creative talent. The recent literature has begun to examine the local determinants of attraction of creative individuals. One of the main factors in this is that the rural is inherently different from the urban, offering quality of life attributes that are unattainable in the urban metropolis.

Furthermore, Verdich (2010) categorised outdoor amenities, downshifting, family, proximity to the natural environment and a strong sense of community as vital quality of life-pull factors. McGranahan (1999) has also published an abundance of material pertinent to the periphery-pull factors for the creative class and for society at large. Generally speaking, quality of life is the main constituent that attracts creative individuals towards more peripheral areas (Bell and Jayne, 2006; Huggins and Clifton 2011; McGranahan and Wojan, 2007; Verdich, 2010; Waitt and Gibson 2009). Outdoor and natural amenities were classified as being important in this regard, which in turn is instrumental in job creation (McGranahan 1999; McGranahan and Wojan 2007; Verdich 2010). Furthermore, Huggins and Clifton (2011) noted that the beauty of the natural environment of the rural played a key role in attracting individuals, something which echoes McGranahan and Wojan (2007) contention that the allure of natural amenities was vital in relation to the same process. Similarly, Deller et al. (2001) and McGranahan (1999) documented that overall patterns of growth and decline in rural areas were largely shaped by the availability of outdoor recreational facilities and natural amenities.

Several studies also refer to the rural as an escape from the hustle and bustle and 'rat-race' of the metropolis (Hamilton and Mail 2003; Hoey 2005) in a type of lifestyle migration. One respondent in Hoey's (2005) study moved to the rural to open up a pie shop having previously worked as an engineer in a large city. He contended that the rural was a type of safe haven for him, exerting a form of liberatory power from the ethically challenging rat race of the urban as he was 'trading away his value system' for his job. In addition, this represents a type of downshifting which Hamilton and Mail (2003) argue should not be trivialised as its effect on our society is much greater than previously imagined. Although downsizing in rural areas may also be a luxury unique to affluent urban individuals who have accrued enough wealth to move to the countryside and 'start over'. This would also explain why several studies report that the creative class of many peripheral areas has an elderly cohort, especially in comparison to the urban (Hoey 2005; Mayes 2010). Furthermore, the therapeutic role of the rural and nature has been cited as another influential quality of life factor (Conradson 2005; Hoey 2009; Lea et al. 2009). Moreover, the slower pace of life is said to be a pleasing antagonism to the hustle and bustle of city life (Hoey 2005). Therefore, the motivations for migration of individuals to peripheral areas is rarely in search of economic affluence nor is that the goal of their enterprises. Hence, their creative endeavours can be seen as linking into non-economic motivated creative practices, which have previously shown to be commonplace in peripheral regions.

Creative talent is key to rural areas and as such, quality of life factors such as those mentioned here must be preserved through policy (Government of Ireland 2008). It is not enough to attract creative talent as it is arguably even more important to retain such individuals as they are imperative to the development of these places. The only discernible retention study concluded that it was cultural facilities, the gastronomy scene and social interaction venues that retained the creative class (Verdich 2010). Admittedly, this was for a rather large rural town and not every town is likely to have such facilities. Therefore, more studies and better policy are needed to analyse phenomenon of the retention of the creative class in peripheral areas. The next section will focus on policy relevant to creative and cultural industries.

3.4 Creative Production Peripheral Regions: Cases Studies

From 2012 to 2014 we collated database of creative industries located in our four case-study regions. The database was compiled through extensive research (outlined in Chapter 1) that used European, national and local statistics agencies, business directories as well as industry-specific resources. Taken together, the database contains almost 6,000 creative businesses across the case-study regions. These include core creative companies, such as advertising, architecture, engineering, craft, design, publishing, film, television, radio, software, computer services, creative arts and cultural recreation activities, as well as businesses that support creative industries such as retailing and printing companies. One general pattern to observe is that creative industries concentrate around areas of higher population in each region. However, creative industries are also dispersed across the rural areas. It is also important to distinguish that creative industries are more concentrated around centres of population in the Kemi-Tornio region of northern Finland and Västerbotten county in Sweden than in the Western Region of Ireland and South East Economic Development (SEED) area in Northern Ireland. The database also identified a presence of creative industry organisations of different types: networks, non-profit associations and state-funded bodies exist to different degrees within the regions, and also display a tendency to concentrate in the largest cities and towns in the Creative Edge partner regions.

3.4.1 The West of Ireland

Arts and creative industries were estimated to directly contribute to 2% of Irish GNP in 2008. When non-direct and direct contribution are combined, the figure rises to 7.6% of GNP in 2008. In employment terms, as a percentage of the total workforce, arts and creative industries account for 2.5% in direct employment, and when non-direct employment is included it amounts to 8.7%. Arts, culture and creative sectors are also highlighted as a growth area that can support Ireland's economic recovery (DKM Economic Consultants 2009). The economic contribution of Ireland's craft sector is also significant. It is a growing sector with a 13% increase in the number of enterprises – a total of 1,696 in 2009. Students of craft are an important skills base for future growth, with 1,787 students of craft identified. The GVA of the sector is estimated at €178 million and the most conservative estimate of employment in craft in Ireland is 5,771.

More broadly defined employment of up to 11,415 people is estimated. The industry is largely composed of microenterprises with up to 10 employees, but a large proportion employs less than five people. It is a geographically dispersed industry, with the greatest proportion (68%) in villages, small towns and rural areas (Indecon 2012).

Indecon (2012) of this Irish creative industries in 2011 finds that is contributes €4.6 billion to GVA, or in other terms, composing approximately 2.8% of GDP. Creative industries have been defined in this report broadly on the UK definition, including the following sectors: film and video; publishing; advertising; software; radio & television and other creative industries. Software is the largest single sector, making up more than half of overall GVA. Other sectors contributing large proportions of the GVA are literature and publishing, valued at €319.7 million, radio and television valued at €296.5 million and advertising valued at €302.7 million. Employment directly created by creative industries is 48,308 and all employment (direct, indirect and induced) 76,862 people. This report also measures the arts sector, and notes the much greater economic contribution of 'creative industries', than if the narrower arts sector is measured. The arts sector is valued at €713.3 million in GVA and employs 20,755 people (direct, indirect and induced) (Indecon 2012).

A number of research reports have demonstrated the economic importance of the creative sector to the Western Region of Ireland. The Baseline Research on the Creative Industries Sector in the Western Region of Ireland (2008) undertaken by Oxford Economics and Creative West by Western Development Commission (2009), focussed attention on social and cultural factors, and the economic value of the sector. In 2008, the turnover was estimated at €534 million and the sector contributed to 11,000 jobs, or one in every 33 jobs in the western region. In terms of structure, self-employment is a common feature, as are micro-companies with less than 10 employees. Businesses with more than 10 employees made up less than 15% of the sector. The highest number of companies was in the music, visual and performing arts sectors, followed by craft, video, film and photography businesses. In terms of economic contribution, creative technology companies (internet and software, digital media and design) accounted for 7% of the total number of businesses, 15% of total direct employment and

25% of turnover. Music, visual and performing arts accounted for 66% of companies, 31% of total direct employment and 21% of turnover. This highlights how different sub-sectors make differing economic contributions (Western Development Commission 2009).

A geographical breakdown of craft enterprises in Ireland shows 22% located in the western region, a total of 374 enterprises (Indecon 2012). At local level, the value of cultural and creative industries has also been highlighted. For example, a survey of just 10 organisations participating in Sligo's Culture Night in 2009 found they have a combined annual turnover of €3.5 million, and employ 46 full-time and 20 part-time and seasonal staff (National Campaign for the Arts 2009). Creative industry clusters have been identified around Galway city, which has a strong technology-based business cluster. Another creative business cluster in digital media exists on the outskirts of the city, in which the Irish language channel TG4 has been an important factor anchoring its development there (Collins and Fahy 2011).

Future growth prospects for the western region's creative industries are potentially strong, especially with the introduction of specific supports for the sector. Collins (2011) conducted an economic impact assessment of the sector in 2010. The report examined a number of growth scenarios, finding that if the 'high growth' scenario was implemented, which would include support for networking, formal networks for specific sub-sectors and the implementation of an export promotion strategy, by 2020 the sector could generate €648,720,000 in direct sales and directly employ 29,720 people. In this context, where projections see the creative sector emerge as having high economic significance, attention needs to focus on the costs of not investing in the sector.

Creative industries are significant in the western region, with a total of 2,466 creative companies identified in the database (see Fig. 3.1). The top three core creative business categories in the western region are architectural and engineering activities, computer programming and consultancy and publishing. Other sectors of significance include advertising, craft, design, creative arts, cultural recreation and television and film. The distribution of creative industries shows a concentration around county Galway, with 41% of all creative industries in the region here. (Galway also has the highest population of counties in the western

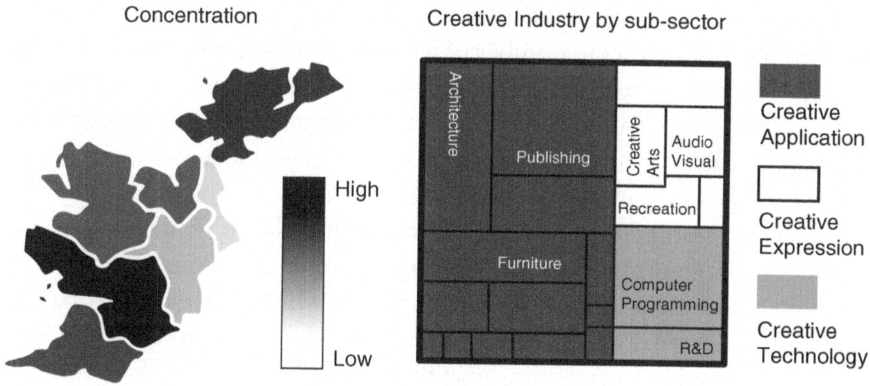

Fig. 3.1 Creative sector of the West of Ireland

region, with near to 30% of the region's inhabitants, it is home to its largest city, Galway) Counties Donegal and Clare have the next highest concentrations, with 17% and 14% of creative business identified concentrated there. The remaining counties have a concentration of 10% or less (Sligo 10%, Mayo 8%, Roscommon 6% and Leitrim 4%).

Of the 62% of companies located in the west that we designate as creative application operations, a high percentage of them are involved in craft production (over 70 companies are working in the ceramics medium and over 80 are registered as jewellers). These are products and services that are high in expressive values, albeit with a more commercial leaning. As previously mentioned the West of Ireland is the most popular of all regions as a tourist destination (attracting close to 2 million visitors in 2015 (Failte Ireland 2016), many of its craft businesses are highly reliant on this tourist trade. Across the region we have businesses registered as trading in the publishing sub-sector, the vast majority of which is the publishing of books and newspapers (though a significant number of companies are publishing software).

The presence of subsidiaries of some of the world's largest technology companies (primarily in the Galway suburbs) cannot fully be appreciated from the number count, but do act as a key driver of the creative economy of the West of Ireland, both directly and indirectly (see Cunningham and Golden 2010; Giblin and Ryan 2012: Green et al. 2001). While more traditional tech sub-sectors like software consultancy and software services are present, there is a growing number of web app developers located across the region. What can be seen in the West of Ireland is a filtration of symbol-laden content out of the traditional cultural sectors, like storytelling and theatre out through to newer creative sectors like film and television and more recently still animation and gaming. This can be seen in a number of guises, from the stop-motion animation companies using Irish folklore as inspiration for children's programming to the gaming companies reinterpreting Irish mythology and using them as the narrative upon which their games are based.

Finally, in terms of the core creative activity as represented by the creative expression companies, overall numbers downplay their relative importance. The West of Ireland, is home to a number of well-renowned writers and performers, one company that might best reflect that is the Druid Theatre company (see below). That is an interesting case of high artistic expression, critical acclaim and commercial success. This all stems from the unique perspective and place of their inception and operation. Another sub-sector of note is the audiovisual cluster situated in Connemara, in the west of county Galway. This cluster (of more than 50 companies) supports the equivalent of 600 employees on a full-time basis and has a turnover of more than €70 million euros annually. Again, as we will see below, what marks this sub-sector, and indeed the sector itself out here and across other regions is the collaborative nature of the way they do business.

Druid Theatre Company

Founded in 1975, the award-winning Druid theatre company forms a central part of the cultural fabric of Galway and the West of Ireland. The company founders met while studying at NUI Galway during the 1970s. Similar to many young companies they struggled to secure production space and a Market/audience. Through their young endeavour they convinced a local business owner to assign them an unused commercial space, 40 years later the internationally renowned Druid theatre sits at the heart of Galway city's cultural quarter.

What marks Druid out as unique in the context of cultural production and theatre-making is their founding remit for celebrating local culture and bringing that to local audiences. In doing this they set out to 'deliberately avoid the well worn track to Dublin' and instead bring

Art to the people of Roscommon, Clare and West Galway. The kind of Art they brought was also different in its place-based authenticity. Responsible to the rebirth of the work of playwrights like JM Synge, as well as nurturing new voices from the West of Ireland (Tom Murphy to Martin McDonagh), Druid theatre had a unique and successful model of celebrating the local in the west and bringing it to international audience and critical acclaim.

The theatre currently supports 10 permanent staff, and produces up to 10 different experiences a year. It has plans to expand its theatre-making space in Galway as well as touring North America, Australia and China. International acclaim has been cemented through Tony awards and the productions of the company are regularly reviewed in key outlets. Druid theatre are an excellent example of a cultural producer inspired by the culture of their peripheral space and transforming that culture into an internationally demanded product.

3.4.2 SEED – Northern Ireland

The Department of Culture, Arts and Leisure (DCAL) (2011) estimates the number of creative businesses in Northern Ireland at 2,200. The size of the sector depends on how it is measured, and another DCAL report (2012) reports 1,197 such enterprises in 2010. Compared to other regions of the UK, Northern Ireland holds the smallest concentration of creative businesses, with 1.4% of all UK creative businesses located here. One-third of all firms in the UK's creative industries are located in London.

Comparing all businesses in Northern Ireland, creative industries are a small sector, at 1.7% of all firms. Most of these businesses are found to have between one and five employees, with 33% employing one, and 42% between two and five employees (DCAL 2012). The sector contracted by 0.91% from 2008 to 2010, but when compared with other industries, it showed a lower rate of contraction (the construction industry shrunk by 10.94% in the same time period). The number of creative industry firms in Northern Ireland fell over the study period, but by just under 1%. Growth in the rest of the UK varied between just under 1.98% and 8.32%. However, comparing growth in turnover with other regions in the UK, Northern Ireland had a rate of 12.09%, above the overall UK rate of growth of 9.85% (Department of Culture, Arts and Leisure (DCAL)).

Employment in creative industries in Northern Ireland is 1.6% of total employment in creative industries in the UK. London accounts for 40.4%, while regions with similar employment levels as Northern Ireland were Wales (1.7%) and the North East (1.4%). Creative industries account for 1.1% of overall employment in Northern Ireland. However, from 2008 to 2010 there was an increase in overall employment in the creative sector year-on-year, and was one of the few UK regions to experience growth each year. It had the second highest employment growth rate (12.3%) in the UK, with Wales (13.4%) having the highest (Department of Culture, Arts and Leisure (DCAL)).

Overall DCAL (2012) shows the scale of the creative industries in Northern Ireland as small when compared to other industries, however, trends in creative industries employment and turnover show growth when compared to other parts of the economy, making it a well-performing sector in the broader economic context. DCAL (2012) identifies scope for further analysis, such as the nature creative businesses clustering and the performance of particular sub-sectors of creative industries. UK Trade and investment describe creative industries as an increasingly important sector for Northern Ireland, citing film, television, digital content, music and performing arts as strong areas. Northern Ireland has also been the location for film and TV productions, such as Game of Thrones (UKTI 2013).

DCAL (2013) statistics show the experience of the arts by adults in Northern Ireland and found 31% of adults participated in arts activities, with textile crafts such as embroidery, crocheting and knitting, and playing a musical instrument, the two arts activities that adults most frequently participated in. Some 78% of adults attended arts events, with attending a film at a cinema the most frequently attended arts event, and attending a museum, a play or drama the next two most frequently attended events. Adults living in the most deprived areas were less likely to participate in arts activities or attend arts events than those living in the least deprived areas.

Our research of peripheral region creative industries in Northern Ireland was confined to the SEED region and within that we identified a total of

838 creative businesses. The top three creative business categories are computer programming and consultancy, architectural and engineering activities and cultural recreation activities. Other creative industry business sectors also of significance in the SEED area are craft, advertising, film and TV, publishing and creative arts.

In terms of geographic concentration, creative industries are most concentrated in the Newry & Mourne local authority area, with 26% of all creative businesses. This is also the most populated local authority area with 100,858 people. The Craigavon local authority area has 21% of creative businesses and is the next most populated area with a population of 94,597. The remaining four local authority areas each have between 10% and 15% of creative industries identified (Ards 15%, Down 14%, Armagh 13% and Banbridge 10%).

Again, it is the application of creativity that keeps most of these operations in business (see Fig. 3.2). Of the 838 industries, we see 42% of them operating out of the creative application sector. Of these nearly 300 companies, we have high numbers in the sub-sectors of architecture and publishing. Showing a similar trend to their southern neighbours, craft textiles and furniture-making account of a high percentage of activity in the sector, jewellery and traditional furniture-making are products that are high in both heritage and authenticity and return values to the region far beyond the economic or commercial. Advertising companies show a relative high presence in the region, with all of them located in the larger settlements.

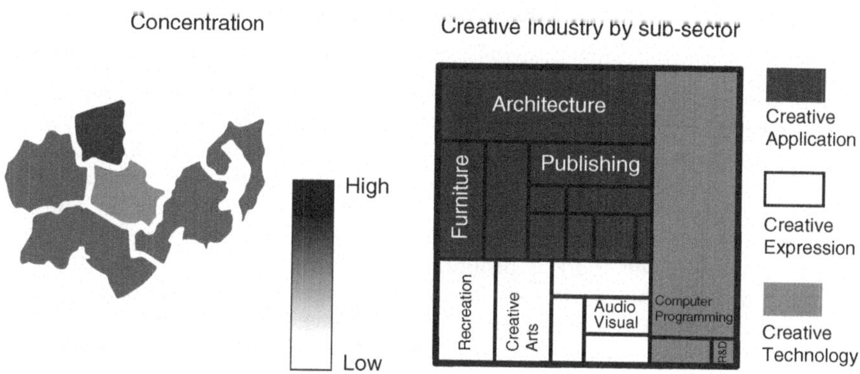

Fig. 3.2 Creative sector of the Southeast of Northern Ireland

Again, as noted above, the presence of engineering activities skews the figures upwards, but the overall trend is similar to other case-study regions.

Overall there is a higher representation of public companies and social enterprises in the creative economy of this region. Community partnerships and cross-border social enterprises speaks to the history of a region that suffered entrenched divisions as part of the political and civil unrest seen across Northern Ireland in the latter part of the twentieth century. Associations and initiatives aimed at moving past these divisions make use of creative expressions in the form of music and language as well as sport.

More than other regions in our study, the creative productivity in the SEED area of Northern Ireland relies on companies working in the creative technology sector. Those specialising in IT services dominate the sector, but there are also a significant number of companies involved in programming and app development. Unlike its counterpart regions in the Republic of Ireland, the SEED area has relatively few international companies acting as anchors for the sector. The sector is populated by small and emerging enterprises, many of which offer a wide range of different products and services across the technology spectrum. Over 30% of SEED's creative industries are in the technology sector.

BNL Productions

One example of a Northern Irish creative business is BNL productions. It's an award-winning Production Company delivering content-rich films, websites, print and motion graphics. It is a young company supporting over 10

employees with a growing experience in producing a multitude of styles and products in variety of medium for large clients in Northern Ireland. BNL's production model is to work alongside marketing departments to provide branded products which aim to inform, promote and sell to clientele. They support full brand creation with print produce film and build it into a tailored website, all in-house. Ostensibly a video production company, they offer a range of services from web and graphic design to App development. Their work is grounding locally by their clients, but their methods of producing and ability to switch between technical offerings places them at an innovative edge. They also have teaching as part of their portfolio, and work with community and commercial organisations reflecting their reach into social enterprise also.

In terms of core creative expression activities, this region is home to 157 companies that describe themselves as operating in this sector. As already referred to the recent HBO box office hit 'Game of Thrones' has done much for the productivity of this sector in the region (likely the full effect of which is not reflected in the 2013 figure here). A growing audiovisual sub-sector is reflected in our figures, a greater number of which are clustering in Co. Down. Obvious also is the presence of radio production and the high number of community radio initiatives in the region. In terms of performing, the presence of a cross-border orchestra and the dominance of community associations add further to the use of creative expression in the region. In terms of more commercially oriented businesses in this core sector, a strong subset of companies acting as amusement and recreation industries account for over one-third of those operating in the sector.

3.4.3 Västerbotten, Sweden

Sweden is a leader in how it has developed its creative and cultural industries. It ranked seventh on the Martin Prosperity Institute's 2015 Global Creativity Index and is renowned for high performance in key areas of the creative economy from design to technology (MPI 2015). Attention began to focus on creative and cultural industries in Sweden in the late 1990s (Skantze and Pihlgren 2012). These industries underwent great transformation in the first decade of the 2000s, with a good general awareness of the concept of creative industries now well-embedded at all levels of Swedish society (Generator Sverige 2011).

Assessing the place of cultural industries in Sweden's economy, based on data from the mid to late 1990s, Power (2002) found it to be a significant, fast-growing part of Sweden's economy with domestic and international success. Moreover, Power (2002) observes that Sweden's cultural industries tend to concentrate in large urban areas, with Stockholm's cultural industry dominating. Sectoral clusters are an important pattern identified, and the smaller the firm, the more likely it is to cluster. However, Power (2002) notes that cultural industries are still significant and play an important role in less urbanised areas, with concentrations also existing in rural areas. National level employment figures can hide how important employment in cultural industries can be in less-urbanised areas. The example of Älmhut is cited, a mostly rural area greatly influenced by cultural industries, and where IKEA was founded in 1947. Particular sectors within cultural industries were found to be concentrated outside of cities, such as furniture, glass, ceramics, cutlery and crafts. Growth in firms at this time was concentrated with small firms employing between one and four people.

Recent figures suggest that creative industries continue to flourish in Sweden. In 2010, creative and cultural industries contributed 3.3% of Sweden's GDP and had a turnover of SEK 285 billion. The number of creative and cultural businesses is rising and increased by an average of 5.4% each year between 2008 and 2010. However, its growth rate of 1.3% per year is less than average business sector growth between 2008 and 2010, which was 2.1%. The 117,000 creative and cultural businesses in Sweden tend to have a small number of employees, with 98% employing between zero and nine people and only 0.1% of these companies employing more than 200 people. Self-employment makes up a large proportion of those working in creative and cultural industries at 83% of total employment. These patterns are not uncommon in Swedish businesses, however the rates of self-employment, and companies employing nine or less people is higher in creative and cultural companies. More people are employed in cultural and creative industries – approximately 146,000, than are employed in the automotive industry in Sweden, (Sternö and Nielsén 2012).

A society with high levels of tolerance and openness, widespread use of technology and a skilled workforce supports Sweden's creative industries (Skantze and Pihlgren 2012). Sweden's creative industries are viewed as well placed for further development and growth. Technological development is strong, with good access to computers and broadband. Sweden is a highly developed country with experience of trading in international markets. There is also a high level of engagement with cultural activities in Sweden, supported by public funding for the arts (Nielsén 2008).

Creative industries have a very significant presence in the Västerbotten region, which is the focus of our study. Creative industries are defined more narrowly in Västerbotten, with creative manufacturing, retailing and scientific research and development excluded from the data collected. Despite this exclusion our database contains 2,154 creative businesses for Västerbotten county. The top three categories of creative business in the county are creative arts, computer programming and consultancy and design and photography. Other significant creative industry business sectors in the county indicated by the database are advertising, film and TV, publishing and cultural recreation (see Fig. 3.3).

The geographic distribution of creative industries in Västerbotten county shows a high degree of concentration in two most populated municipalities. Umeå (117,524 population) is the most populated municipality in Västerbotten county and 61% of creative industries are found to be concentrated here. Skellefteå (71,831 population) is the second most populated municipality and 21% of creative industries are found to be concentrated here. Lycksele, is next (12,348 population) and is home to 2.6% of creative industries. The remaining 12 municipalities (Vännäs, Åsele, Bjurholm, Dorotea, Malå, Nordmaling, Norsjö, Robertsfors, Sorsele, Storuman, Vilhelmina and Vindeln) each have between 0.5% and 2.7% of creative industries identified in the database.

With the exclusion of retail and the more 'making' oriented activities of cultural production, the creative application sector for the region carries relatively less weight compared to other regions in this study. That said,

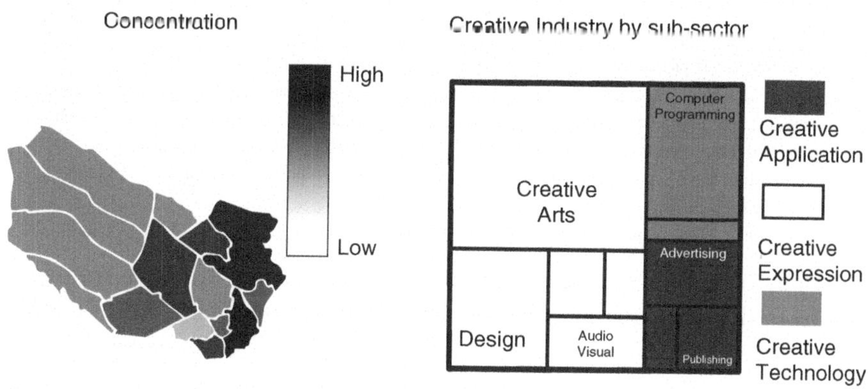

Fig. 3.3 Creative sector of the Vasterbotten, Sweden

with over 300 companies in this sector it still has a significant presence in the creative economy of the region. Significant sub-sectors here are publishing (especially book publishing – similar to the West of Ireland we see many publishers specialising in the native language/regional dialect) and a cluster of companies in Umea are in the advertising sub-sector.

Over 17% of the creative production of the region is classed as creative technology. There is evidence of the presence of a number of clusters in the field of animation and gaming. The vast majority of producers are involved in programming and programme development in the area of apps and games/audiovisual content. Another trait of the companies in this sector is their multifunctionality, with many spreading across the creative spectrum into creative application (advertising and brand development) and creative expression. Indeed, it is the overlap with the latter that defines the creative technology sector here. This can be seen through a Skellefteå-based company called North Kingdom.

North Kingdom

Established in 2003, this award-winning 'experience design' company employs close to 40 people in the north of Sweden. Its unique selling point is the use of technology (from augmented reality to 3D design) to create a unique brand for its customers. Some of these include world-leading brands from Coca Cola to Lego, and in all international business accounts for 56% of its work. They employ what is termed 'gamification' to help their clients sell better experiences. This ranges from small app-based games that revolve around the client's product or services to fully immersive augmented reality depictions of the products themselves. Interestingly, in the context of peripheral creative economies, they do not see their location as a hindrance to their commercial success citing the fact that they have access to the same technology as all their major competitors. As such, North Kingdom are expressive value retailers operating in a technology sector that is highly reliant on the application of design to serve their customers.

Again, owing to different national accounting methods, the region is unique in the sense that over 65% of its creative industries are in the creative expression sector. (The relative size of this figure is skewed somewhat by the inclusion of industries that in other regions were categorised as creative application (notably craft industries), and are included in the creative expression sector for the Swedish Creative Economy.) The presence of the strong digital media clusters around the two main settlements in the region is also reflected in the fact that the region is home to 170 companies in the audiovisual sub-sectors (nearly one third of which are involved in sound recording and music publishing). The presence of nearly 300 performing arts organisations is reflective of an extremely vibrant sector in the region. More specifically this reflects a significant music scene in both metropolitan areas as well as a number of musicians and producers dispersed around the region.

3.4.4 Kemi-Tornio, Finland

Again a different state authority defines the creative economy slightly differently. Finnish definitions of the creative economy are more broad than their western neighbours in Sweden, with national accounting pointing to a positive trend of year on year growth. The most recent figures show that 'culture' accounts for more than 4% of all employed persons and 3% of value add in the Finnish national economy in 2011. The majority of the value added of cultural activities comes from two industries: newspapers, periodicals and news agencies (18.4%), and advertising (11.1%) (www.creative-edge.eu).

A 2014 study on *Direct copyright revenue streams in creative industries in Finland* (2014) shows direct copyright revenue streams increasing by 45% from 2008 to 2012 Koskinen and Muikku 2014). The biggest growth has taken place in computer games (78%) and in software and databases (56%). Of the total copyright revenue streams software's share was 62.4% and that of computer games 11.8%. The latter point is reflected in Finland's ranking as the fifth most creative economy in the world according to the Global Creativity Index (Martin Porsperity Institute 2015). Helping it achieve this position is the relative strength of the Finnish technology sector as well as the performance of its educational institutes and educational attainment levels of its populations.

Located in Lapland province in northern Finland, Kemi-Tornio is a small region made up of five municipalities: Tornio, Kemi, Tervola, Keminmaa and Simo. The Lapland Regional Council describes the province as having rich natural landscape, distinct culture and strong creativity. The province has a population of 195,000, and 59,847 of the total population is located in the Kemi-Tornio region (Regional Council of Lapland 2012; Statistics Finland 2013). The Kemi-Tornio region accounts for the second largest number of people employed in the Lapland province, with the highest number employed in the Rovaniemi region (Regional Council of Lapland 2012). The region is classed as a regional centre in Lapland province and is served by Kemi-Tornio airport. The area is also known as Sea Lapland and has developed a tourism experience around its climate of ice, snow and frozen seas in wintertime. Industry in the region includes forestry, mining and agriculture.

Located on the Bothnian Arc, Kemi and Tornio are two cities in the region, and Tornio is twined with the Swedish city Haparanda. Tervola is a mainly rural area and important industries are agriculture, forestry and the mining of rock and metal. Based in Bothnian Bay, Keminmaa is located on the mouth of the Kemijoki River. Processing of wood and plastics are important industries in Keminmaa. Simo is known for salmon fishing, which is a long tradition because of rich stocks along the coast and in the Simojoki river. Fishing tourism is important to the area, as well as forestry and agriculture (Regional Council of Lapland 2013).

The Lapland Regional Council is important in developing regional policy to support creative industries in the overall Lapland region, and its sub-regions, such as Kemi-Tornio. A theme of the Regional Strategic Programme for Lapland is promoting creativity. Among a number of strategies of the Lapland Regional Council is the Strategy for Creative Industries 2008–2013. This strategy highlights the importance of design in enhancing competitiveness and adding value to products, but also as a critical area for overall creative industry development in the region. The Lapland Design Programme 2011–2015 has been developed, coordinated by the University of Lapland and developed in consultation with stakeholders, and aims to promote and develop the design sector across Lapland through a variety of initiatives. Design is a theme integrated in Kemi-Tornio's regional development programme for creative industries during 2009–2013, and high-tech and industrial production companies in the region now have a greater focus on design (University of Lapland 2011). Regional and sub-regional development in Lapland focusses on collaboration across industry sectors, such as between tourism and creative industries (Regional Council of Lapland 2012, 2013). Supporting education in creative industries, the Culture and Media Arts Department of Kemi-Tornio University of Applied Sciences provides practically focussed education programmes in fine arts and media.

This small sub-region of Lapland in northern Finland is found to have 476 creative businesses (see Fig. 3.4). The top three creative business categories are architectural and engineering activities, advertising and market research, and computer programming and consultancy. Other significant creative business sectors are design and photographic activities, film and TV, publishing and creative arts. The region has a population of 59,847, with just over 44,000 living in the Kemi and Tornio municipalities combined. It is in these two municipalities that the creative industries are concentrated, with 40% concentrated in Kemi and 49% in Tornio. Keminaa, with a population of just over 8,500, is home to 8% of the region's creative industries.

Making use of the broader definition of the creative economy, Finnish account of productivity is more comparable to that of the Irish and UK regions. With a nearly two thirds of all creative industries located in the creative application sector, we see more of a similarity between this Lapland region and the West of Ireland and SEED sectoral breakdowns. Similarly, this sector is somewhat skewed by the presence of engineering activities in their architectural services sub-sector. That said, some architectural activities

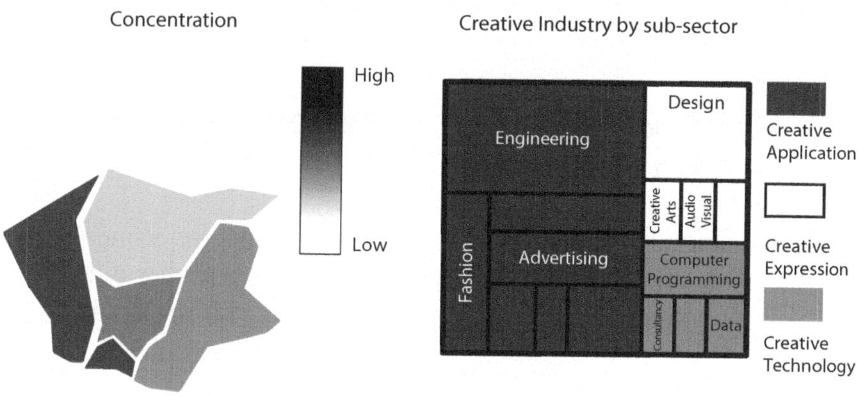

Fig. 3.4 Creative sector of the Kemi-Tornio, Finland

are of note in the region, namely the work of *Rauno Rousnansuu Ltd* and their world famous Kemi Snowcastle, a temporary structure erected each year.

With perhaps one of the smallest creative sectors of all case-study regions, creative technology accounts for 13% of all creative producers in the region. More than half of these companies are involved in computer programming activities, while the remainder are split between IT services and computer consultancy. The presence of Lapland University can be seen as important to the development of the sector in the Arctic circle.

Related to this is the presence of a number of creative expression companies in the audiovisual sub-sector. Many of whom are located close to the university campus. Photography is the largest sub-sector amongst these companies, likely in part inspired by the unique landscape and lighting offered by the region's northerly location. Performing arts and other amusement/recreation activities are under-represented in the region, likely owing to its low population density.

SunSaa

Also inspired by the region and its weather is a start up company in the advertising sub-sector named SunSaa. Located in Rovanemi this company uses innovative software to offer weather reactive advertising solutions. Their core concept is that advertising that is in tune with immediate consumer needs allows sellers to more effectively target consumer markets. A small company operating in the Arctic Circle SunSaa sells to international clientele.

3.5 Creative Industries in Peripheral Regions: A Firm Perspective

To further illuminate the distinctiveness of the creative economy and industries we take a firm level perspective to explore further differences and commonalities. Under the auspices of the Creative Momentum[2]

[2] Creative Momentum is co-funded by the EU Interreg Northern Periphery & Arctic (NPA) Programme 2014–2020. The NPA is a cooperation between nine programme partner countries;

project a survey of 200 companies located across the northern periphery of Europe was carried out in 2015. One of the key findings from this survey is that much more that unites than divides them. This survey has highlighted some key messages with respect to how unique cultural production on the periphery is and how it is something that adds far more beyond the economic portfolio of a region (Fig. 3.5).

In analysing and reflecting further on the survey findings we summarise the following that highlights the uniqueness of cultural production in periphery from a firm perspective. It also further reinforces the non-economic benefits of the creative economy to these regions.

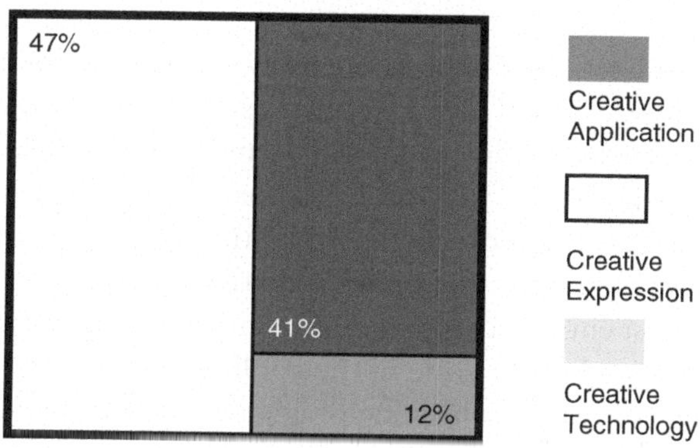

Fig. 3.5 Survey respondents by sector

Finland, Ireland, Sweden, the United Kingdom (Scotland and Northern Ireland), Faroe Islands, Iceland, Greenland and Norway. The NPA 2014–2020 is part of the European Territorial Cooperation Objective, supported by the European Regional Development Fund (ERDF) and ERDF equivalent funding from non-EU partner countries. The authors would like to thanks NIall Drew (Armagh City, Banbridge and Craigavon Borough Council) for administering the survey.

3.5.1 Small and Productive

Little surprise that the creative economy of peripheral areas is dominated by small, indeed microenterprises. Over 58% of the respondents are one-person operations, with nearly 90% having less than five employees. The nature of the type of production and business models employed (see Chapter 4) lend itself to small workforce/one-person operation. In many cases, individuals are inspired by the pursuit of artistic gain (the artists versus the entrepreneur) and see that as an individual pursuit. We also see from other studies (Harvey et al. 2012) that many creatives, from visual artists to musicians, pursue their craft on a part-time basis.

3.5.2 Scale of Producers and Employees

Creative expression sector companies show the largest amount of one-person operations (65% of all CE industries are one-person operations). This figure is dominated by visual artists and photographers and these pursuits that are individual in nature. Companies with higher numbers of employees specialise in audiovisual production. In the creative application sector, the near two thirds of industries operating as one-person entities are almost entirely comprised of members of the crafts sub-sector. On the opposite end of the scale in the application sector are advertising and marketing companies with much higher average employee numbers. The creative technology sub-sector has a much higher average employee head count, with less than 40% of respondents acting as one person operations (usually in digital media/web design) while some of the animation and gaming companies in these peripheral regions employ over 50 people. Again, the type of product being produced in these larger operations requires a greater number of producers. Advertising and games development require a raft of different talents to bring the product to market. While these companies are relatively fewer compared to the single-employee operations, they tend to produce the more marketable products, ones that while high in expressive values bring with them the higher commercial returns.

3.5.3 Sharing and Caring

While the vast majority of these industries and their small nature means that more than half work from home, close to one in five of these peripherally located industries operate out of shared spaces. These range in type from hot desk facilities in business innovation centres, to artist studio collectives and newly established creative hubs. These shared spaces are defined by collective services agreements, with collaborative practices either expected or encouraged as part of tenancy. This has been the focus of much analysis in the creative economy literature (see Evans 2009; Rusk 2011; Comunian et al. 2015), and the promotion of creative hub spaces has become popular in policymaking circles over the past five years.

The sectoral breakdown shows that those in the expression and technology sectors are most likely to find themselves in shared spaces, the former in art studio collectives, the latter in creative hubs. Creative expression has the highest percentage creatives working from home, while those in the area application are most likely to work from commercial premises that are either owned or privately rented. The level of home-based workers speaks to the commonalities already identified above and elsewhere (Andersson 2012; MacRobbie 2015) between this set of industries and the practices of cottage industries of the pre-industrial era.

One more unique element that was alluded to in the above case studies was the amount of time spent in pursuit of non-commercial ends. The degree of overlap with the social economy becomes more obvious when industries report on activity carried out beyond the commercial. According to respondents a small percentage are registered as non-profit operations but close to half have recorded a significant time spent with community pursuits. This ranges from teaching to public art projects. In the creative expression sector these figures are higher, but they are also above average in the creative technology sector.

3.5.3.1 Exporting: Orientation and Ambition

67% of respondents reported selling their produce internationally. The highest rates of exports are seen in the more commercial sub-sectors of

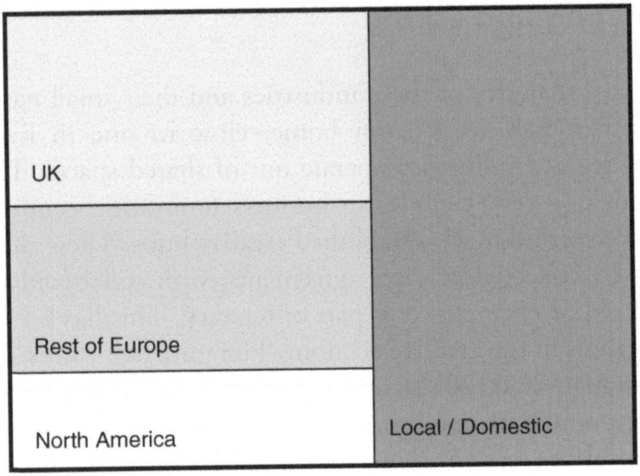

Fig. 3.6 Market destinations

application and technology (those in design, digital design and app development). For any set of industries that are predominantly micro-enterprises, this high level of internationalisation is impressive. Very few other sectors show such a high rate of exporting from one-person operations. Taken in the context of trends identified in Chapter 2, we see that the produce of these industries, which is laden with expressive values and authenticity is in increasing demand.

Interesting also is where this produce reaches its consumer. Overall, it is a trend of the periphery selling to the core. The major markets are the big European countries and the North American market (Fig. 3.6). Again this is supported by trends identified already. The allure of the peripheries produce, notably in the area of craft and design, it's authentic and how they sit against the mass produced that flood major markets can be seen as explanatory here. How these products reach the market also shows the unique business approaches/models adopted by the creatives. Owing to the nature of the produce, 15% of products go through the route of a distributor, exhibitions and craft shows are used by expression and application creatives. Technology and the use of the internet is cited by more than half of all respondents with a significant number declaring that online sites such as Etsy and eBay are useful access routes. Another small but increasingly significant aspect of creative exports from peripheral regions is the growth of creative tech companies servicing the needs of major international clients. The Swedish example referred to in the previous section is supported by the fact that the creative tech sector export 40% of their produce to North America with a significant amount of that tender quote contracts with their partners. This is also evidence of the prevalence of business-to-business selling, something we will explore further in the next section.

The export figures are as impressive as the intention of those that do not yet export. Of the one third of respondents that do not currently export, 71% expressed a desire to do so in the near future. This is evidence of a dynamic sector in pursuit of growth opportunities and counters the labelled moniker of 'lifestyle enterprise' placed on many of these small operations. Creative expression enterprises had the highest percentage of those who do not export that to not wish to export in the future, again, the nature of the produce and the production process that is guided more by artistic than commercial success is explanatory here. When asked to explain the main barriers to the export market, respondents cite a lack of information/knowledge, time and growth stage of their organisation as the main impediments. Previous work shows a change here that has been influenced by the roll-out of broadband further into and across the more peripheral European regions. WDC (2009) cited the lack of technological infrastructure as among the primary concerns for non-exporting creatives in the West of Ireland.

3.5.3.2 Mentoring and Collaboration

The survey included an open ended question on how best to improve on their current predicaments. In analysing these responses there were unified views conveyed. While those in the technology sector made the case for more training and upskilling to keep a pace with the rapid advances in technology, those in creative expression sought more mentoring from others that had successfully pursued work in their area, while those in application expressed a need for more networking opportunities. What unifies all three sub-sectors is a desire to connect with other creatives. To collaborate, for the purposes of training or upskilling or through commercial projects of an international scale was uniformly expressed as key to future success. This is one further trait that marks the creative economies of the periphery as unique. The desire to collaborate and pursue business models of comparative advantage amongst seemingly competing entities helps demarcate this group. Much of this can be explained by their geography, often remote, there is an obvious want for a connection to help keep these concerns up to industry and market standard. But the production and selling of creative produce is unlike other products and services. The expressive nature of the produce that often times comes about through artistic process makes of a unique market. A market where replicability is almost impossible (Aran jumpers need to come from Aran; Swedish design needs to be Swedish; Finnish folk music can only come from Finland). Also expected the nature of the production techniques, ones that rely on methods that could have been in place for centuries, necessitates the use of collaborative methods. We will explore this more in the final chapter, but state here that tradition, method and craft are evident in the pursuits of the creatives on the edge of Europe. It is a case now of how those unique elements can help enable them to sustain and thrive into the future.

3.6 Conclusions

Thanks to the extensive and dedicated work of researchers the world over, the fact that the creative economy is a growing entity is well known in policy circles and beyond. In this chapter we have set out to add to the growing literature that is making the case for that growth not taking place solely within the limits of the worlds larger cities. In our case-study regions we see evidence of a vibrant creative economy, one that is responding to the changing nature of consumer demand. It succeeds because of its place and not in spite of it. Particular focus on individual businesses from theatre companies to app developers help make the case for the creative economy of peripheral areas being worthy of further attention, not just from academics but from policy makers as well.

Together with insights from Chapter 2, we are trying to better understand how the creative economy exists in more rural and peripheral areas. We have key learnings that point to the fact that more rural-based creative economies exist inside the traditional market model, but beyond it as well. The creative industries here serve as building blocks of community development and maintaining distinct peripheral identities. They use their environment as a unique resource, in the guise of inspiration, the landscape is not altered, but instead acts as an infinitely renewable resource that helps answer increased demands for authenticity, heritage and narrative laden produce. The social impacts of the creative economy are magnified in the peripheral setting. Here we get to gauge the extra economic effects of creativity at the more local scale. This is the topic that requires further work, but work that is important in shaping how creative industries grow in less urban areas.

Beyond proving the existence of the economy outside of the 'core' what our analysis proves is that creative pursuits in the periphery are very different. Too often this is assumed as an overly romantic visions of lonely artists, rather our work shows the vibrancy of these pursuits can match those of urban ones. As we will explore further in the following chapter, what really differentiates the peripheral from their urban counterparts is not just their produce but their modes of production. We tracked the rise of the sharing economy and collaborative consumption, often times these are identified as new phenomena, in actuality, they are not, rather they are the revival of practices that have been undone by more recent market-oriented practices. The lived memory of collaborative economies in more peripheral areas puts them in the ideal position to make the most from practices that technology has helped us rediscover.

Bibliography

Adorno, T., and M. Horkheimer. 2002. *Dialectic of enlightenment*. California: Stanford University Press.

Andersen, L. 2010. Magic light, silver city: The business of culture in Broken Hill. *Australian Geographer* 41(1): 71–85.

Anderson, C. 2012. *Makers: The new industrial revolution*. New York: Crown.

Asheim, B. T. and H. K. Hansen. 2008. The creative class, people climate and business climate: Knowledge bases, variety of capitalism and social capital. In H. K. Hansen (Ed.), *The Urban turn—and the location of economic activities*, (pp. 227–259). Lund: Lund University.

Asheim, B., and H. K. Hansen. 2009. Knowledge Bases, Talents, and Contexts: On the Usefulness of the Creative Class Approach in Sweden. *Economic Geography* 85(4): 425–42.

Atkinson, R., and H. Easthope. 2009. The consequences of the creative class: The pursuit of creativity strategies in Australia's Cities. *International Journal of Urban and Regional Research* 33(1): 64–79.

AuthentiCity. 2009. *Durham region cultural mapping project*. Durham, Canada: Economic Development and Tourism.

AuthentiCity. 2010. *Windsor/Essex cultural mapping project*. Windsor, Canada: Essex Community Futures Development Corporation.

Banks, M., A. Lovatt, J. O' Connor, and C. Raffo. 2000. Risk and trust in the cultural industries. *Geoforum* 31(4): 453–64.

Banks, M. 2007. *The politics of cultural work*. Basingstoke: Palgrave Macmillan.

Becker, H. 1982. *Art worlds*. Berkeley: University of California Press.

Bell, D. 1976. The coming of the post-industrial society. *The Educational Forum* 40(4): 574–79. Taylor & Francis Group.

Bell, D., and M. Jayne. 2006. *Small cities: Urban experience beyond the metropolis*. London: Routledge.

Bell, D., and M. Jayne. 2010. The creative countryside: Policy and practice in the UK rural cultural economy. *Journal of Rural Studies* 26(3): 209–18.

Bennett, D. 2010. Creative migration: A Western Australian case study of creative artists. *Australian Geographer* 41(1): 117–28.

Bilton, C. 2010. Manageable creativity. *International Journal of Cultural Policy* 16(3): 255–69.

Blau, J. R. 1989. *The shape of culture*. Cambridge: Cambridge University Press (CUP).

BOP Consulting (2009) *Creative clusters 2008 conference report*. London: BOP Consulting.

Boschma, R. 2005. Proximity and innovation: A critical assessment. *Regional Studies* 39(1): 61–74.

Bouchard, D. 2009. *Museums, cultural heritage and dialogue in Northern Ireland: Strategies for divided societies*. Council of Europe: Heritage and beyond.

Brennan-Horley, C., and C. Gibson. 2009. Where is creativity in the city? Integrating qualitative and GIS methods. *Environmental Planning A* 41(11): 2595–2614.

British Council. 2010. *Mapping the creative industries: A toolkit.* London: British Council.

Brooks, D. 2000. *Bobos in paradise: The new upper class and how they got there.* New York: Simon & Schuster.

Brown, A., J. O'Connor, and S. Cohen. 2000. Local music policies within a global music industry: Cultural quarters in Manchester and Sheffield. *Geoforum* 31(4): 437–51.

Cabras, I., and G. Bosworth. 2014. Embedded models of rural entrepreneurship: The case of pubs in Cumbria, North West of England. *Local Economy,* 0269094214544276.

Cairncross, F. 1997. *The death of distance.* London: Texere Publishing Limited.

Cairncross, F. 2001. *The death of distance: How the communications revolution is changing our lives.* Boston MA: Harvard Business Press.

Casellas, A., and M. Pallares-Barbera. 2009. Public-sector intervention in embodying the new economy in inner urban areas: The Barcelona experience. *Urban Studies* 46(5–6): 1137–55.

Castells, M. 1996. *The rise of the network society. Vol. 1 of The information age: Economy, society and culture.* Blackwell: Massachusetts and Oxford.

Caves, R. E. 2000. *Creative industries: Contracts between art and commerce.* London: Harvard University Press.

Christen, K. 2006. Tracking properness: Repackaging culture in a remote Australian town. *Cultural Anthropology* 21(3): 416–46.

Clark, D. 2009. Crunching creativity: An attempt to measure creative employment. *Creative Industries Journal* 2(3): 217–30.

Collins, P. (2011) *An economic impact assessment of the Creative Sector in the west of Ireland.* Ballaghadereen: Western Development Commission.

Collins, P., J. Cunningham, A. Murtagh, and J. Dagg. 2014. *The creative edge policy toolkit.* Galway, Ireland: The Whitaker Institute.

Collins, P. 2014. *Galway is Film: A bid for UNESCO city of film.* Economic Impact Assessment.

Collins, P., and F. Fahy. 2011. Culture and creativity: A case study from the West of Ireland. *Cities* 28(1): 28–35.

Collis, C., S. Freebody, and T. Flew. 2013. Seeing the outer suburbs: Addressing the urban bias in creative place thinking. *Regional Studies* 47 (2): 148–60.

Comunian, R., A. Gilmore, and S. Jacobi. 2015. Higher education and the creative economy: Creative graduates, knowledge transfer and regional impact debates. *Geography Compass* 9(7): 371–83.

Comunian, R., and A. Faggian. 2011. Higher education and the creative city. Handbook of creative cities. from http://dx.doi.org/10.4337/9780857936394.00016.

Connell, J., and B. Rugendyke. 2010. Creating an authentic tourist site? The Australian Standing Stones, Glen Innes. *Australian Geographer* 41(1): 87–100.

Conradson, D. 2005. Landscape, care and the relational self: Therapeutic encounters in rural England. *Health & Place* 11(4): 337–48.

Cooke, P, and K. Morgan. 2001. *The associational economy: Firms, regions, and innovation* Oxford: Oxford Press.

Crane, D. 1989. *The transformation of the Avant-Garde: The New York Art World, 1940–1985*. Chicago: University of Chicago Press.

Crang, P. 1997. Cultural turns and the (re)constitution of eco- nomic geography: Introduction to section one. In *Geographies of economies*, ed. R. Lee and J. Wills, 3–15. London: Arnold.

Cunningham, James A., and William Golden. 2010. National innovation system of Ireland. *Wiley Encyclopedia of Management*. doi: 10.1002/9781118785317.weom130051.

Currid, E. 2006. New York as a global creative hub: A competitive analysis of four theories on world cities. *Economic Development Quarterly* 20(4): 330–50.

Currid, E., and S. Williams. 2010. The geography of buzz: Art, culture and the social milieu in Los Angeles and New York. *Journal of Economic Geography* 10: 423–51.

Curtis, R. A. 2010. Australia's Capital of Jazz? The (re)creation of place, music and community at the Wangaratta Jazz Festival. *Australian Geographer* 41(1): 101–16.

De Propris, L., C. Chapain, P. Cooke, S. MacNeill, and J. Mateos-García. 2009. *The geography of creativity*. London: NESTA.

Deller, S. C., Tsai, T. H. S., Marcouiller, D.W., and English, D. B. 2001. The role of amenities and quality of life in rural economic growth. *American Journal of Agricultural Economics* 83(2), 352–365.

Department of Culture, Arts and Leisure (DCAL). 2011. *Creative industries economic estimates for Northern Ireland*. Belfast: DCAL.

Department of Culture, Arts and Leisure (DCAL). 2012. An analysis of creative industries in Northern Ireland. Belfast: DCAL.

Department of Culture, Arts and leisure (DCAL). 2013. Experience of the arts by adults in Northern Ireland. Available at: http://www.dcalni.gov.uk/arts_chs_2012-13_bulletin.pdf (Accessed 18 October 2013)

DiMaggio, P. 1987. Classification in art. *American Sociological Review* 52(4): 440.

Direct copyright revenue streams in creative industries in Finland, 2014.

DKM Economic Consultants. 2009. *Economic impact of the arts, culture and creative sectors*. Dublin: DKM Economic Consultants.

Donegal County Council. 2009. Cultural Connections: Strategic Plan For Cultural Services Division Donegal County Council 2009–2014. Available at http://www.donegallibrary.ie/media/donegal library/contentassets/files/English_lowres.pdf

Donegal County Council. 2010. *Cultural connections: Strategic plan for cultural services division donegal county council 2009–2014*. Donegal: Donegal County Council.

Dos Santos, B. L. 1991. Justifying investments in new information technologies. *Journal of Management Information Systems* 7(4): 71–89.

Drake, G. 2003. This place gives me space': Place and creativity in the creative industries. *Geoforum* 34(4): 511–24.

Dunbar-Hall, P., and C. Gibson. 2004. *Deadly sounds, deadly places: Contemporary aboriginal music in Australia*. Seattle: UNSW Press.

Dunphy, K. 2009. *Developing and revitalizing rural communities through arts and creativity: Australia*. Vancouver: Creative City Network of Canada.

Ernst and Young. 2015. *Cultural times: The first global map of cultural and creative industries*. Paris: CISAC.

Evans, G. 2009. From cultural quarters to creative clusters–creative spaces in the new city economy. *The sustainability and development of cultural quarters: International perspectives. Institute of Urban History, Stockholm, 3259*.

Faggian, A., R. Comunian, S. Jewell, and U. Kelly. 2013. Bohemian graduates in the UK: Disciplines and location determinants of creative careers. *Regional Studies* 47(2): 183–200.

Failte Ireland. 2016. *Preliminary Tourism Facts 2015*. Dublin: Failte Ireland.

Felton, E., C. Collis, and P. Graham. 2010. Making Connections: Creative industries networks in outer-suburban locations. *Australian Geographer* 41(1): 57–70.

Florida, R. 2002. *The rise of the creative class*. New York: Basic Books.

Florida, R. L. 2005. *The flight of the creative class*. New York: Harper Business.

Freire-Gibb, L. C., and K. Nielsen. 2014. Entrepreneurship within urban and rural areas: Creative people and social networks. *Regional Studies* 48(1): 139–53.

Generator Sverige. 2011. The Creative Industries Sweden. Report available at culturefighter.eu/centres-factories-incubators-amp-initiatives/how-they-work/generator-sverige

Giblin, M., and P. Ryan. 2012. Tight clusters or loose networks? The critical role of inward foreign direct investment in cluster creation. *Regional Studies* 46(2): 245–58.

Gibson, C., Chris Brennan-Horley, and Jim Walmsley. 2010. Mapping vernacular creativity: The extent and diversity of rural festivals in Australia. In *Spaces of vernacular creativity: Rethinking the cultural economy*, eds. T. J. Edensor, D. L. Steve Millington, and Norma M. Rantisi, 89–105. London: Routledge.

Gibson, C., and C. Brennan-Horley. 2006. Goodbye Pram City: Beyond inner/outer zone binaries in creative city research. *Urban Policy and Research* 24(4): 455–71.

Gibson, C., and J. Connell. 2004. Cultural industry production in remote places: Indigenous popular music in Australia. In *Cultural Industries and the Production of Culture*, eds. D. Power and Allen J. Scott, 243–58. London and New York: Routledge.

Gibson, C., & Kong, L. 2005. Cultural economy: A critical review. *Progress in Human Geography* 29(5), 541–561.

Glaeser, E. L., S. S. Rosenthal, and W. C. Strange. 2010. Urban economics and entrepreneurship. *Journal of Urban Economics* 67(1): 1–14.

Government of Ireland. 2008. *Building Ireland's smart economy a framework for sustainable economic renewal.*

Green, R., J. Cunningham, I. Duggan, M. Giblin, M. Moroney, and L. Smyth. 2001. The boundaryless cluster: Information and communications technology in Ireland. *Innovative Clusters*, 47.

Hamilton, C., and E. Mail. 2003. *Downshifting in Australia. A sea-change in the pursuit of happiness.* Canberra: The Australia Institute.

Hansen, H. K. 2007. Technology, talent and tolerance—the geography of the creative class in Sweden. *Rapporter och Notiser* 169. Department of Social and Economic Geography, Lund University.

Hansen, H. K., and T. Niedomysl. 2008. Migration of the creative class: Evidence from Sweden. *Journal of Economic Geography* 9(2): 191–206.

Hardhill, I., P. Benneworth, M. Baker, and L. Judd Eds. 2006. *The rise of the English regions*. Oxford: Routledge.

Harvey, C., H. Hawkins, and N. Thomas. 2012. Thinking creative clusters beyond the city: People, places and networks. *Geoforum* 43: 529–39.

Hesmondhalgh, D. 2013. *The Cultural Industries*, Third Edition. London: SAGE.

Hesmondhalgh, D., and A. C. Pratt. 2005. Cultural industries and cultural policy. *International Journal of Cultural Policy* 11(1): 1–13.

Hoey, B. A. 2005. From Pi to Pie: Moral narratives of noneconomic migration and starting over in the postindustrial midwest. *Journal of Contemporary Ethnography* 34(5): 586–624.

Hoey, B. A. 2009. Pursuing the good life: American narratives of travel and a search for refuge.

Huggins, R., and N. Clifton. 2011. Competitiveness, creativity, and place-based development. *Environmental Planning A* 43(6): 1341–62.

Indecon. 2012. *Assessment of the economic impact of the arts in Ireland: Arts and culture scoping research project submitted to the arts council*. Dublin: Indecon.

Jayne, M., Gibson, C., Waitt, G., and Bell, D. 2010. The cultural economy of small cities. *Geography Compass* 4(9), 1408–1417.

Johnson, L. 2009. *Cultural capitals: Revaluing the arts, remaking urban spaces*. Burlington VT: Ashgate Publishing Company.

Kenyon, P., and A. Black. 2001. *Small town renewal: Overview and case studies*. Canberra: Rural Industries Research and Development Corporation.

Kerr, A., and A. Cawley. 2012. The spatialisation of the digital games industry: Lessons from Ireland. *International Journal of Cultural Policy* 18(4): 398–418.

Kong, L. 2005. The sociality of cultural industries. *International Journal of Cultural Policy* 11(1): 61–76.

Koskinen-Olsson, T., and Muikku, J. 2014. Direct Copyright Revenue Streams in Creative Industries in Finland. Saatavilla <http://www.copyrightsociety.fi/TU1302_Direct%20Copyright%20Revenue%20Streams_final%20%282%29.pdf/>

Landry, C. 2000. *The creative city. A toolkit for urban innovation*. London: Earthscan.

Lash, S., and J. Urry. 1994. *Economies of signs and space*, Vol. 26. New York: Sage.

Lazzeretti, L., Capone, F., & Seçilmis, I. E. 2016. In search of a Mediterranean creativity. Cultural and creative industries in Italy, Spain and Turkey. *European Planning Studies* 24(3), 568–588.

Lea, J. 2008. Retreating to nature: Rethinking 'therapeutic landscapes'. *Area* 40(1): 90–98.

Lea T., Luckman S., Gibson C., Fitzpatrick D., Brennan-Horley C., Willoughby-Smith J., Hughes K. 2009. *Creative tropical city: Mapping Darwin's creative industries.* Research report. Charles Darwin University, Northern Territory Government and Tourism NT, Darwin.

Lippard, L. 1997. *The lure of the local.* New York: The New Press.

MacLeod, G. 2002. From urban entrepreneurialism to a "Revanchist City"? On the spatial injustices of Glasgow's Renaissance. *Antipode* 34(3): 602–24.

Markusen, A. 1996. Sticky places in slippery space: A typology of industrial districts. *Economic Geography* 72(3): 293–313.

Markusen, A. 2010. Organizational complexity in the regional cultural economy. *Regional Studies* 44(7): 813–28.

Martin Porsperity Institute. 2015. *The Global Creativity Index 2015.* Available at. martinprosperity.org/content/the-global-creativity-index-2015/

Mateos-Garcia, J., and H. Bakhshi. 2016. *The Geography of Creativity in the UK: Creative Cluser, Creative People and Creative Networks.* London: Nesta.

Mayes, R. 2010. Postcards from somewhere: "Marginal" cultural production, creativity and community. *Australian Geographer* 41(1): 11–23.

McGranahan, D. 1999. *Natural Amenities Drive Rural Population Change.* Washington, DC: Economic Research Service, US Department of Agriculture.

McGranahan, D., and T. Wojan. 2007. Recasting the creative class to examine growth processes in rural and urban counties. *Regional Studies* 41(2): 197–216.

McGranahan, D. A., T. R. Wojan, and D. M. Lambert. 2011. The rural growth trifecta: Outdoor amenities, creative class and entrepreneurial context. *Journal of Economic Geography* 11(3): 529–57.

McKee, A. 2013. The power of art, the power of entertainment. *Media, Culture & Society* 35(6): 759–70.

McRobbie, A. 2015. Is passionate work a neoliberal delusion? Retrieved 12 November, 2015, from <https://www.opendemocracy.net/transformation/angela-mcrobbie/is-passionate-work-neoliberal-delusion>

Molotch, H. 2002. Place in product. *International Journal of Urban and Regional Research* 26(4): 665–88.

Molotch, H. 2003. *Where stuff comes from: How toasters, toilets, cars, computers, and many other things come to be as they are.* New York: Routledge.

Mossig, I. 2011. Regional employment growth in the cultural and creative industries in Germany 2003–2008. *European Planning Studies* 19(6): 967–90.

Munoz, C.L., Wood, N.T., & Solomon, M.R. 2006. Real or blarney? A cross-cultural investigation of the perceived authenticity of Irish pubs. *Journal of Consumer Behaviour* 5(3), 222.

Myers, F. R. 2002. *Painting culture: The making of an aboriginal high art.* London: Duke University Press.

Nathan, M., A. Pratt, and A. Rincon-Azner. 2015. *Creative economy employment in the EU and UK: A comparative analysis.* London: Nesta.

National Campaign for the Arts. 2009. Artists and arts workers in Sligo unite to support the campaign. Available at http://ncfa.ie/news/artists_and_arts_workers_in_sligo_unite_to_support_the_campaign (Accessed October 2014)

NESTA. 2016. http://www.nesta.org.uk/publications/geography-creativity-uk#sthash.DIybiEvB.dpuf).

Nielsén, T. 2008. *The ERiBA model: An effective and successful policy framework for the creative industries.* Stockholm: The Knowledge Foundation.

O'Connor, J. 2007. *The cultural and creative industries: A review of the literature (Report for Creative Partnerships).* London: Arts Council.

O'Connor, J. 2010. *The cultural and creative industries: a literature review. Creativity, culture and education.*

O'Connor, J. 2015. Intermediaries and imaginaries in the cultural and creative industries. *Regional Studies* 49(3): 374–87.

Oakley, K. 2009. The disappearing arts: Creativity and innovation after the creative industries. *International Journal of Cultural Policy* 15(4): 403–13.

Oxford Economics. 2008. *Baseline research on the creative industries sector in the Western Region of Ireland.* Belfast: Oxford Economics.

Peck, J. 2005. Struggling with the creative class. *International Journal of Urban and Regional Research* 29(4): 740–70.

Piore, M. J., and C. F. Sabel (1984). *The second industrial divide: Possibilities for prosperity.* New York: Basic books.

Power, D. 2002. "Cultural industries" in Sweden: An assessment of their place in the Swedish economy. *Economic Geography* 78(2): 103.

Pratt, A. 2008. Creative cities: The cultural industries and the creative class. *Geografiska Annaler: Series B – Human Geography* 90(2): 107–17.

Pratt, A. C. 1997. The cultural industries production system: A case study of employment change in Britain, 1984–91. *Environmental Planning A* 29(11): 1953–74.

Pratt, A. C. 2004. Creative clusters: Towards the governance of the creative industries production system? *Media International Australia Incorporating Culture and Policy* 112(1): 50–66.

Pratt, A. C. 2007. 'Imagination can be a damned curse in this country': Material geographies of filmmaking and the rural. In *Fish Robert, Cinematic countrysides*, (pp. 127–146). Manchester UK: Manchester University Press.

Pratt, A. C. 2012, November. A world turned upside down: The cultural economy, cities and the new austerity. In *Proceedings of the regional studies association winter conference*, 13–19.

Prideaux, B. 2002. Building visitor attractions in peripheral areas? Can uniqueness overcome isolation to produce viability?. *International Journal of Tourism Research* 4(5): 379–89.

Rebanks Consulting Ltd and Trends Business Research Ltd, 2009.

Regional council of lapland. 2012. Lapland in Figures 2012–2013. Available at: http://www.lapland.fi/en/lapinliitto/c/ document_library/get_file?folderid=931431&name=DI FE-16378.pdf (Accesses 10 december 2013)

Regional Council of lapland. 2013. http://www.lapland.fi (Accessed 10 december 2013).

Ritzer, G., and N. Jurgenson. 2010. Production, consumption, prosumption the nature of capitalism in the age of the digital 'prosumer'. *Journal of Consumer Culture* 10(1): 13–36.

Rusk, M. 2011. Design thinking, enterprise and innovation: Strategies for stimulating creative hubs and making an impact on city regeneration. In Cai, Jun, Liu, Jikun, Tong, Gabriel Y.L. and IP, Anthony K.C. (Eds.), *Design management: Toward a new era of innovation* (pp. 20–27). Hong Kong: Innovation and Design Management Association. ISBN 978-988-15984-1-7

Rutten, R. 2016. Beyond proximities The socio-spatial dynamics of knowledge creation. *Progress in Human Geography* 41(2): 159–177.

Rutten, P., F. Van Oort, and G. Marlet. 2011. *Creative industries as a flywheel.* Amsterdam: Amsterdam Economic Board & Creative Amsterdam.

Schlesinger, P. (2007). Creativity: From discourse to doctrine? *Screen* 48(3): 377–87.

Scott, A. 2001. Capitalism, cities, and the production of symbolic forms. *Trans Inst Br Geog* 26(1): 11–23.

Scott, A. 2005. *On Hollywood: The place, the industry.* Princeton, New Jersey: Princeton University Press.

Scott, A. J. 2010. The cultural economy of landscape and prospects for peripheral development in the twenty-first century: The case of the English Lake District. *European Planning Studies* 18(10): 1567–89.

Skantze and Pihlgren. 2012. Lagesrapport om den kreativa sektorn. Stockholm: Generator Sverige.

Stam, E., J. P. J. De Jong, and G. Marlet. 2008. Creative industries in the Netherlands: Structure, development, innovativeness and effects on urban growth. *Geografiska Annaler B* 90(2): 119–32.

Statistics Finland. 2013. Population structure. Available at: http://www.stat.fi/til/vaerak/tau_en.html (Accessed 13 November 2013).

Sternö, J., and T. Nielsén. 2012. Kulturella och kreativa näringarna 2012: statistik och jämförelser. Stockholm: Volante.

Storper, M., and R. Walker. 1989. *The capitalist imperative: Territory, technology, and industrial growth.* Oxford: Blackwell.

Stratton, J. 2008. The difference of Perth music: A scene in cultural and historical context. *Continuum* 22(5): 613–22.

Strom, P., and R. Nelson. 2010. Dynamic regional competitiveness in the creative economy: Can peripheral communities have a place?. *The Service Industries Journal* 30(4): 497–511.

Tarja Koskinen-Olsson & Jari Muikku: Direct Copyright Revenue Streams in Creative Industries in Finland. An Evaluation. The Finnish Copyright Society /The Finnish Copyright Institute Publications No. 31 (2014).

Throsby, D. 2008. Modelling the cultural industries. *International Journal of Cultural Policy* 14(3): 217–32.

Throsby, D., and V. Hollister. 2003. Don't give up your day job: An economic study of professional artists in Australia. Australia Council Report, Surry Hills N.S.W.

Turok, I. 2004. Cities, regions and competitiveness. *Regional Studies* 38(9): 1069–83.

UKTI. 2013. *UK trade and investments annual report.* London.

UNCTAD. 2013. Creative Economy Report 2013 Special Education Widening Local Development Pathways, United Nations Development Programme (UNDP), One United Nations Plaza, New York, NY 10017, USA and the United Nations Educational, Scientific and Cultural Organization (UNESCO), 7, place de Fontenoy, 75352 Paris 07 SP, France. http://www.unesco.org/culture/pdf/creative-economy-report-2013.pdf

UNCTAD. 2015. *Information Economy Report 2015: Unlocking the Potential of E-Commerce for Developing Countries.* Geneva, United Nations.

United Nations Development Programme (UNDP)/United Nations Conference on Trade and Development (UNCTAD). 2010. *Creative Economy.* Report 2010. Geneva and New York, NY: UNDP and UNCTAD.

University of Lapland. 2011. *Lapland design Programme 2010–2015*. Available at:http://www.lapinmuotoiluohjelma.fi/loader.aspx?id=93770b7f-2454-4334-a122-ad93002a1f80

Verdich, M. 2010. Creative Migration? The attraction and retention of the creative class in Launceston, Tasmania. *Australian Geographer* 41(1): 129–40.

Waitt, G., and C. Gibson. 2009. Creative small cities: Rethinking the creative economy in place. *Urban Studies* 46(5–6): 1223–46.

Warren, A., and R. Evitt. 2010. Indigenous Hip-hop: Overcoming marginality, encountering constraints. *Australian Geographer* 41(1): 141–58.

Western Development Commission. 2009. Creative West. The Creative Sector in the West of Ireland. Western Development Commission.

Woods, M. 2011. Winning and losing: The changing geography of Europe's rural areas. *European Urban and Regional Studies* 13(3): 282–83.

Woods, M. 2015. Reconfiguring places: Wealth and the transformation of rural areas. In J. Beaverstock, I. Hay (Eds.), *International Handbook of Wealth and the Super-Rich* (pp. 264–286). Elgar Original Reference Series Edward Elgar Publishing.

Woods, M. 2017. (In press) Creative ruralities. *Journal of Arts and Communities*.

4

Doing Business Creatively: Business Models and Policy

4.1 Introduction

In the previous chapters we have focussed on the unique approaches to consuming and producing culture. We have provided some insights into how the creative economy and industries in peripheral regions are distinct. In Chapter 3 we saw that creative firms in peripheral regions are ambitious, export orientated and want to interact and engage with others in their industry to learn and create.

In this chapter we explore the different approaches to doing business employed by creative industries, notably those located in peripheral areas and the types of supports that are necessary to enable the future growth of the creative economy there. The business models and the business supports of the creative industries need to reflect the unique offering of these enterprises. The nature of the produce, its narrative laden and expressive value nature, together with the unique mix of commercial and non-commercial incentives means that a different approach to supporting these industries is required.

P. Collins, J.A. Cunningham, *Creative Economies in Peripheral Regions*, DOI 10.1007/978-3-319-52165-7_4

4.2 Creative Industries and Business Models

Business models (BM) are now one of the main tools used by businesses and nascent entrepreneurs, and have received growing attention in the academic literature particularly in the fields of strategy, entrepreneurship and innovation (see Baden-Fuller and Managematin 2013; Casasesus-Masanell and Ricart 2010; Gately and Cunningham 2014; Teece 2010). The term Business Model (BM) has been conceptualised and redefined in many ways in the current literature. One of the more prevalent definitions has been that of Osterwalder et al. (2005: 3) who proposed it as a 'conceptual tool that contains a set of elements and their relationships and allows expressing the business logic of a specific firm'. Teece (2010) argued that the objective of a BM is to delineate how a particular business distributes value to consumers, persuading customers to pay for value and translating those payments into income. As such a BM offers an architecture and organisation which outlines revenue and profit sources for a particular enterprise.

From the previous chapter and from our engagement with creative industry enterprises their approach to value and what is now termed their business models appear to be different. To understand how business models relate to creative industries we carried out an evaluation of recent published literature on the topic of business models. First, a search was conducted in ISI Web of Science, using the search terms 'business models' AND 'creative industry'/'creative economy'. The search was restricted to the discipline areas of economics, economic geography management and business. We focussed explicitly on journal articles, excluding book reviews and editorials. A total of 201 results were obtained, and those that (1) in English, (2) contained empirical work, (3) published in the last 15 years and (4) contained cultural or creative industries as a meaningful entity were selected for further analysis. The resulting 62 empirical studies form the core of that we draw on for this section.

In recent years the term 'business model innovation' has garnered increased attention. Casadesus-Masanell and Zhu (2013: 464) state that: 'at root, business model innovation refers to the search for new logics of the firm, new ways to create and capture value for its stakeholders, and focuses primarily on finding new ways to generate revenues and define value propositions for customers, suppliers, and partners'. Consequently, business model innovation often affects the whole enterprise (Amit and Zott 2001). Empirical observations suggest that imitation is abundant with established firms often learning about new BMs from newcomers and respond by partially or fully implementing these innovations into their enterprise.

Digital technology has been key in allowing for business model innovation. Li (2015) distinguishes between three different intensities of BM change due to implementation of digital technology (DT): enhance (existing ways of doing things); extend (or supplement traditional products or processes through DT); transform (the way things are done with DT).

With respect to creative industries Moyon and Lecocq (2014) classify three different types of business model innovation: value-network extension, value proposition bundling and new resources and competencies valorisation. Value-network extension involves establishing partnerships with companies outside the traditional boundaries of a particular industry, with the intention of creating alternative value sources. Somewhat interrelated is value proposition bundling which constitutes enhanced revenue capture from the sales of complementary products or services from the value-network extension. Lastly, new resources and competencies valorisation involves the implementation of what are termed '360-degree' strategies to capture revenue from every activity in which artists participated (at least in the example of the record industry) (Moyon and Lecocq 2014).

4.2.1 Defining Creative Industries Business Models

Several studies have attempted to classify creative industry BMs under diverse but often interrelated headings. One of the first major attempts was undertaken by Nielsen (2008) who defined three major BMs; mass-produced and scalable content products; live-based experience goods and; service-based inputs to other products as value enhancers.

The first is premised upon the possibility of leveraging on the mass production of creative output through the application of Intellectual Property Rights. In this category, ownership of the content is fundamental and content may be directly transmitted to consumers or indirectly through third-party brokers. The subjective worth and project-based disposition of these products are aspects that differentiate it from more traditionally manufactured products. As such, this grouping comprises video games, filmed entertainment, print publishing, recorded music, fashion and designer goods and reproduced art. Therefore, it is seen most frequently in the creative application and creative expression sectors. Live-based experience goods centre around direct, jointly creative encounters with the consumer which includes theatre, festivals and concerts and is premised upon the uniqueness of experience (creative experience). Lastly, in the third category (service-based inputs to other products as value enhancers) creativity functions as an input good to increase the value of another product such as advertising, design consultancy or architecture (creative application and technology sectors). The service provider delivers a one-off service to the client towards a specific client brief, with the client usually retaining ownership of the rights after production (Nielsen 2008).

More recently Svejenova et al. (2015) distinguished between two different types of BM (albeit with a focus on the haute cuisine industry). She argues that depending on their motivation, scale and scope of their activities, creative entrepreneurs vary in the denomination of BM they institute and manipulate. For instance, those BMs with the creative endeavour as its hub are defined as workshops. Here, the pursuit of opportunities is centred on those that permit artistic expression, innovation and learning, in which expansion is neglected in favour of R&D (creative expression sector). As such, the workshop BM is not motivated by capital concerns but rather by experimentation, discovery and the development of new ideas or methods. With this in mind, it can be argued that the customer segment of the workshop model is the profession itself. Svejenova et al. argue that freedom for expression and experimentation was a major incentive behind the restaurant elBulli, which was characterised by a novel and risky style of cooking.

The other BM highlighted by these authors is the enterprise BM, which is more oriented towards growth and profitability than the workshop model. Instances include chefs who pursue both scope and scale, engaging in internationalisation and diversification of their businesses, opening restaurants in dissimilar but fashionable cities worldwide. Svejenova et al. (2015) cite the example of the 'durable luxury' high-end restaurant concept offered by Alain Ducasse which compete for the much coveted Michelin stars regularly (traits more commonly associated with the creative technology and application sectors). What these two business models emphasise is that the business models of creative endeavours is highly influenced by the particular motivations of the creative entrepreneur.

In relation to more core or cultural entities, the European Network on Arts-Cultural Management and Cultural Policy Education (ENCATC 2013) underline the potential of the cellular model. The externally oriented version of this has the board functioning as an enabler, meaning the focus is on cells (these can be teams, working units etc.) working alone or in collaboration. This model depends on online networks and technology in order to function properly. Traditional governance models are described as unlikely to survive if they persevere with advancing an internalised perspective. A customer orientation is a viable alternative as it prioritises the consumer experience (creative expression). An equally worthwhile substitute, albeit more externally oriented, is the societal orientation. Here, art organisations attempt to contribute to the well-being of citizens, using the arts as a vehicle to make a real difference. The ENCATC also highlight the most extreme version, the wiki orientation, whereby people can help choose and partake in their experiences with cultural organisations.

Furthermore, Sapsed et al. (2015) identified several different types of creative industry BMs in their analysis of the Brighton Creative Digital and IT companies. Amongst those considered very important by the firms were 'work for hire' (the producer delivers work for a client over a definite period and the client keeps the IP), 'commissioned' (the producer delivers work for a client over a definite period, keeping the IP), 'retainer model' (a client pays you to work for an indefinite or continual period) and the 'platform' (providing a platform for UGC). Other BMs identified were freemium, paid search, performance-related payments and derivate fee. These derivative fees and platforms are used by the web portals sector, with paid search used by digital agencies, as well as Knowledge Intensive Business Services, which employ a number of different business models (creative technology). The retainer model was highlighted as being important in the digital agencies, marketing services and the digital technologies sector.

In examining the online content industry Lyubareva et al. (2014) identified three major types of BM: participative; distribution and editorial. In the participative category, revenue sources include advertising and sponsorship with User-Generated Content (therefore participative evidencing prosumption) and content from external producers key. Content may be consumed either by streaming or download with the BM functioning on a multisided market, offering content to consumers for free but selling audience access to advertisers. The distribution category integrates web sites targeting specific market segments who produce unique content. Revenue is sourced by selling content to users while other content is free. This revenue stream is often complemented by donations or public funding. Moreover, it avails of both digital dissemination as well as physical distribution. The latter model (editorial) habitually sells content for offline consumption (i.e. renting), accompanied by a DRM to restrict usage. Similar to the distribution model, advertising and sponsorship are rarely seen as viable sources of revenue. Importantly, the authors acknowledge that there is a plethora of intermediate companies that offer original content and supply it for free without UGC or external content (Participative + Distribution) or companies who supply original and external content (Distribution + Editorial). This mixed or portfolio approach to the BM is something that is becoming increasingly apparent in the creative industries as a whole.

4.2.2 Business Models in the Creative Industries

One of the dangers of business models is their blind adoption from one sector to another. Hearn et al. (2007) suggest that it would be ill-advised to uncritically embrace business models imitative of other industry sectors without allowing for the particular dynamic of the creative industries. Some authors (Dumcke 2015: 5; Svejenova et al. 2015) have argued that studies on BMs in the creative and cultural sector embody 'a helicopter perspective' with relatively little amounts of pertinent literature when juxtaposed with other economic sectors. Compounding this is the fact that relevant literature has tended to focus upon the more commercial end of the continuum (video games, film, music, etc.) (Dumcke 2015). Thus, comparatively little is known about new BMs in the core creative or creative expression industries, for instance. Yet there is value in studying the BMs across the creative economy. As Guercini (2014) argues, a firm's BM dictates the logic, data and other information through which it creates and delivers value to its customers. Thus, a key element of BMs in creative industries is how well they manage to capture and deliver value by leveraging the results of a firm's creativity (ibid.). In their introduction to a special issue entitled *Business Models in Creative Industries*, Warnier and Runfola (2014) argue that the design and implementation of effective BMs can assist creative businesses in surmounting conflicts between the creative process (innovation) and organisational processes (efficiency). The authors contend that this is facilitated by the reciprocal influence of creativity and organisation. Thus, competent organisation can augment creativity and creativity can, in turn, foster novel organisational arrangements. In specific reference to rural areas, the European Commission (2010) Green Paper stated that new BMs can help bring innovation and sustainability to traditional forms (i.e. craft /creative application) and result in economic viability.

However, Dumcke's (2015) analysis of the BMs of creative and cultural organisations demonstrates their heterogeneous nature. This analysis shows that many of these industries are in constant flux given the experimentation with and application of novel BMs. Yet, no all-encompassing BM exists for all businesses collated under the umbrella term creative and cultural industries. Indeed, this is a point that we will return to in the latter half of this chapter when looking at policy supports. Following a similar logic, Marsland and Krump (2014: 13) argue: 'We have always asserted that the idea of a singular model for all is absurd in a field in which there is such enormous variety of working processes, curatorial approaches and intentions. We believe that there are many formats and approaches that work and, when allowed to appropriately extend from the values, goals and working processes of the artists, represent effective new ways of working.'

Indeed, this multiplicity of BM opportunities and options is something which is echoed by the UK Technology Strategy Board (2009: 18) and contend that 'the purely linear business model is giving way to a much more interwoven environment' characterised by 'a much more rapid evolution of product development and consumption'. Jones et al. (2015) and Svejenova et al. (2010) argue that changes in the BMs of creative industries are driven by entrepreneurs whose identity and passion drives product creation. The former contend that these producers rely on a small set of clients and patrons to support new creative products, which tend to be small or limited. While a host of opportunities and options exist for BM innovation in the creative industries, the Green Paper by the European Commission highlights the challenging nature of maintaining business under a traditional BM while managing the transition to new BMs still under development.

4.2.3 Project-Based Organisation in the Creative Industries

Another type of BM has emerged within creative industries, which Fuller et al. (2011) argue revolves around entrepreneurial and often unorthodox collaborations, with numerous large, small and micro-businesses converging for a single project, then disbanding and forming new alliances for subsequent projects. This is what is known as project-based organisation (PBO) and is increasingly relevant in creative endeavours, especially when such industries are starting out (Dumcke 2015). Given that the creative sector in characterised by uncertainty, Ebbers and Wijnberg (2009) contend that the PBO is an increasingly common form of short-term organisation that can help foster innovation and diffuse uncertainties.

This further expanded by DeFillippi (2015) and their chapter on project-based organisations (PBOs) in the DCMS-defined creative industries. DeFillippi argues that studies demonstrate that theatre production (Uzzi and Spiro 2005; Eikhof and Haunschild 2007), movies (Sydow and Staber 2002), videogames (Ayoama and Izushi 2003; Cadín et al 2006), music (Lorenzen and Fredricksen 2005), advertising campaigns (Grabher 2002; Hallgen and DeFillippi 2014) and software (Grabher 2004) all satisfy the conditions necessary for PBOs. DeFillippi further argues that creative industries demonstrate the flexibility and ability of project-organised temporary systems and generate new knowledge. Ebbers and Wijnberg

(2009) indicate that the Dutch project-based film-making industry is characterised by transactional labour contracts. Grabher's (2002) study of the advertising industry in Soho, London has found that concentration of the industry has developed an agile ecology for organising projects in which teams of advertising firm 'creatives' can work in partnership with other resource suppliers from the media, public relations, or design firm sectors to collaborate on advertising campaigns and associated support media materials. While many projects are based on pre-existing relationships and trust, Delmestri et al. (2005) suggest the need for project organisations to draw upon new relationships in order to provide new creative combinations of experience and perspective.

Project-based collaboration is discernible in the study of theatre production by Marsland and Krump (2014: 11) who state that the Why Not Theatre in Toronto is pioneering a non-integrated, multi-organisational producing and mentoring format, known as intergenerational collaborative producing. Indeed, the authors note that '(i)n Canada, there is much interesting work happening in mid-sized and larger venue-based theatres in terms of adapting new producing structures; however, it was difficult to locate specific formal literature on this.' Similarly Sapsed et al.'s (2015) study on the Creative Digital and IT industry cluster in Brighton highlighted that many of the companies organised themselves around project-based business models, such as work for hire or commission-based models. Indeed, these were often considered more important than non-project based models. The report by Filmby Aarhus et al. (2011) underlines the rising inclination of new business models and value chains to be premised on cooperation among firms across the creative industries and beyond. These can often involve cooperation with research and educational institutions, private businesses or stimulated by the city or regional authorities in order to support and organise the local/regional development of the audiovisual/creative sectors.

Nowhere is the PBO more apparent than in the changing patterns of working methods highlighted by Dumcke (2015). Emphasising the continued emergence of co-working spaces, innovation labs and start-up accelerators, Dumcke (2015) contends that these milieus constitute an answer to the challenge of changing working methods and patterns in the creative and cultural industries. He also references the case of Berlin where grassroots, co-working, company-owned and research and university affiliated labs, as well as incubators and accelerators allow temporary or permanent collaboration to flourish.

4.2.4 The Portfolio Approach to the Business Model in Creative Industries

A significant trend in the increasing adoption of the portfolio model, using digital technology to combine different business models within the same organisation and managing them as a portfolio (Li 2015). According to the literature the implementation of the portfolio model has proliferated in the creative industries. The portfolio model also allows a company to focus on a more traditional aspect of their particular industry while simultaneously adopting a non-dominant approach to the market, which enhances the possibility of profits by filling a niche. Van Andel et al. (2012: 6) argue: 'navigating away from the dominant business model orientation in the market can deliver a potential source of competitive differentiation and provide conditions for a company to become successful'. In Li's (2015) study, digital technology was key in facilitating the deployment of several BMs. The author cites how some enterprises pooled features of new digital BMs with traditional BMs to create supplementary income and extend their reach and influence. For instance, a digital printing company collaborated with independent authors to create personalised children's books, generating extra revenue for that firm to pursue its main activity: digital printing.

Furthermore Li (2015) also highlights the example of a major music company that gave away music through free downloading in order to sell merchandise and live performance for selected artists; switching from selling music to selling events. The company experimented with the 'pay as much as you like' model, giving customers the opportunity to decide how much they would be willing to pay, this enabled the company to maximise revenues (leveraging the willingness of loyal fans to pay) while maintaining and expanding the fan base.

Moreover, Van Andel et al. (2012) argue that the creative industries' business models are characterised by this portfolio approach, as demonstrated by employing Nielsen's three categories of creative industry BMs (creating content, delivering a live-based experience, providing a value-enhancing service to other products). Thus a musician can be both a content producer and a provider of live-based experience products. Similarly in the gaming industry, the majority of enterprises and individuals work on producing their own content. However, a portion also exists that develops custom-made, often educational games for clients. Thus, Van Andel et al. (2014) argue that they focus on a different orientation within the framework as they aspire to create a made-to-order value enhancing service to clients. As such these examples evidence that in creative industries there is a dominant focus on business model, but another secondary focus also exists.

A study on the video game, music and television industries also corroborates ideas of the portfolio model (see Searle 2011). In relation to the former, Dynamo Games combines three games development BMs: mobile games for publishers; games for sale via iTunes and online games for Facebook. Thus, this unique combination allows them to capture different segments of the market. Heist Records, a music company accesses the market by combining three distinct BMs to capture and deliver value (performing musicians; artists' representation; and music for games). Witnessing the plight of physical sales in music, their BM seeks alternative routes to the market via computer games and social media. Another company Clash Music does not exhibit any focus on recorded music, accessing the market through non-dominant entry points which are based around a monthly magazine. Lastly, Tern TV chooses to focus on lifestyle and factual content for television and storytelling for digital platforms, thus intertwining two BMs: television production and digital content production. As such, it provides an exemplar of a company combining a traditional BM with a new, digitally-enabled BM (ibid.).

The value of the portfolio model in the creative industries has not received much attention. However, Sapsed et al.'s (2015) study of the Brighton and Hove Creative Digital and IT Industries cluster indicated that companies employing more than one BM (i.e. The portfolio model) experienced greater profit and innovation than those which only utilised one.

4.3 Illustrative Creative Economy Business Model Innovation

From the previous section we see that there is a significant variety of business models and business model innovation evident in the creative economy and industries. Project organisation and portfolio business models seem to be more prevalent in this industry given the nature of the work within the creative economy. Owing to the variety and proliferation we have taken some illustrative creative economy business model innovation to illuminate it and to highlight how these BM are challenging conventional thinking and the status quo with respect to creative expressive, application and technologies

4.3.1 Creative Expression

4.3.1.1 Museums

The majority of creative and cultural organisations have embraced some degree of innovation in their business models. Museums provide an excellent illustrative example in this regard. Amsellem (2013) argues museums need to imagine new BMs to alleviate their reliance on subsidies, with internationalisation touted as a potential resolution. Moreover, Amsellem (2013) proffers several alternatives, including the co-produced exhibition BM which offers a varied catalogue, stimulates intellectual resources by bringing together scientists and historians, and pools costs and creates economies of scale. An example is the exhibition 'Matisse, Cézanne, Picasso . . . L'aventure des Stein' which was displayed in Paris, New York and San Francisco, thus combining many resources. In this manner, the coproduction allowed them to save 65% on transportation items from the initial budget. An alternative is the co-organised exhibition which has an identified technical producer and represents a collaboration between several museums, one of which accepts full financial responsibility.

Moreover, in relation to the world-renowned Louvre in Paris, Coblence and Sabatier (2014) and Jones et al. (2015) note how the new BM of the museum is premised upon a global network of museums with new branches opened in Lens and Abu Dhabi, with plans to rotate the collections. Jones et al. (2015) contend that the most successful museums have embraced some grade of innovation in their BMs – such as crowdsourcing ideas for exhibition, using IT to engross visitors in displays and offering 3D models of popular artefacts on the web as to increase the museum's influence outside the physical boundaries.

4.3.1.2 Cultural Heritage

Other organisations have engaged in creative business model innovation measures in order to uncover new revenue sources. A Report by the Horizon 2020 Expert Group on Cultural Heritage includes case studies in which innovative financing, novel methods of governance, unified landscape management, public private partnerships, crowd-sourced funding and various other innovative and creative measures have been taken to release the locked-up potential of Europe's heritage. The case study for Italy represents an example of a crowdfunding platform for cultural heritage. The organisation is a community where lovers of Italy interact and contribute to the protection of the country's unique art and culture. Crowdfunding was used to source financing for relevant projects. For example, in their first crowdfunding endeavour the group raised funds to create an aseismic pedestal that will ensure the safety of a prized piece of art (Francesco I d'Este's bust by Gian Lorenzo Bernini) from earthquake damage (European Commission 2015). While common in most of the creative industries, Dumcke (2015) argues that crowdfunding or crowdsourcing is most discernible in museums, cultural heritage, music and cinema. The ENCATC (2013) document argues that Kickstarter, the main crowdfunding platform has had more than 4.5 million people pledge over $723 million that has gone to funding more than 45,000 creative projects since its launch in 2009.

4.3.1.3 Theatres, Operas, Orchestras

Continuing with the creative expression industries, theatre organisations have also implemented some innovations to their business models. A NESTA (2010) report details how digital streaming of the National

Theatre (NT Live) attracted both intranational and international audiences. The popularity of the service is evidenced by the estimate that 50,000 saw the streamed (live or shortly after) production of Phédre. Some cinemas have collaborated with the National Theatre to stream their productions live. NESTA conclude that NT Live attracted audiences of lower incomes than the theatre. Thus business model innovation is enabling the participation and engagement of new audiences in theatre. Other theatres are collaborating to maximise shared resources and knowledge bases. Marsland and Krump (2014) state that the WhyNot Theatre in Toronto is pioneering a non-integrated, multi-organisational producing and mentoring format, known as intergenerational collaborative producing. Similarly, the report by Arts Action Research (2012) highlights how Peculiar Works Projects (New York) has been utilising an integrated combination format approach where at least three artists combine and collaborate to produce their projects for the past 20 years. The report by Marsland and Krump (2014) also indicates some novel approaches to acquiring environments for theatre production, with one group able to develop a 'pop-up' art-colony through crowdfunding.

The innovations to the business model in theatre are also discernible in the opera and orchestra milieus. Dumcke (2015) argues that technological progress has enabled operas and orchestras to record their productions, which can then be channelled through digital platforms to stream them to a broader assemblage (Berlin Philharmonic and the New York Metropolitan Opera). An example from May 2015 is the inauguration of the Opera Platform, supported by the Creative Europe Programme. The website links the cultural broadcaster, ARTE, and fifteen opera companies in Europe. The Platform facilitates the online streaming of performances which are subtitled in six languages and supplemented with extra content. Furthermore, the Brussels Philharmonic developed classical music ringtones to promote their own label (ENCATC 2013) with twelve ringtones experiencing over 10,000 downloads in three days. The organisation has also embarked on a novel investment scheme where investors purchase and lend a high quality violin to the orchestra. After a period of five years the investor can decide to reinvest or sell the instrument on the market (given its value will have increased in the meantime).

4.3.2 Creative Application and Technology

4.3.2.1 Content Industries (Music, TV)

As has been well documented, the traditional business models of the content industries have been the most influenced by the emergence of online alternatives. The contrast in revenue sources between the more traditional BMs and the contemporary BMs provide a lens through which one can conceptualise the change. Jones et al. (2015) argue that the revenue sources of content industries' BMs have moved from selling to consumers to selling to advertising and introducing membership fees for consumers. Examples include streaming models such as Netflix and Spotify who source their revenues from membership fees rather than purchase or rental. The key driver of Spotify's BM is its value proposition. Comparable to that of both the iTunes Store and YouTube, it features an abundance of readily available music, either for free (with the support of advertising) or with added benefits available through subscription plans. The Filmby Aarhus et al. (2011) report presents an extensive analysis of new audiovisual business models, with specific attention given to revenue models.

There have been changing BMs in the content industries (see Li 2015). For example, digital technology allowed Nine Inch Nails to release their album Ghosts I-IV with different pricing packages. Moreover, Radiohead released an album based on the 'pay as much as you want' model. Similarly, the Leading to War documentary film maker released the file for free download but also via DVD for purchase on Amazon. In these examples, the value proposition in terms of the product offering and the revenue model are transformed, as is the value architecture of the business model employed (Li 2015). He also references the 'wisdom of the crowd' concept, which has inspired several new BMs, including that of Slice the Pie. This website allows users to rate and ultimately decide which bands are offered recording contracts. This allows customers and investors to invest in artists they like, which reduces the risk for companies signing these artists, given they already have a following. These examples embody Lyubareva et al.'s (2014) contention that traditional BMs often focussed on a single revenue model whereas today the majority of online BMs can find and employ multiple sources of revenue (Subscriptions, advertising, premium etc.) and business models.

In terms of live music, the report by Berklee College of Music (2013) highlights some innovative adjustments to the business models of festivals. Some festivals have internationalised their offerings with Lollapalooza debuting in Santiago, Chile and in Sao Paolo, Brazil in 2011 and 2012, respectively. Similarly, Sónar, founded in Barcelona has been internationalised as Sónar on Tour which has featured festivals in Canada, America, Reykjavik, Tokyo, Cape Town, amongst others. The same report highlights how the music publishing industry diversified its sources of revenue by reaching arrangements with mobile partners, app developers, streaming services, greeting cards, film and other sources outside the traditional model. These strategies resonate with Moyon and Lecocq's (2014) value network extension and value proposition bundling forms of business model innovation.

Changing consumer behaviour – prosumption – has also induced innovations in the business models of content industries. Dumcke (2015) notes how digital tools have enabled the emergence of the prosumer (although she doesn't explicitly use that term) given consumers can now generate and publish their own content. This is especially apparent in the book publishing industry where self-publishing has become a viable platform for budding authors. Dümcke furthers her argument by arguing that there are increasing amounts of BMs based on such User-Generated Content (videos, blogs, forums, podcasts, social media, photography, wikis etc.).

The sheer diversity of BMs available to the creative industries results in high levels of experimentation and change. A NESTA Report (2010) claims that although some sectors are more advanced than others, businesses are exploring a wide range of novel platforms and strategies to reach audiences and generate revenues. Moreover, Searle (2011) noted how some interviewees' BMs changed every three months. Lyubareva et al. (2014) argue that constant BM innovation and experimentation is a key source of competitive advantage. Thus, Fuller et al. (2011) contend that to remain fit over time, creative industries must constantly organise for novelty in anticipation of industry change, particularly in high velocity industries where uncertainty is high.

In terms of future research, more investigation is needed on the business models of creative industries in general. The 'helicopter perspective' will not benefit the sector as a whole and nor will the concentration of studies on the more commercial end of the creative and cultural continuum.

Figure 4.1 constitutes a reflection on the emerging business models evident in our reading of the literature. Represented as such they mark a clear difference to general business approaches. As referred to throughout this book there are a number of key external influencers here, notably the role being played by technological diffusion as well as the broader phenomenon of collaborative consumption/production. Taking what is unique about the creative sector in terms of changing patterns of consumption and the unique traits of its produce we can see how both these internal and those external factors are coming together to create a different approach to doing business.

The use of technology has brought consumers and producers of culture together in distinct ways. As referred to above, technology and

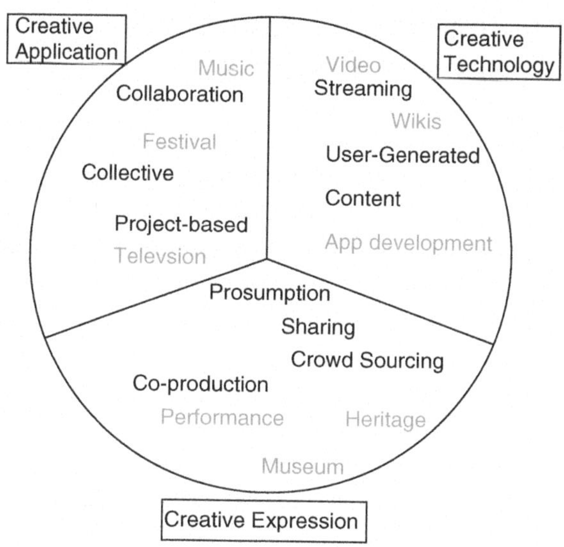

Fig. 4.1 Emerging business models across the creative sectors
Source: Derived from systematic review of the literature

increased collaboration is serving to lower the barrier between the consumers and producers. In many ways too, the relationship is being pushed beyond the marketplace. From instances of co-production up to increasing user-generated content we are witnessing a rise in models that non-commercial in their guise. From crowdsourcing to shared spaces creative industries (and industries beyond the creative sector) are pushing the boundaries of business beyond solely economic concerns.

While this is of consequence to the general understanding not just of the creative economy, but of the changing nature of the economy more generally, it is of key importance in considering creative industries in peripheral areas. In the following section we will turn our attention to the policy approaches being taken towards supporting these industries in more remote regions. Any policy that will promote the sustainability of creative economies there will need to be mindful of the emerging patterns identified in the literature and summarised in Fig. 4.1. A recognition and support of the different approaches taken to doing business there is the key to supporting its future development.

4.4 The Policymaking Challenge for Peripheral Regions

A variety of policy approaches exist to support creative and cultural industries. However this does not make devising policy a straightforward process. One of the key messages of UNCTAD's 2010 Creative Economy report is that: 'Each country is different, each market is special and each creative product has its specific touch and splendour. Nonetheless, every country might be able to identify key creative industries that have not yet been exploited to their full potential so as to reap developmental benefits. There is no one-size-fits-all prescription; each country should formulate a feasible strategy to foster its creative economy, based on its own strengths, weakness and realities.' The policymaking challenge for creative and cultural industries exists everywhere because all places have resources that can be capitalised on. However, at the country level, developing creative industries would also benefit from attention to their different contexts, such as large cities, small cities and rural areas. The need for a shift in the scale of policymaking in creative and cultural industries is a key theme in cultural policy research. Cities have received much attention, and there is a need for a shift in focus. The Creative Edge project is concerned with the peripheral perspective, which also encompasses the small city and rural agendas.

Below a general overview of policy strategies for creative and cultural industries is outlined. A number of key challenges for creative and cultural industry policymaking are identified. However, policy must not just consider broad policy issues, but also be focussed on addressing issues that arise in different contexts. Therefore, the peripheral perspective is considered in detail, with challenges and issues first outlined, before then moving on to present some areas of potential future policy direction. The discussion also presents policy initiative examples and policy approaches that have addressed similar challenges.

4.4.1 Policymaking Instruments, Challenges and Frameworks

Policy is a package of instruments. Like other industries policy makers use a variety of policy instruments to support the creative sectors. The application of these tools can vary in different context and in some instances these policy instruments are not used as national or regional authorities have not prioritised the industry. Types of instruments typically contained in cultural development strategies, in combinations of one or more, such as (Throsby 2010):

- The provision of infrastructure
- Finance and investment providing access to start-up or working capital
- Capacity-building at local level encouraging people's active participation in arts and culture
- Inter-jurisdictional cooperation with cross-departmental and agency cooperation in different areas
- Support for the core of creative arts which also supports the broader cultural and creative industries underpinning cultural production

Policy areas that can support the creative economy, identified by the UNCTAD (2010: 260) include:

- Mapping of inventories of cultural assets and creative industries
- SME business development and finance (e.g. microfinance)
- Promote creative clusters to stimulate collaboration, innovation and linkages
- Copyright awareness and legislation
- Support for artists and the arts, both direct (e.g. taxation, social security) and indirect (e.g. private sector support, training, professional associations, laws)
- Conservation of tangible and intangible cultural heritage
- Expansion of digital capacity and know-how
- Domestic and export market development (e.g. quality, brands, trade facilitation)
- Better articulation between creative industries and tourism objectives
- Education, vocational training and business skills development
- Industry assistance (e.g. investment incentives, tax concessions, bilateral agreements, co-production contract negotiation etc.)

However, effective policy development that facilitates creative and cultural industries reaching their growth potential is more complex than just selecting a range of policy instruments. The need for a more holistic, multifaceted and strategic approach is identified. A set of broad challenges face policy makers when devising creative and cultural industry policy to ensure it best serves the contexts in which it is applied. In the next part of this chapter some of the broader policy issues are outlined and discussed, which are relevant to all contexts.

4.4.1.1 General Policymaking Challenges

The 2010 European Commission (2010) Green Paper *Unlocking the potential of cultural and creative industries* identifies a number of challenges for the further development of cultural and creative industries. The first challenge is that the correct enablers are put in place so entrepreneurs can experiment and innovate, and have access to funding and the correct mix of skills. Enablers that provide new spaces for experimentation might be in the form of collaborations between institutions, the arts and academia, or through meeting places and laboratories where creative and cultural entrepreneurs can experiment and innovate. Clusters are also identified as an ideal organisational structure to facilitate cooperation between businesses. The need for innovative financial instruments and better access to finance is also identified as an important enabler. Matching creative industries skills needs and education provision is another enabler for growth. These enablers should foster the correct kind of environment so that cultural and creative industries can flourish towards their potential.

The second major challenge identified by the European Commission (2010) Green Paper is that the local and regional creative and cultural industry environment should be developed as a launch pad for the global success of these industries. The role of cultural and creative industries in regional development should be taken into account in the design of policies at the local level, and not seen as a luxury policy option, but a part of social and economic development. Cross-European knowledge-sharing is also highlighted as important in regional development of cultural and creative industries. Mobility of cultural and creative entrepreneurs and facilitation of cultural exchanges is another factor highlighted as important from this respect. The third challenge highlighted is to catalyse the spillover effects of creative and cultural industries in wider social and economic contexts. For example, these industries can contribute to an innovation-friendly economic environment. In addition, strong cultural resources improve a place's attractiveness for living and working.

The challenges highlighted in the Green Paper are reflected to a large extent in the EU Open Method of Coordination Expert Working Group on Cultural and Creative Industry's (OMC-EWG-CCI) framework for development of creative and cultural industries. This framework is based around three aims, which can be summarised as:

- Creating the correct preconditions
- Supporting existing and emerging businesses
- Harnessing the spillover effects for wider society and economy

The first part of the framework, creating the preconditions and a favourable environment for developing creative and cultural industries, may take the form of raising awareness, developing strategic alliances and better understanding of creative and cultural industries through mapping studies. The second part, strengthening creative and cultural industries, can be through measures such as developing networks and clusters, increasing access to finance and introducing measures supporting business incubation. The final part, harnessing the spillover effects of creative and cultural industries for society and the economy, can be implemented through tourism, regional development, lifelong learning, social and business innovation.

This assessment of policy instruments and frameworks has shown that to fully capitalise on creative and cultural industries, policy must engage with creative and cultural industries in a number of ways. Policy should focus on existing creative and cultural industries, but it should also focus on creating the correct environment for creativity to flourish, while also capturing the additional benefits of the existence of creative and cultural industries, beyond their primary effects. This approach is even more fundamental in the context of sustainably and effectively developing rural and peripheral creative and cultural industries. Because creative and cultural industries are less concentrated in peripheral places, to most effectively develop their full potential, this three-pillar approach – creating the best preconditions, supporting existing industries and harnessing the spillover effects – is important.

In the next part of this chapter we focus on some more specific aspects of creative and cultural industry policymaking. We begin by focussing on some general issues not linked to all contexts, but also consider policy issues from the peripheral and rural creative industry perspective.

4.4.2 The Urban Fixation

In previous sections, we noted that, oft in the peripheral creative economy, non-economic values were of more significance than their solely economic counterparts. Given the permeation of urban bias from studies to policy, it is of no surprise that policy is regularly fixated on the latter. Throsby (2010) and Frey (2007) acknowledge the need for both economic and non-economic indicators to achieve a full account of the value of culture. Similarly, Lilley and Moore (2013) argue that for too long, a purely economically motivated model, viewing money as a sole measure of value, has dominated the policymaking sphere when conferring the value of culture. Moreover, Hesmondhalgh and Pratt (2005) add that culture and creative policy need to contribute towards social cohesion and community development. In an Irish context, Collins and Fahy (2011) regarded the creative and cultural mantra of Galway as fitting with the urban entrepreneurial approach in which urban and economic values took precedence over cultural. Similarly, developers are often closely connected to city redevelopment agencies and their interests often dominate cultural planning outcomes (Markusen and Gadwa 2010; Strom 2003; Zukin 1995) with thinly veiled real estate revaluation attempts also discernible (Kunzman, 2004).

The increasing pressure for an economic value of culture within relevant policy has been documented. Viewing creative economies solely in terms of physical wealth is anachronistic, as it disregards the considerable presence of social and cultural values. Furthermore, several researchers have argued that an economic focus suborns the integrity of the case for culture and consequently a loss of what represents cultural value and a misguided belief that what can be gained from linking arts, culture and creative activities to innovation is more than counterbalanced by what would be lost from such sector-specific attention (Oakley 2008; Oakley 2009; O'Connor 2009). Thus, and in line with Markusen and Gadwa (2010), despite the interest and momentum of cultural industries, policy has often been legislated without the benefit of a solid evidence or a data-based approach (Lilley and Moore 2013). Moreover, when it has, it has often been similar to a 'Trojan Horse' (Garnham 2005) in that it is imbued with hidden intentions that hinder the development of the cultural and creative industries. Cultural values underpin the creative industries, and retaining a central focus on harnessing and promoting culture and creativity in wider society is a vital focus for policy.

4.4.3 One Size Fits All Approach to Policy and Instruments

The belief that creative economies were unique to urban areas has consequently impacted heavily on the scarcity of policy relating to peripheral and rural areas. Indeed, this was epitomised at the start of the millennium by Griffiths (2001) who contended that culture-led development of the previous two decades was essentially engrossed with the urban. Thus echoing Bell and Jayne's (2004) contention of the 'urban script', creative economy policy measures for peripheral areas become little more than a facsimile of the same policy implemented in the urban area. Scott (2006) refers to this translation of urban policy onto a rural context as urban cognitive cultural economies. Additionally, Huggins and Clifton (2011) document the ramifications of such translation, which they categorise as 'detrimental' to the competitiveness of rural and peripheral areas. They suggest this urban-biased policy has had a fundamental role in the increasing divide in competitiveness between the ex-urban periphery and the metropolis itself.

Correspondingly, similar caution is issued by Strom and Nelson (2010) in a Swedish context who, in line with Huggins and Clifton (2011) characterise such policy as being imbued with the 'where's it at' mentality, not wholly different to the idea of buzz mentioned earlier. Moreover, Mahroum et al. (2007: 2) argue that economic development policy has understood cities as innate representatives of competition and growth, in the process overshadowing the capacity and capability of rural areas: 'Years of urban-focused policy initiatives have implicitly treated them more as dormitories or playgrounds for urban-dwellers rather than as areas in their own right. Recent innovation policies have tended to reinforce this stereotype by their concentration on urban areas and implicit neglect of rural areas.' Thus, with regard to possible future policy it is essential that it not be found upon what Currid and Williams (2010: 455) note are 'general conclusions about the cultural industries across disparate geographies'.

From the above it is perceptible that policy makers had disregarded the advantages of incorporating the potential of more ruralised areas to maximise the competitiveness of peripheral areas into economic development strategies (Huggins and Clifton 2011). Furthermore, the Petrov (2007) is of the opinion that some small cities and towns in the UK could prosper from particular policy instruments to draw creative industries, albeit in a dissimilar manner than that observed in metropolitan centres. Particular policy measures should pursue an evidence-based empirical approach, which would allow it to overcome the weakness and inadequacy of some original data sources (i.e. Census data) (Pratt 1997). In addition, as creative industries as Coe (2000: 394) notes 'are embedded in networks and institutions that are socially constructed and culturally defined', the development of the sector is shaped by the geography and networks in which it is embedded (see Felton et al. 2010). In other words, it is essential to understand the dynamics of locality at play before devising strategic measures, even more apparent when one considers that creative industry research bears the imprint of the context from which it stems (Gibson and Klocker 2004). Therefore, in line with Felton et al. (2010), supporting and sustaining creative industries in ex-urban localities becomes a task of devising different strategies to those discernible in metropolitan areas. According to Scott (2006) and Mossig (2011), failure to do so combined with the implementation of urban-influenced government policy will result in few winners and numerous losers, the preponderance of the latter found in rural areas.

4.5 The Policymaking Process

One central issue in policymaking is the diverse nature of creative and cultural industries. This trait adds a fundamental challenge for policymaking. What is important is an awareness of what Gibson and Kong (2005) term the 'polyvalency' of the sector, i.e. it has many facets and forms, and policy design approaches should begin with a strong awareness of this fact. Also because of the diverse nature of creative industries, responsibility for policy development can be unclear. Nielsén (2008) highlights how the needs of creative industries can fall between areas of responsibility, and primarily between the areas of industry, culture and education. UNCTAD's 2010 Creative Economy report states that policy must recognise the multidisciplinary nature of the creative economy, which has economic, social, cultural, technological and environmental linkages, requiring inter-ministerial action at the national level. It is recommended that the nature of policies themselves should be specific, and not generic, and neither top-down nor bottom-up but a mixture of both, with a range of stakeholders, such as the public sector, private sector and civil society involved in the process. Policies also must aim to achieve multifaceted aims, and not just focus on economic needs, but also the impact of creative economies on local communities, in areas such as education and cultural identity. UNCTAD's (2010) Creative Economy Report also recommends that action at one particular level should not be prioritised, but community, municipality and national level targeted plans of action are all important. The message for policy-making here is that devising policy must take into account the diverse nature of the creative and cultural industries. There should also be cross-ministerial cooperation in policy development, and engagement with stakeholder groups.

4.5.1 Evidence-Based and Data-Driven Policy and Organisations

One way to account for the diversity of creative and cultural industries in policy development is to better understand the sector. The need for policy to be driven by data on cultural and creative industries is increasingly highlighted (UNCTAD 2010; Lilly and Moore 2013). Sub-sectors of creative industries have specific needs and understanding these can inform more strategic policy (Generator Sverige 2011). Analysis of data on cultural and creative industries allows for policymaking to be informed by real world patterns of development. For example, cultural mapping of data can identify cultural hotspots. These hotspots or 'event enclaves' were identified by Currid and Williams (2010) where clusters of industries are found in similar locations. Evidence like this can also help inform the extent to which particular sectors of creative industries should be the focus of policy.

In their recent provocation, Bakhshi and Cunningham (2016: 4) call for a move away from the 'conflation of culture with creative industries' which they claim has been detrimental to both creative industries and cultural policy in the UK. The propose the production of government statistics that support a better definition of creative industries and the cultural sector. They point to the Australian experience and suggest that official statistics would 'allow both cultural and creative activity to be taken full account of, acknowledging both the substantial overlap between the two areas of activity, as well as dealing as best as possible with well understood challenges that tend to underestimate the extent of cultural activity (for example, the extent of voluntary labour in the cultural sector)'.

Creative and cultural industries in rural and peripheral places are not well understood, but some particular traits have been identified. Characteristics of rural creative business highlighted by Bell and Jayne (2006) include that working from home is a dominant trend. The arts, crafts and antiques sectors are found to have a strong connection with the tourist economy. Cross-sector working within creative industry sectors is more important in some sectors than others, and found to be important in advertising, publishing and architecture. In the Italian context, creative industries are not just found concentrated in urban locations, but for some creative industry sectors, a more complex geography is found. For example, Bertacchini and Borrione (2013) find content and service-based creative industries (e.g. audiovisual, advertising, publishing) are found to concentrate in urban areas, while industrial design and craft-based industries had a more complex geographic distribution pattern, showing a strong presence in traditional centres of craft production, especially in municipalities of the 'Third Italy'. Craft and artisan production is present in many rural European regions, and the challenge for many European countries is to revitalise these rural traditions in the context of creative economy development. Bell and Jayne (2006) also highlight different roles for creative industry sectors in rural areas. Some creative sectors have higher economic value than others, such as advertising, architecture, publishing, TV and radio, while others, such as craft, arts and antiques, are of greater importance symbolically, based in local traditions and culture. Policymakers also face the challenge of balancing social, cultural and economic goals in developing rural and peripheral places, and developing the correct balance of creative industries should then contribute to more sustainable development. Evidence can help guide the direction of creative and cultural industry policy in rural and peripheral places. However, much more work in this area is needed.

There is also more than one role for cultural and creative industry data. It can be used to inform policy, but it can also be used by creative industries and culture organisations themselves as a tool that proves their importance definitively. Lilley and Moore (2013) highlight how 'big data' can improve the accountability of how public funds are used in the arts, showing that funding for the arts is not a subsidy without return, but is an investment. In creative and cultural organisations, better use of data can bring a number of benefits, such as financial, operational, and increase in social impact. Lilley and Moore (2013) call for 'data-driven decision-making', and argue that arts and culture organisations should make being a data-driven organisation a strategic objective of their organisation. It is also argued that data-driven decision-making does not replace human wisdom and experience but enables better decision-making. Using data alongside stakeholder insights can improve human decision-making.

In recent years, the importance of evidence is increasingly recognised. In England, for example, Regional Development Agencies have invested in research to identify clusters and sectors of significance (Taylor 2006). DACL (2012) conducted an analysis of creative industries in Northern Ireland to better understand the dynamics and performance of the sector and to inform policymaking and make informed policy decisions. The UK Department for Culture Media and Sport set up the Creative Industries Task Force and it produced the Creative Industries Mapping Document in 1998 that mapped creative industries around 13 sub-sectors of creative industries. This was the first attempt to map creative industries at the national scale (British Council 2010). This mapping exercise is seen as important in the value of the creative sector becoming recognised in the UK. It progressed understanding of the sector and informed policy. It was particularly useful to creative industries for advocacy as an authoritative statement about the value of creative industries (Taylor 2006). Other countries, for example Australia, have published culture statistics, showing the contribution of culture to the economy

(Australian Bureau of Statistics 2013a). Also in 2013, the Australian Bureau of Statistics published a feasibility study on producing cultural and creative satellite accounts for Australia, to find that a reasonable level and quality of statistics are available to make this possible. The paper also considers how to measure the contribution of culture and creative activity, which would comprise measuring economic activity in industry supply chains, activity in selected occupations outside those supply chains, volunteer services and output supported by charitable contributions. It is also suggested that 'culture' and 'creative' activity should be measured separately (Australian Bureau of Statistics 2013b).

Putting this policymaking tool into practice is easier said than done. It needs collaboration between policy makers, research institutes and industry, as well as programmes of support for such work (Taylor 2006). Developing an evidence base to inform policy is not a simple process. Resources are needed to support work that can produce well-informed research, and accurate and reliable statistics. For example, the German Federal Ministry of Economics and Technology has established the Cultural and Creative Industries Initiative of the Federal Government that has as a monitoring mechanism for reporting on current economic data of the culture and creative industries. There is also a need for a comprehensive approach and for consistency in how data is gathered (Lilley and Moore 2013). This point has significance in national contexts, that an agreed definition of creative and cultural industries is applied by different research institutes involved in producing key evidence and statistics. Internationally agreed definitions, such as at the EU level, would facilitate more cross-national comparison. Also, in the context of UK regional development, Taylor (2006) raises the issue that definitions must meet a range of perspectives on the role of creative industries as an economic development tool. Taylor (2006) argues that more clarity is needed in regional development policy objectives on the relationship between arts and culture and the creative industries, and believes cultural and economic development objectives have become muddled, with potentially creative industries being overly idealised and an over-valuing of the economic value of the arts.

Efforts are increasing to develop common frameworks for culture statistics. UNESCO published its revised framework for cultural statistics in

2009. This is also a concern receiving attention at EU level. The European Statistical System Network on Culture (ESSnet-Culture) working group has been established to revise the existing European framework for culture statistics, to improve on methods currently used to collect culture statistics, and to better encompass the complexity of the cultural sector. Its final report in 2012 makes recommendations and provides practical tools for EU member states. This includes the definition of a list of cultural NACE codes and a ranking of their cultural link and is composed of a list of 29 4-digit classes of the NACE Rev.2. Of these, 22 are entirely cultural in content while 7 are mainly cultural. NACE or Nomenclature des Activités Économiques dans la Communauté Européenne is a pan-European classification system that groups organisations according to their business activities.

4.5.2 Considering Rural and Peripheral Needs for Context-Based Policy

Where creative and cultural industries are located should be considered in policy. Attention to creative and cultural industries has had an urban bias, which has left definitions too narrow and not capturing the complexity and diversity that exists in other contexts (Jayne et al. 2010). For example, research has examined the creativity embedded in rural festivals, suggesting it is less commercially-driven and a more socially-embedded type of creativity. Rural festivals are found to be small, quirky, organised by charities or local committees working with limited resources and relying on volunteers (Gibson et al. 2010). Experts have warned against the application of the same policy measures in rural and peripheral contexts, calling for greater understanding of creative and cultural industries in these contexts (Bell and Jayne 2006; Ström and Nelson 2010). Gibson and Kong (2005: 550) argue that interpretations of the cultural economy have become normative and script like. This 'script' reads as follows: 'Contemporary capitalism is characterised by more recently dominant forms of accumulation, based on flexible production, the commodification of culture and the injection of symbolic "content" into all commodity production. Some places do better than others from this: those that have highly skilled, creative, innovative, adaptive workforces, sophisticated telecommunications infrastructures, interesting and diverse populations, and relatively low levels of government interference in regulating access to markets, as well as lifestyle attractions, restaurants and arts institutions to attract the new "creative class". In order to compete in the new cultural economy, places should seek to implement particular policy initiatives: encourage cultural industry clusters, incubate learning and knowledge economies, maximize networks with other successful places and companies, value and reward innovation, and aggressively campaign to attract the "creative class" as residents.'

Furthermore, Gibson and Kong (2005: 552) warn that there is a danger that can emerge from this, that the complexities of place, and the knowledge of local actors is not integrated in policy development: 'An obvious danger in the emerging model of academic-knowledge to policy traffic is one of assuming singular "recipes" for success in transforming places, based on the advice of experts and advisors not well enough grounded in places to account for the more complex and contested geographies they contain.' More holistic models of policy development are needed to design policy in tune with the needs of peripheral rural places. Collaborative policymaking, such as demonstrated by the ERIBA model (discussed further below), is one potentially fruitful approach. Fuller appreciation of the assets available in peripheral places is also needed. For example, in the urban context, Throsby (2010: 133) argues that cities can be understood as a collection of capital assets, physical assets (buildings, economic infrastructure), natural capital (natural resources and ecosystems), human capital (skills, capacities of inhabitants) and cultural capital (tangible and intangible cultural assets). In this context, urban development projects can make a number of interventions in these categories, to create new assets, to improve efficiency of existing assets or to restore, recycle or reuse old assets. Understanding rural and peripheral places in this way could also help devise policy that works from available resources. While there is potential for developing creative and cultural industries in peripheral places, they also face challenges. Identifying these, and ways to reduce their impact, is an important issue for better policy development for creative and cultural industries.

One issue for creative and cultural industries in peripheral places is that their culture and creativity is not well understood and is perhaps blemished by stereotypes, while many cities have a more positive creative image. The distinctiveness of creative and cultural industries in cities has been described as being made up of a diversity of culturally-rich districts and clusters of creative industries that exude a buzz and energy. This all makes for more attractive cities. Strong arts and culture in cities is said to improve their attractiveness, making them more inviting places to live or visit. Festivals, cultural events and cultural facilities, such as a significant museum or cultural symbols including significant buildings or structures, can contribute to making places more attractive. Creative and cultural industries in peripheral and rural places also have their own distinctive traits, but have not received as much focus as the urban creative and cultural tale. Rural creative economies also have a story to tell, but this can be overshadowed by stereotypes of rurality. An Arts Council of England (2005) report highlights the need to move beyond outdated impressions of what is rural, to acknowledge the diversity of the arts in rural areas, and also to recognise this by building policy that specifically supports rural needs (Ibid 2005). Rural creativity has been characterised as diverse, quirky, specialist and authentic. Cultural policy recommendations for rural areas in Finland recommend developing rural areas on the basis of diversity, and as a 'countryside of creative contrasts' (Cultural Theme Group of Rural Policy Committee 2011). Therefore an important part of developing cultural and creative industries in rural and peripheral places is to work to change perceptions of these places (Bell and Jayne 2006). The strong creative image of urban places, and negative associations with peripheral places can draw creative talents away from the periphery and towards the city. Part of the challenge for peripheral places is to recreate themselves. Festivals can be one tool to contribute to this.

In Gibson et al. (2010) assessment of the nature of rural creativity, they argue rural festivals should gain more attention from regional development policy makers. They observe the breath and diversity of festivals in rural areas, including sporting, agricultural, music and arts festivals. Festivals can be part of coordinated regional development strategies, but were most often non-commercial and rooted in the community, and not about producing material goods. While non-commercial, they still generate significant income for rural places. An important point observed is that this form of creativity differs from creative industry policy research that can focus on attracting creative industries to places, but this form of creativity is said to focus on producing an authentic cultural experience. Festivals are touted as an example of a potential joined-up policy initiative for rural areas, where connections between the food, tourism and creative industries can be jointly promoted (Bell and Jayne 2006). They also increase the visibility of creativity, which is an important factor in the perception of the vibrancy of places (Bennett 2010). Constructed correctly, their value can extend beyond festival days (Curtis 2010).

Peripheral places also face a number of other specific challenges to overcome to develop their creative and cultural industries (Andersen 2010; Bennett 2010; McGranahan and Wojan 2007). They need to retain and attract creative talents to live and work in them. High youth out-migration is a challenge as young people move away to gain education or employment, and creative workers can be lured to big cities because of the vibe they emulate. Remoteness itself is also an issue and the physical distance from cities and events. The time and cost of travelling to the periphery also adds a difficulty in attracting people, and selling products and services from the periphery. Other disadvantages include a lack of funding sources, low consumer spending power in local markets, a lack of critical mass of skilled professional people to network with in the locality, and limited paid work opportunities to sustain a living (Andersen 2010). These are a diverse range of issues and some more challenging to overcome than others. However, some of the attributes of peripheral places that can be a disadvantage, such as remoteness, can be reconstructed as an attractive attribute of peripheral places. Creative workers can be lured to peripheral places, their rural areas, small towns and cities because of their attributes, such as offering a quieter, slower pace of life, where there is a sense of peace, tranquility, solitude and freedom. This different pace of life is described as offering a better quality of life, where its slower pace brings fewer stresses and accessibility to natural landscapes for recreation and inspiration. Marginality can be negotiated and overcome to some degree, and remoteness and marginality can become part of the attractiveness of place. Peripheral places have been described as offering a distinct, quirky experience, and an alternative to the fast-changing fashions and trends that can be a factor in more urbanised creativity. Creative and cultural industries in rural and marginal areas are identified as less commercially-driven, with greater connections to community and a greater focus on social goals. Locating in the periphery can also bring economic benefits such as cheaper office and studio rents and, general, a lower cost of living (Gibson 2010; Andersen 2010; McGranahan and Wojan 2007).

Evidence also suggests that care is needed not to overvalue the potential of developing strong creative and cultural industries in peripheral areas (Petridou and Ioannides 2012). They are not a panacea for economic development issues in peripheral places and strategies aiming to develop strong creative and cultural industries may not be suited to all parts of peripheral places. Argent et al. (2013) caution that rural development strategies may overemphasise the role of creative workers in economic development, but do acknowledge they are an important component of rural revitalisation, in that their presence is important as innovative, entrepreneurial people, creating less tangible social and cultural benefits. Their research finds that the presence of creative workers does impact on business growth, however it does not have a substantial effect, and is comparable to other sectors. However places differ, and research in rural USA by McGranahan and Wojan (2007) shows that the presence of the creative class did have a positive effect on employment growth. Importantly, however this research also makes other important distinctions. It is also suggested that not all rural areas will be attractive to creative workers. Attractive rural places should have particular traits, such as adequate services, natural amenities, attractive landscapes and outdoor recreation opportunities. Other attributes particular to this area of study highlighted are a rich cultural heritage, an active arts community and local norms that do not impose conformity and restrict creativity. The research also makes other useful observations. The rural creative class is attracted to more densely populated rural counties. Compared to the urban creative class, this rural creative class is found to be older and, more often, to be married (McGranahan and Wojan 2007). Moreover, Argent et al. (2013) also argue a certain critical mass of economic, social and cultural activity is needed to attract the creative worker. They are drawn to the more attractive rural places, and not just any rural place. Peripheral places focussing development around culture and creativity should have specific natural, physical and cultural capital, or make increasing this capital a central part of the development strategy for peripheral places.

4.6 Policy Approaches

Approaches to creative and cultural industry policy development and policy initiatives that work to overcome challenges and issues raised are the focus of this section. We aim to provide a set of tools for policy development geared towards addressing the general deficiencies in policy, as well as being focussed on the particular needs of peripheral places.

4.6.1 Working to Overcome the Challenges of a Diverse Industry – Policy Process

The need for collaboration between policy makers and stakeholders in culture, industry and education to develop effective policy is a central consideration highlighted earlier in this chapter. This makes policymaking challenging, with different agendas to consider. However, the design of the policy process can help address these issues for effective policy development. Collaboration is an important part of the policy development process, but can also inform industry development (see Fig. 4.1).

Emerging from the Knowledge Foundation in Sweden, the FUNK policy model is designed around collaboration to address the diversity of agendas raised by creative and cultural industries. The 'FUNK' policy model promotes collaboration between research (F), education (U), private sector (N) and culture (K). The aim is that collaboration occurs between these actors, applied in sectors of the 'experience economy' to facilitate their growth. The policy model is designed to be applicable at both national and local levels, to the experience economy as a whole, or specific sectors. The process of collaboration between the FUNK players is intended to develop strategies help overcome some of the challenges faced by the diverse creative industries, that is composed of micro-businesses and multinationals, new and established businesses and the need to internationalise for growth. Collaboration as part of the FUNK model involves both developing policy strategies and also more concrete collaboration (Knowledge Foundation 2008).

The ERIBA model emerged from adaptation of the FUNK model. It was applied in Hultsfred in Sweden to develop business activities around an annual rock festival, and found to be successful in this case. Based on the Hultsfred case study, the ERIBA or E (Education and training), R (Research), I (Industry), B (Business), A (Arts/Culture), model emerged, with focus on creative industries, rather than the experience economy. The central emphasis again is on collaboration between these key elements to identify needs, pinpoint measures to address them and implement the measures in collaboration between all players. Measures developed are focused on each of the ERIBA areas in order to stimulate economic growth. It is also noted that this is not a completely new concept, but is likened to the 'quadro helix' concept where there is interaction between industry, the public sector, academia and the arts in policy development (Nielsén 2008). In 2007, the ERIBA model was applied in seven Swedish locations, focussing on places where a particular industry had the strongest supports. The result was seven industry-specific growth proposals. While each sector had its differences, there were also similarities, and the proposals were merged to form a national strategic plan summarised in ten focus areas that form a common foundation for collaboration in creative industries (Nielsen 2008) (Box 4.1).

Box 4.1 Collaboration between creative industries

DinoLab

Collaboration between groups such as industry and academia can also go beyond the policy formulation process. DinoLab or Digitala Idéplatser Norr is a Swedish initiative that aims to strengthen the audiovisual industry in northern Sweden. It aims to increase opportunities for creative entrepreneurship and businesses, develop new knowledge and high-level competences, support academic research, and develop of new technology as well as new combinations of technology. A number of academic researchers work on the project from Umeå University and the Skellefteå Campus of the Luleå University of Technology. DinoLab operates an 'ideas forum' where the public are invited to submit ideas for DinoLab to consider developing as projects. It supports workshops for the audiovisual industry and has implemented a number of projects to support the industry in northern Sweden. Among these is the piloting of a prototype called 'The Creature', an experimental concept for gaining instant feedback from audiences, and increasing engagement between the speaker and audiences at events, through screen-based devices, such as smartphones and tablets.

www.dinoprojektet.se

4.6.2 Supporting Creativity and Culture by Creating an Enabling Environment

One theme among the general policy needs identified earlier in this chapter is creating the correct kind of environment for creativity to flourish in society. This includes facilitating entrepreneurship, innovation and creativity. There is a danger in developing creative industries that too much focus is placed on the commercial, enterprise side of creative industries, at the expense of culture (Generator Generator Sverige 2011). Pratt (2004) also identifies a tension between the broad cultural sector and creative industries. The cultural sector is described as traditionally having a not-for-profit focus, placing cultural products before profit. However creative industries have a different starting point: they aim to profit from their creativity, and profit and creativity go hand in hand. There is a debate that if there is too much of a focus on commodities, assets and profit in cultural and creative industries, this will have a negative impact on the arts from the perspective of artistic creation and authenticity. The challenge is for the cultural and creative industries, to innovate and retain authenticity, without overcapitalising on creativity at the expense of authenticity (Pratt 2004; Oakley 2009). What is termed 'culture-based creativity', to think imaginatively and laterally, to challenge and break conventions, has been described as an essential feature of the post-industrial economy. And for it to emerge, the correct environment must be created (European Commission 2009). Initiatives such as Arts in Action at the National University of Ireland, Galway, that help to promote arts and culture among students, can contribute to this. Another initiative that supports a creative society and economy is Fab Labs, which promote creativity with a focus on innovation and entrepreneurship (see Box 4.2). Culture underpins the creative industries, and retaining a central focus on harnessing and promoting culture and creativity in wider society is also an important focus for creative and cultural industry policy. And while challenging to maintain, it is the strength on which the industry rests.

Box 4.2 Initiatives supporting creativity and culture

Arts in Action

Arts in Action is a creative arts programme run by the College of Arts, Social Sciences and Celtic Studies at the National University of Ireland, Galway (NUIG). The programme aims to promote a greater awareness of the performing arts among students and increase their engagement with them. It includes a practice-based class, 'Exploring the Indigenous Arts', for US visiting students to NUIG exploring Irish music, song and dance. Arts in Action also organises a series of performances throughout the academic year featuring music, dance, drama and poetry readings. This includes a free lunchtime concert series open to all members of the NUIG community. This removes the cost barrier to arts engagement. The programme also helps to promote the rich arts and cultural heritage in the west of Ireland. The 2013–2014 Arts in Action performance programme focusses on young, emerging performers and legends of traditional Irish music. The focus is also on performers from the west of Ireland, such as from counties Sligo, Donegal, Leitrim, Mayo and Galway.
www.nuigalway.ie/artsinaction

Fab Labs

A Fab Lab or fabrication laboratory is a community space that helps people turn creative ideas into real products. Professor Neil Gershenfeld at Massachusetts Institute of Technology first developed the idea. Fab Labs aim to provide the environment, skills and technology to enable people to experiment and innovate, thereby encouraging entrepreneurship and creativity. They also have an educational role by providing training. Innovative products that have emerged with the help of Fab Labs include a tracking system for sheep with the use of mobile phones in Norway, and a truck refrigeration system powered by the vehicles exhaust in Ghana. There is a global network of 150 Fab Labs, two of which are in Northern Ireland, in Belfast's Ashton Centre and Derry's Nerve Centre. Equipment includes open-source design software and a selection of computer-controlled machines, such as 3D printers, laser cutters and milling machines. Commercial projects can also make used of Fab Labs, but eventually move beyond the Fab Lab space (Fab Labs NI 2013). Fab Labs don't just benefit creativity in the community, but are also a resource for creative industries.

Craft Northern Ireland has collaborated with Northern Ireland Fab Labs to offer craft businesses a digital design and fabrication training programme (Craft Northern Ireland 2013).

www.fabfoundation.org
http://fab.cba.mit.edu/
www.fablabni.com

4.6.3 Working Together Nationally and Cross-Nationally

An important part of support for creative businesses is facilitating their networking and cooperation. In the context of peripheral areas and creative and cultural industries, this has been highlighted as particularly important. For example, Petridou and Ioannides (2012) argue that fostering culture and creativity are valuable regional development tools, but also that in peripheral contexts, limited resources make cooperation a necessity to effectively capitalise on the potential of creative and cultural industries. Cooperation can occur between individuals from the same sector, for example artist's cooperatives. Bottom-up, creative and cultural industry-led cooperation is said to be especially important in peripheral areas. Cooperation at different levels across different creative and cultural industry sectors and between regional and local governance bodies is also important.

Examples of such cooperation in peripheral places include the Lodge, a network of internet, film and game companies based in the northern Swedish city of Skellefteå in Västerbotten county. The network includes companies such as North Kingdom, Hello Future, Dreamfield and Arrowhead Game Studio. The companies have worked together on international projects with big name companies such as Adidas, Disney and Toyota. The Lodge does not just collaborate commercially, but also acts as a representative organisation for creative industries in the area (Västerbotten Investment Agency 2013).

International cooperation not only opens up the potential for development of new knowledge and business collaboration networks, but also potentially greater access to export markets, as cross-national cooperation between Nordic counties has demonstrated. Internationalisation and export strategies of cultural and creative industries in EU member states differ in their levels of engagement with export and internationalisation.

The engagement of Nordic agencies with each other to create a regional Nordic 'brand' to promote the growth of cultural and creative industries and move into international export markets, is cited as an example of a good regional policy and the benefits of working across national boundaries (Mercer and Staines 2013). Different examples of international collaboration in creative industries are discussed in Box 4.3.

Research has pointed to the need for new business models to facilitate different kinds of relationships between creative businesses (European Commission 2010; ENCATC 2013). Cooperatives and social enterprises can play a part, but newer and more dynamic business models are also important. In the context of culture organisations, the European Network on Arts-Cultural Management and Cultural Policy Education (ENCATC) (2013) point to models such as the cellular model where an organisation is governed by series of 'cells' or task forces, and the network model where there is cross-organisational collaboration, both public and private. Business models that involve creative businesses in different parts of the production chain also could enable creative industries to capture more of the economic value created by their products (European Commission 2010). In the context of technological evolution and digitisation, new business models are needed in many creative industries most affected by the digital world (Skantze and Pihlgren 2012). E-commerce and online social media communities also offer an opportunity for peripheral creative businesses as marginality is less of a challenge in building networks and connecting with distant markets online.

Box 4.3 Initiatives to promote working together nationally and cross nationally

Kilkenny Design Workshops

To reflect on a historical example, Kilkenny Design Workshops Ltd (KDW) helped develop the Irish craft and design industry. KDW was an Irish government-owned industrial design consultancy, and the first organisation of this type set up by a government. It was established in 1963 and abolished in 1988. Set up in response to the findings of the 1961 Scandinavian report on Irish design, it also shows the value of international expertise to offer insight on national problems. The legacy of the KDW is considered to exist to the present day, with its influence still felt in Irish craft practice and design culture. Deliberate emphasis was placed on craft-based industries during the formative years of KDW, seen to be where innovation starts,with traditional craft products where the cultural characteristics of a country can emerge. Reviving traditional craft skills, increasing awareness of the importance of design and designers were aims of the consultancy. The focus was on craft, which was considered the area where public engagement with design and designers could most easily occur, thereby increasing public awareness. It focussed on education, upholding good standards and innovation in design and promoted international export development (Marchant and Addis 1985).

FilmArc

An international network across parts of northern Finland, Norway and Sweden, FilmArc works to strengthen the audiovisual sector in these regions. The network has built up a considerable base, with over 300 businesses and 400 freelancers now part of the network. The key goal of the FilmArc network is to help audiovisual creative businesses to develop and internationalise. It directly supports businesses by providing funding for up to half of the costs of, for example, contracting an expert consultant, developing marketing materials, translating a script, running a pilot project, or attending a conference, festival or professional training course. It runs a series of educational workshops and master-classes, which have been led by some of the most successful and talented people in the Scandinavian and European film and TV business. The network is made possible by the cooperation of film organisations in the regions, such as FilmCamp in Norway, the POEM Foundation in Finland, Filmpool Nord and Film i Västerbotten in Sweden (FilmArc 2013).

http://filmarc.net/

KreaNord

Coordinated by the Nordic Council of Ministers, KreaNord is an example of an international cooperative effort across the Nordic region. It aims to support the Nordic region to become one of the leading regions of the global creative economy through engaging government, industry and experts in developing the creative economy. Countries collaborating in KreaNord are Sweden, Norway, Iceland, Finland, Denmark and the Faroe Islands. Among its initiatives is a grants programme that supports projects with an international focus, commercial potential, thereby aiming to increase the competitiveness of the Nordic creative industries. It funds specific projects such as the Nordic Game Programme that facilitates children and young people access Nordic computer games and the Creative Business Cup, a global competition for creative business entrepreneurs. KreaNord also operates an investor network that assists creative industries to access capital (KreaNord 2011).

www.kreanord.org
www.kreanordinvestors.org

MyCreativeEdge

MyCreativeEdge is a website developed through the Creative Edge project that provides creative industry businesses, freelancers and jobseekers, in all the Creative Edge partner regions the opportunity to showcase their work at no cost. MyCreativeEdge also provides an avenue for consumers and businesses to explore creative products and creative suppliers from across Europe's northern edge. The sectors showcased on the site include advertising and publishing, architecture, arts, crafts, design, digital media, fashion and jewellery, film and video, music and theatre, photography, software and gaming and TV and radio. Creative business and freelancer members of MyCreativeEdge each have their own profile page in the 'Creative Showcase' section of the site. The 'Employ a Creative' section allows young creative talents to promote their skills to potential employers. There is also a members' area, the MyCreativeEdge Forum, providing networking opportunities, opening national and international links between creative businesses.

www.mycreativeedge.eu
www.creative-edge.eu

4.6.4 Promoting the Periphery as an Attractive Place

Challenges identified as inhibiting the development of creative and cultural industries in peripheral places are the image and associations made with the periphery, and the migration of creative workers to cities. However, working directly on these issues as policy concerns could help overcome problems they create. Some policy initiatives are identified in Box 4.4. The rise of cultural and creative industries in rural areas has been linked with a broader trend towards a desire for a counter-urban lifestyle. The periphery also has its advantages, and it can be directly promoted as an attractive place. For example, Gibson and Kong (2005) link the growth of visual arts in Broken Hill, a remote part of Australia, to its landscape and cheap housing rents that artists with unstable incomes could afford to rent. In developing the creative economy, a central challenge for the peripheral place is to retain a greater proportion of its creative talent, and also attract creative talent (Bennett 2010; Argent et al. 2013). Bennett (2010) identifies that migration of creative artists (focussing on music, visual arts and film) is driven by push and pull factors. Push factors include lack of opportunity to sustain a full-time career, and isolation in their profession. Pull factors attracting creative artists away from peripheral places include more established industries and clusters in other places. However, migration also has its drawbacks. It is financially risky if employment is not secured before moving, and networks must be built up, which are vitally important to securing work as a creative artist. Networks, both personal and professional, are also left behind. Migration can be an option taken out of necessity and not choice. Push factors can be also be negated to a certain extent. For example, Bennett (2010) highlights how smaller markets can provide a means for early career creative entrepreneurs to connect with their professional fields. It is also argued that those who have migrated should be facilitated to stay connected with where they migrated from, as their success can contribute to how their home-place is perceived. The use of virtual networks can connect creative talents in a local area with national and international networks of creative talents who have migrated. This can re-frame such migration more positively and facilitate those people to remain involved as 'active agents in the cultural life and image of our cities and regions' (Bennett 2010: 126). Focussing on place can play more than one role in development strategies for creative industries. Aspects of place can also be used as a promotional tool for creative products. For example, Andersen (2010) highlights how creative artists from Sweden, Australia and the USA use aspects of place, landscape, culture, tradition and their marginality, that are all rooted in place to inform their products, and market them to consumers.

Box 4.4 Snow Castle of Kemi

A strong cultural infrastructure, such as culturally iconic buildings, museums and theatres add to the attractiveness of place. One innovative building that is climatically and culturally linked to place is the Snow Castle of Kemi in the Kemi-Tornio region of northern Finland. It also features a Snow Chapel where events such as weddings and christenings can be held. It represents architectural skill in how it uses snow as a building material. Creativity and imagination like this can increase the attractiveness of peripheral places.

http://www.visitkemi.fi/en/snowcastle

goNORTH

Festivals can positively impact the cultural perception of a place, such as arts, music and literary festivals. But creative industry-focussed festivals also have potential in peripheral places. GoNORTH is Scotland's creative industry festival, held in its most northerly city, Inverness, and free to attend. The festival runs workshops for creative industry professionals, film screenings and a creative industry showcase. Other peripheral places also have the potential to showcase and celebrate their creative industries in a similar way.

http://gonorthfestival.co.uk/

Creative Hubs

Vacant buildings in towns and villages can be turned into a resource when innovative thinking is applied. The Creative Hub concept puts life back into vacant buildings by facilitating creative businesses to access unused commercial premises on a non-profit basis. This provides businesses with access to premises at a low cost and also enriches towns and villages putting life back into their streets. Craigavon Borough Council, member of South East Economic Development in Northern Ireland developed a number of Creative Hubs in Northern Ireland through the Creative Edge project. To facilitate the development of Creative Hubs, public meetings were held in Northern Ireland to engage with interested stakeholders, such as potential landlords and creative business tenants. The first of the Creative Hubs to launch was the Lurgan Creative Hub that began in March 2013. Three more Creative Hubs at Armagh, Banbridge and Newry have also been developed through the Creative Edge project. A model to facilitate replication of the Creative Hub concept in other places is also being developed by Craigavon Borough Council, available through the Creative Edge website.

www.creative-edge.eu

Look West

Place promotion is not a novel idea and an initiative of the Western Development Commission in Ireland, Look West, promotes the western region of Ireland as a place to live, work and do business. Less stress, lower cost of living, a better quality of life, a wealth of leisure activities and low pupil to teacher ratios are highlighted as benefits of living in the west of Ireland. As a place to set up a business or develop a career, the west is touted as being easily accessible, having a variety of business supports and strong business sectors such as life sciences, engineering and green energy. Look West operates a company directory of businesses in the western region and a skills register, collecting information on the skills and education of people interested in moving west. The initiative launched in 2004 and interest is growing with traffic on its website increasing year-on-year (Western Development Commission 2013). Similar initiatives have potential to focus on the periphery as a creative place to live and set up a creative business.

www.lookwest.ie

The Donegal Diaspora project

Reaching out to a global community with a connection, or interest in, county Donegal in the western region of Ireland is the aim of the Donegal Diaspora project. The project also has development goals, aiming to encourage inward investment. The network of people is also viewed as a resource that can be tapped into to develop skills and knowledge in the county to support its social, economic and cultural development. Similar initiatives linking creative talents who have migrated, back to their home-place could also benefit the cultural and creative image attached to the periphery.

www.donegaldiaspora.ie

4.6.5 Capturing the Spillover Potential of Creative and Cultural Industries

Cultural industries are systematically related, and growth in one sector within this industry can lead to growth in others, for example furniture production and design (Power 2002). In the Swedish rural context, and based on the experience of the furniture industry, a growth pattern has been observed, where growth occurs around a single large firm or a cluster of firms. Diversity in rural cultural industries is also observed, and this is seen as a positive part of how cultural industries should be structured in rural areas: 'Diversity and small scale may not produce global brand names like IKEA, a more generalised spread of activities and organisational forms may be beneficial to rural/remote areas by supporting a healthy tourist industry' (Power 2002: 119). The presence of creative industries in less urbanised and rural areas is therefore potentially more important than their actual presence immediately represents. It can lead to spin-off developments in other sub-sectors of creative industries, and wider industry sectors. Box 4.5 outlines one example of how wider economic benefits can be captured from integrating artisan craft and tourism.

Box 4.5 Capturing the connection between craft and tourism

Économusée

Économusée can facilitate capturing the tourism potential from the presence of craftspeople in peripheral places. It supports rural enterprise development by facilitating artisan craft businesses to develop infrastructure allowing them to serve the tourist market, offering direct experience of local culture and produce (Heanue, McIntyre & Heneghan). The Économusée concept was first developed in Québec, Canada to help artisan businesses capitalise on their cultural tourism potential. Artisan businesses use traditional techniques and therefore can be understood as a living, working museum. Économusée have an exhibition and gallery space where artefacts and information on the history and contemporary application of the artisan craft are displayed. Central to the Économusée concept is that the artisan craft maker can be observed at work in the workshop space where demonstrations of craft in practice are carried out. The term Économusée is protected by copyright and businesses must meet eligibility criteria and go through four-stage approval process before they can used the term to promote their business.

www.economusee.eu

4.7 Research Agenda

This work calls for a greater recognition of the prevalence of the creative economy outside of the major cities. It does so by contending that it exists as a different entity to its urban counterpart. We recognise that changing consumption patterns are bringing with them a greater demand for goods and services endowed with experiential values. The values that are produced in the periphery are different to those in the urban, they have a different relationship with their place and evidence higher social and authenticity traits imbued in the cultural output of the periphery. As such we are calling for a better understanding of how culture and goods more general are consumed. Price competition will always be telling in the market but the profusion of non tangible traits, those that contain less quantifiable characteristics are the ones that warrant closer attention. Therefore more attention needs to be paid to how these are changing our patterns of consumption. This is not just a focus on the role of cultural consumption, rather it requires a broader understanding of how all consumption is becoming increasingly cultural.

How creative industries exist in peripheral areas requires more attention. We now have an understanding of the main barriers that these endeavours face, they do not differ drastically from other industrial sectors located in similar settings, but they are unique in their relationship with their place. We can understand that many peripheral creative industries exist in place by accident of geography (founders grew up in the area, etc.) but more research is required on those that are spatially embedded in their place through inspiration (landscape, the allure of the rural) and those that embedded in their place via network anchoring (see Collins and Grimes 2008) whereby they existence of similar industries (within and without of the same subsector) is dependent on their mutual relationships (increased co-dependence via collaboration). This is an area of particular interest in how it goes against the orthodox model of business location in an era of globalisation.

Much is known about the problems that peripheral locations bring (access to market, poor infrastructure etc.) but more needs to be understood about how the peripheral can be leveraged for competitive advantage. Often dismissed as 'one offs', through a number of case studies contained in this volume we can see a degree of commonality in the traits of successful creative enterprises. Primary amongst these are their ability to hop scales. By this we mean that they can remain local while succeeding in the global. This is a key factor of success and can be seen across the creative spectrum from visual art and theatre to app development and graphic design. In an age of mass production and standardisation, these important facets enable companies and their produce to stand out and gain a better market share. Cases of using the periphery to demarcate themselves, using the periphery to inspire a fresher view (artistically or entrepreneurially) needs to be highlighted and better understood.

Location is where lines intersect on a map, but place is something that is much more complex. In an effort to better understand the place inhabited by the peripherally located creatives we have tried to gain a better understanding of their supporting ecosystem. Our attempts to map the cultural infrastructure of these regions in one small step towards a much bigger undertaking involving a true understanding of the necessary ecosystem in place to support creative endeavour. We would recommend a robust and complete mapping of all traits of the creative economy/activity evidenced in place. An effort to do such would lend a much better understanding to the key impediment and enablers of success within the region. This is an exercise that can be carried out across all regions (urban and peripheral) in order to gain a better understanding of a new economy that is becoming increasingly important.

In our final chapter we went some of the way to better elucidating how creative businesses carry out their work. More work needs to be done on the different types of business models that creative industries use. Questions need to be answered on what approach best suits which circumstance. Our highlighting of the importance of collaborative approaches is something that also requires further investigation. We understand the need for businesses in more remote areas to collaborate with each other to ensure a better outcome for all (sharing transport costs, utilities, etc.) but we have witnessed something different in the creative sector. We need a better understanding of whether the kinds of practices, co-production, competitors working together or deliver on a product are unique or are they an evolution in the general approach to conducting business.

This book hopes to add to the growing debate on the importance of the creative economy to peripheral areas. It does so by highlighting a number of interesting case studies that point to interesting trends that could have relevance far beyond the boundaries of the creative economy.

4.8 Conclusion

Cultural and creative industry policy is a diverse area, and responsibility for action can be unclear. But this is not an optional policy agenda, it is one that all places can benefit from developing. One message for policy makers is that devising policy must take into account the diverse nature of the creative and cultural industries and engage cross-ministerial cooperation and stakeholder engagement throughout the policy process.

In addition, the need for a shift in the scale of policymaking in creative and cultural industries is a theme emerging from research. Cities have received much attention, and there is a need for shift in focus towards developing other perspectives, such as rural and peripheral agendas.

We have focussed on the peripheral perspective, and found that creative and cultural industry polices can help support the development of the creative economy in peripheral places in a number of ways. The wider policy context on national levels sets up the broad framework for how the creative economy is supported in peripheral places. The best approach should create the correct preconditions, enable culture and creativity to develop, support existing and emerging businesses and harness the spillover effects for the wider society and economy. In addition, from the peripheral perspective, working together nationally and cross-nationally, as well as promoting the periphery as an attractive place, are important considerations for policy. Central to future policy development should remain that local actors and local knowledge is utilised in the policy development process at regional and local levels.

In this book we have set out to analyse the current state of the creative industry in peripheral regions by focussing on four regions in the north-western periphery of Europe. Through an analysis of evolving patterns of consumption as well as an appreciation of different ways of producing we have made the case that the creative economy is unique relative to others, and that the creative economy of peripheral regions is unique relative to its urban counterpart. Though a broad summation is not really apt for this section, we hope to conclude by reiterating the uniqueness of peripheral locations for creative and cultural production.

Ultimately, the accounting methods used by the vast majority of state agencies do a disservice to the burgeoning creative economy. Place differentiation must move beyond the traditional socio-economic or industrial base indicators to truly understand how and why certain places succeed where others fail. In understanding the birth of a new (creative/cultural) socio-economic paradigm, traditional variables come up short. Here we have gone some of the way by trying to tie the provision of cultural infrastructure to the prevalence of creative activity. Poets and writers have long tried to capture the distinctiveness of places, their spirit or personality, making use of more scientific thinking, Alfred Marshall speaks of 'industrial atmosphere', but we believe that the true culture of a place, it's depth and its potential can be pointed to by a more imaginative use of statistical fact. Thus we see the fact that a strong network of local theatres existing in the west of Ireland has much to say about the region's relative international success in theatrical production. We contend that these 'softer factors' can be grasped by more novel accounting methods (numbers of YouTube uploaders, rates of prosumption, rates of sharing etc.).

We know that this has broader implications beyond the creative economy to the affect the social and economic wealth of places more generally. In an increasingly globalised world, competing on harder factors, tax rates, educational attainment etc., while important can also lead to a race to the bottom. The softer factors are those that are much harder to emulate, those are the ones upon which regions, even, if not especially, peripheral ones can compete. In a similar way, it is the unique geography of a place, one that is steeped in those soft factors that determines its cultural produce. Geographic cultural self-selection builds market for a particular type of good. Locality constrains through prior accumulations of physical and cultural infrastructure. Be this the family design craft of Northern Swedish Sammi people or the Arann jumpers of the west of Ireland, a history of consumption and a recognition of quality ensures better produce demanded beyond the region in the more globalised world.

Cultural attractiveness in the face of the place homogenising tendencies of globalisation forces is key to the potential of peripheral places and their produce. The cultural infrastructure of a place is not just important for attracting greater tourist revenues but for forming the basis of more robust, place based creative industries. We know that the history of art is a regional story, be that the Bauhaus movement or Irish literature. What regions need to concern themselves with is how their cultural infrastructure can create a regional style. So the productions chosen by local theatres, or the courses offered by local educational institutions play a role in the development of this. Support of this is identity forming and aides in the process of place making; key facets for sustaining creative activity in peripheral places.

The economic geography of the modern world is a story of how products have become ingrained in their place. This story is most easily recognised through consumer products from the technologies of Silicon Valley to the fashion of Milan. These products rely how their expressive, the material and the organisational elements connect to their place. This is part of the real policy gap that exists in legislating for the more culturally imbued products and services of our time. The soft infrastructure, the atmosphere, the taboo and traditional character of places determine success in cultural production. In this book we have set out to start to set the gaze of policy makers more in this direction in supporting the creative development of the periphery.

While being mindful of the fact that the presence of creative industries in a peripheral region will not act as the immediate solution to entrenched problems of the periphery, we argue that a broader recognition of their potential is necessary. We recognise this through the coincidence of new patterns of cultural consumption of innate traits of more rural regions. These can be surmised is the terms above or recognised as simply the presence of authentic in an increasingly inauthentic world. The provision of correct infrastructure to support the creative economy does more than encourage the development of new industries. As noted above, the key building blocks for creative sectors are also key factors in ensuring the attractiveness of places. What is necessary for all agents of local development to acknowledge is the changing nature of attractiveness. What we have learned throughout this study is that the place attractiveness and policies promoting place attractiveness from tax incentives to subsidised rents for industry, have, in general, looked at the issue from the wrong perspective, that of commercial concerns. This is of course part of the wider neoliberal experiment that sees economic development as the first stepping stone in place development. We argue that this is an approach that was apt for a bygone (industrial) era. What we see is that making places attractive to people is the first step that needs to be taken in place development. This is the new reality that policy needs to better understand: businesses follow people, and people go where it is most attractive. The story of San Francisco and its oft cited liveability might seem a far remove from that of peripheral European regions looking to sustain themselves. We would argue that the conditions for success of that world city and the development of the neighbouring Silicon Valley provide key lessons. San Francisco provides the cultural infrastructure and the attractiveness that brings the talent that sustains Silicon Valley. That is why companies chose to set up there. It is the fundamental part of the 'atmosphere' or the milieu that has been referred to by many of the leading business thinkers. These are the factors that peripheral regions, those for which the homogenising forces of liberalisation has yet to reach, need to focus on to ensure their own future sustainability.

Bibliography

Amit, R., and C. Zott. 2001. Value creation in e-business. *Strategic Management Journal* 22(6–7): 493–520.

Amsellem, R. 2013. International touring exhibitions: Toward a profitable business model for exhibitions? *The Journal of Arts Management, Law and Society* 43(1): 36–57.

Andersen, L. 2010. Magic light, silver city: The business of culture in Broken Hill. *Australian Geographer* 41(1): 71–85.

Argent, N., M. Tonts, R. Jones, and J. Holmes. 2013. A creativity-led rural renaissance? Amenity-led migration, the creative turn and the uneven development of rural Australia. *Applied Geography* 44: 88–98.

Arts Action Research. 2012. *The emerging narratives in the arts: A special report from arts action research*. New York: Arts Action Research.

Arts Council England. 2005. Arts Council England and communities living in rural England–a position statement. Available at http://www.artscouncil.org.uk/sites/default/files/download-file/Position_statement-The_Arts_Council_and_communities_living_in_rural_England_April_14.pdf

Australian Bureau of Statistics. 2013. Australian National Accounts: Cultural and Creative Activity Satellite Accounts. Available at http://www.abs.gov.au/AusStats/ABS@.nsf/MF/5271.0

Australian Bureau of Statistics. 2013a. The economic contribution of culture. Available at: http://www.abs.gov.au/ ausstats/abs@.nsf/latestProducts/5271.0.55.001Media%20 Release12013 (Accessed 10 September 2013).

Australian Bureau of Statistics. 2013b. Discussion paper: cultural and creative Activity Satellite Accounts, Australia. Available at: http://www.abs.gov.au/ausstats/abs@.nsf/ mf/5271.0.55.001 (Accesses 10 october 2013).

Ayoama, U., and I. Izushi. 2003. Hardware gimmick or cultural innovation? Technological, cultural, and social foundations of the Japanese video game industry. *Research Policy* 32(3): 423–44.

Baden-Fuller, C., and V. Mangematin. 2013. Business models: A challenging agenda. *Strategic Organization* 11(4): 418–27.

Bakhshi, H., and S Cunningham. 2016. *Cultural policy in the time of the creative industries*. London: Nesta.

Bell, D., and Jayne, M. 2004. *Afterword: Thinking in quarters*. City of quarters: Urban villages in the contemporary city, 249–256.

Bell, D., and M. Jayne. 2006. *Small cities: Urban experience beyond the metropolis*. London: Routledge.

Bennett, D. 2010. *Creative Migration: A Western Australian case study of creative artists. Australian Geographer* 41(1): 117–28.

Berklee College of Music, V. 2013. *New business models in the music industry*. Valencia: Berklee College of Music.

Bertacchini, E., and P. Borrione. 2013. The geography of the Italian creative economy: The special role of the design and craft based industries. *Regional Studies* 47(2): 135–47.

British Council. 2010. *Mapping the creative industries: A toolkit*. London: British Council.

Cadin, L., F. Guérin, and R. DeFillippi. 2006. HRM practices in the video game industry: Industry or country contingent? *European Management Journal* 24(4): 288–98.

Casadesus-Masanell, R., and J.E. Ricart. 2010. From strategy to business models and onto tactics. *Long Range Planning* 43(2): 195–215.

Casadesus-Masanell, R., and F. Zhu. 2013. Business model innovation and competitive imitation: The case of sponsor-based business models. *Strategic Management* 34(4): 464–82.

Coblence, E., and V. Sabatier. 2014. Articulating growth and cultural innovation in art museums. *International Studies of Management & Organization* 44 (4): 9–25.

Coe, N. M. 2000. The view from out West: Embeddedness, inter-personal relations and the development of an indigenous film industry in Vancouver. *Geoforum* 31(4): 391–407.

Cohendent, P., and L. Simon. 2007. Playing across the playground: Paradoxes of knowledge creation in the videogame firm. *Journal of Organizational Behaviour* 28: 587–605.

Collins, P., and F. Fahy. 2011. Culture and creativity: A case study from the West of Ireland. *Cities* 28(1): 28–35.

Collins, P., and Grimes, S. 2008. Ireland's Foreign-Owned Technology Sector: Evolving Towards Sustainability? *Growth and Change* 39(3), 436–463.

Craft Northern Ireland. 2013. FabLabs and Craft NI announce. Available at: http://craftni.org/opportunities/fablab-and-craft-ni-announce-first-dedicated-digital-fabrication-programme-for-the-ni-craft-industry (Accessed 12 December 2013).

Currid, E., and S. Williams. 2010. The geography of buzz: Art, culture and the social milieu in Los Angeles and New York. *Journal of Economic Geography* 10: 423–51.

Curtis, R. A. 2010. Australia's Capital of Jazz? The (re)creation of place, music and community at the Wangaratta Jazz Festival. *Australian Geographer* 41(1): 101–16.

Department of Culture, Arts and Leisure (DCAL). 2012. *An Analysis of creative industries in Northern Ireland.* DCAL: Belfast.

DeFillippi, R. 2015. Managing Project-Based organization in creative industries. In *The Oxford handbook of creative industries,* eds. C. Jones, M. Lorentzen, and J. Sapsed, 268–83. Oxford: University of Oxford Press.

Delmestri, G., F. Montanari, and A. Usai. 2005. Reputation and strength of ties in predicting commercial success and artistic merit of independents in the Italian feature film industry. *Journal of Management Studies* 42: 975–1002.

Dumcke, C. 2015. *New business models in the Cultural and Creative Sectors (CCSs).* Geneva: European Expert Network on Culture.

Ebbers, J., and N. Wijnberg. 2009. Latent organizations in the film industry: Contracts, rewards and resources. *Human Relations* 62(7): 987–1009.

Eikhof, D., and A. Haunschild. 2007. For art's sake! Artistic and economic logics in creative production. *Journal of Organizational Behaviour* 28: 523–38.

ENCATC. 2013. Responding to the crisis with culture: Towards new governance and business models for the cultural sector. *ENCATC Policy Debate,* Brussells. 5 July 2013.

European Commission. 2010. *Unlocking the potential of cultural and creative industries.* Brussels: European Commission.

European Commission. 2015. *Getting cultural heritage to work for Europe: Report of the Horizon 2020 Expert Group on Cultural Heritage.* Brussels: European Commission.

European commission. 2009. The impact of culture on creativity. Available at: ec.europa.eu/culture/documents/study_impact_cult_creativity_06_09.pdf (Accessed on 24 March 2013)

Fab Labs NI. 2013. www.fablabni.com (Accessed 12 december 2013).

Felton, E., C. Collis, and P. Graham. 2010. Making Connections: Creative industries networks in outer-suburban locations. *Australian Geographer* 41(1): 57–70.

FilmArc. 2013. http://filmarc.net/ (Accessed 12 December 2013).

Filmby Aarhus, Alexandra Institute and High Tech Accelerator Innovation Center University of Lodz Foundation. 2011. *Report on business models, value chains and business development services in the audiovisual/creative industries: Cases of the Łódź and Małopolska provinces and West Denmark*. Lodz: University of Lodz.

Frey, B. S. (2007). *What values should count in the arts? The tension between economic effects and cultural value*. Cambridge: Beyond Price, Cambridge University Press (CUP), 261–269.

Fuller, T., L. Warren, and S. J. Normal. 2011. Creative methodologies for understanding a creative industry. In *Entrepreneurship and the creative economy: Process, policy and practice*, eds. C. Henry and A. De Bruin, 79–96. Surrey: Edward Elgar.

Garnham, N. 2005. From cultural to creative industries. *International Journal of Cultural Policy* 11(1): 15–29.

Gately, C., and J. Cunningham. 2014. The contributions and disconnections between writing a business plan and the start-up process for incubator technology entrepreneurs. *Academic Entrepreneurship: Creating an Entrepreneurial Ecosystem (Advances in Entrepreneurship, Firm Emergence and Growth, Volume 16) Emerald Group Publishing Limited* 16: 197–241.

Generator Sverige. 2011. *The creative industries Sweden*. Report available at culturefighter.eu/centres-factories-incubators-amp-initiatives/how-they-work/generator-sverige

Gibson, C. 2010. Guest Editorial – Creative geographies tales from the margins. *Australian Geographer* 41(1): 1–10.

Gibson, C., Chris Brennan-Horley, and Jim Walmsley. 2010. Mapping vernacular creativity: The extent and diversity of rural festivals in Australia. In *Spaces of vernacular creativity: Rethinking the cultural economy*, eds. T. J. Edensor, D. L. Steve Millington, and Norma M. Rantisi, 89–105. London: Routledge.

Gibson, C., and N. Klocker. 2004. Academic publishing as 'creative' industry, and recent discourses of 'creative economies': Some critical reflections. *Area* 36(4): 423–34.

Gibson, C., and L. Kong. 2005. Cultural economy: A critical review. *Progress in Human Geography* 29(5): 541–61.

Grabher, G. 2002. Cool projects, boring institutions: Temporary collaboration in social context. *Regional Studies* 36(3): 205–14.

Grabher, G. 2004. Learning in projects, remembering in networks? Communality, sociality, and connectivity in project ecologies. *European Urban and Regional Studies* 11(2): 103–23.

Griffiths, R. 2001. Neighbourhood renewal: The contribution of arts and culture. *Danish building and urban research/European urban research association conference "Area-based initiatives in contemporary urban policy"*, Copenhagen.17–19 May 2001.

Guercini, S. 2014. Profiting from creative performance and business models over time: The case of the Italian design industry. *International Studies of Management & Organization* 44(4), 26–42.

Hällgren, M., and DeFillippi, R. 2014. Tensions of creativity in temporary organizing. In: Advancing research on projects and temporary organizations / [ed] Lundin, R & Hällgren, M, Copenhagen Business School Press, 2014

Hearn, G., S. Roodhouse, and J. Blakey. 2007. From value chain to value creating ecology: Implications for creative industries development policy. *International Journal of Cultural Policy* 13(4): 419–36.

Hesmondhalgh, D., and A. C. Pratt. 2005. Cultural industries and cultural policy. *International Journal of Cultural Policy* 11(1): 1–13.

Huggins, R., and N. Clifton. 2011. Competitiveness, creativity, and place-based development. *Environmental Planning A* 43(6): 1341–62.

Jayne, M., Gibson, C., Waitt, G., and Bell, D. 2010. The cultural economy of small cities. *Geography Compass* 4(9), 1408–1417.

Jones, C., M. Lorenzen, and J. Sapsed. 2015. Creative industries: A typology of change. In *The handbook of creative industries*, eds. C. Jones, M. Lorenzen, and J. Sapsed, 3–32. Oxford: Oxford University Press.

KreaNord. 2011. http://www.kreanord.org (Accessed 12 December 2013)

Kunzmann, K. R. 2004. An agenda for creative governance in city regions. *Disp – the Planning Review* 40(158): 5–10.

Li, F. 2015. Digital technologies and the changing business models in creative industries. *2015 48th Hawaii International Conference on System Sciences*. University of Hawaii, Manoa, Institute of Electrical and Electronics Engineers.

Lilley, A., and P. Moore. 2013. *Counting what counts: What big data can do for the cultural sector*. London: Nesta.

Lorenzen, M., and L. Fredericksen. 2005. The management of projects and product experimentation: Examples from the music industry. *European Management Review* 2(3): 198–211.

Lyubareva, I., Pierre-Jean Benghozi, and T. Fidele. 2014. Online business models in creative industries. *International Studies of Management & Organization* 44 (4): 43–62.

Mahroum, S, J Atterton, N Ward, A M Williams, R Naylor, R Hindle, and F Rowe. 2007 *Rural innovation*. London: National Endowment for Science, Technology and the Arts.

Marchant, N., and Addis, J. 1985. *Kilkenny design: Twenty-one years of design in Ireland*. London: Lund Humphries Publishers Ltd.

Markusen, A., and A. Gadwa. 2010. Arts and culture in urban or regional planning: A review and research agenda. *Journal of Planning Education and Research* 29(3): 379–91.

Marsland, J., and G. Krump. 2014. *The changing theatre landscape: New models in use by theatre artists, groups and organizations*. Ontario: Canadian Public Arts Funders (CPAF).

Matarasso, F. 2007. Common ground: Cultural action as a route to community development. *Community Development Journal* 42(4): 449–58.

McGranahan, D., and T. Wojan. 2007. Recasting the creative class to examine growth processes in rural and urban counties. *Regional Studies* 41(2): 197–216.

Mossig, I. 2011. Regional employment growth in the cultural and creative industries in Germany 2003–2008. *European Planning Studies* 19(6): 967–90.

Moyon, E., and X. Lecocq. 2014. Rethinking business models in creative industries: The case of the French record industry. *International Studies of Management & Organization* 44(4): 83–101.

NESTA. 2010. *Beyond live, digital innovation in the performing arts*. London: NESTA.

Nielsen, T. 2008. *The ERIBA model: An effective and successful policy framework for the creative industries*. Stockholm: The Knowledge Foundation.

O'Connor, J. 2009. Creative industries: A new direction? *International Journal of Cultural Policy* 15(4). 387–402.

Oakley, K. 2008. Any answer as long as it's right: Evidence-based cultural policymaking. Making Meaning, Making Money, 18–41.

Oakley, K. 2009. The disappearing arts: Creativity and innovation after the creative industries. *International Journal of Cultural Policy* 15(4): 403–13.

Osterwalder, A., Y. Pigneur, and C. L. Tucci. 2005. Clarifying business models: Origins, present, and future of the concept. *Communications of the Association for Information Systems* 16(1): 1.

Petridou, E., and D. Ioannides. 2012. Conducting creativity in the periphery of Sweden: A bottom-up path towards territorial cohesion. *Creative Industries Journal* 5(1): 119–37.

Petrov, A. N. 2007. A look beyond metropolis: Exploring creative class in the Canadian periphery. *Canadian Journal of Regional Science* 30(3), 451–474.

Pratt, A. C. 1997. The cultural industries production system: A case study of employment change in Britain, 1984–91. *Environmental Planning A* 29(11): 1953–74.

Pratt, A. C. 2004. The cultural economy a call for spatialized 'production of culture' perspectives. *International Journal of Cultural Studies* 7(1): 117–28.

Pratt, A. C. 2005. Cultural industries and public policy: An oxymoron? *International Journal of Cultural Policy* 11(1): 31–44.

Power, D. 2002. "Cultural Industries" in Sweden: An Assessment of their Place in the Swedish Economy. *Economic Geography* 78(2), 103–127.

Sapsed, J., P. Nightingale, J. Mateos-Garcia, G. Voss, R. Camerani, A. Coad, J. Byford, and S. Miles. 2015. *The Brighton Fuse*. Brighton: Brighton-Sussex Universities.

Scott, A. 2006. Entrepreneurship, innovation and industrial development: Geography and the creative field revisited. *Small Business Economics* 26(1): 1–24.

Searle, N. 2011. *Changing business models in the creative industries: The cases of television, computer games and music.* Newport: UK Intellectual Property Office.

Skantze, J., and Pihlgren, J. 2012. *Lägesrapport om den kreativa sektorn.* Generator Sverige: Stockholm.

Staines, J., & Mercer, C. (2013). Mapping of Cultural and Creative Industry Export and Internationalisation Strategies in EU Member States. Available at https://papers.ssrn.com/sol3/papers.cfm?abstract_id=2261595

Strom, E. 2003. Cultural policy as development policy: Evidence from the United States. *International Journal of Cultural Policy* 9(3): 247–63.

Strom, P., and R. Nelson. 2010. Dynamic regional competitiveness in the creative economy: Can peripheral communities have a place? *The Service Industries Journal* 30(4): 497–511.

Svejenova, S., Planellas, M., and Vives, L. 2010. An individual business model in the making: A chef's quest for creative freedom. *Long Range Planning* 43 (2), 408–430.

Svejenova, S., B. Slavich, and S. Abelgawad. 2015. Creative entrepreneurs: The business models of Haute Cuisine Chefs. In *The handbook of creative industries*, eds. C. Jones, J. Sapsed, and M. Lorenzen, 184–99. Oxford: Oxford University Press.

Sydow, J., and U. Staber. 2002. The institutional embeddedness of project networks: The case of content production in German television. *Regional Studies* 36(3): 215–27.

Taylor, C. 2006. Beyond advocacy: Developing an evidence base for regional creative industry strategies. *Cultural Trends* 15(1): 3–18.

Teece, D.J. 2010. Business models, business strategy and innovation. *Long Range Planning* 43(2): 172–94.

Throsby, D. 2010. *The economics of cultural policy*. Cambridge: Cambridge University Press.

UK Technology Strategu Board. 2009. Collaborative Business Models. Available at https://www.gov.uk/government/publications/collaborative-working-and-mergers-an-introduction-cc34/collaborative-working-and-mergers-an-introduction

United Nations Conference on Trade and Development (UNCTAD). 2010. *Creative Economy Report 2010*. United Nations: Geneva. Available at: http://unctad.org/en/Docs/ditctab20103_en.pdf (Accessed on 4 February 2013).

Uzzi, B., and J. Spiro. 2005. Collaboration and creativity: The small world problem. *American Journal of Sociology* 111: 447–504.

Van Andel, W., K. Vandenbempt, and P. Kenis. 2012. "What makes Creative Companies 'Jump': An explorative study into successful business models for Creative Industries." Retrieved 14 December 2015, from http://www.turas-cities.org/uploads/biblio/document/file/134/Study_into_successful_business_models_for_Creative_Industries.pdf.

Västerbotten Investment Agency. 2013. Creative Industries Overview: Facts and Figures Available at: http:// viaVästerbotten.se/sectors/creative-industries/overview/ (Accessed 25 November 2013).

Warnier, V., and A. Runfola. 2014. Why study business models in creative industries? *International Studies of Management & Organization* 44(4): 3–8.

Western Development Commission. 2013. Look West. Available at: http://www.wdc.ie/regional-development/lookwest/ (Accessed 12 December 2013)

Zukin, S. 1995. *The cultures of cities*. Oxford, UK: Blackwell Publishers.

Index

P. Collins, J.A. Cunningham, *Creative Economies in Peripheral Regions*, DOI 10.1007/978-3-319-52165-7

D

Q

R

The manufacturer's authorised representative in the EU is Springer Nature Customer Service Centre GmbH, Europaplatz 3, 69115 Heidelberg, Germany. If you have any concerns regarding our products, please contact ProductSafety@springernature.com

Printed and bound by CPI Group (UK) Ltd, Croydon, CR0 4YY
22/09/2026
02221070-0002